# Media Production

*Media Production* is an introductory student guide to radio, TV and film production techniques. Illuminating the step-by-step process from conception to delivery, from coming up with the initial ideas, through planning, research and editing, this book creates a guided structure to help students learn about media production. Aimed at those producing radio, film or TV projects for the first time, this book offers relevant advice which takes account of the context in which students work and the type of equipment available to them. Supported by online resources, this textbook provides templates, notes and exercises to help students prepare for their own projects.

**Amanda Willett** is a Producer who has worked for many years with BBC Learning and has extensive experience of creating educational materials for TV and for online use.

# Media Production

## A Practical Guide to Radio and TV

**Amanda Willett**

Routledge
Taylor & Francis Group

LONDON AND NEW YORK

First published 2013
by Routledge
2 Park Square, Milton Park, Abingdon, Oxon OX14 4RN

Simultaneously published in the USA and Canada
by Routledge
711 Third Avenue, New York, NY 10017

*Routledge is an imprint of the Taylor & Francis Group, an informa business*

*British Library Cataloguing in Publication Data*
A catalogue record for this book is available from the British Library

*Library of Congress Cataloging in Publication Data*
A catalog record for this book has been requested

ISBN: 978–0–415–53531–1(hbk)
ISBN: 978–0–415–53532–8(pbk)
ISBN: 978–0–203–08372–7(ebk)

Typeset in Baskerville
by Keystroke, Station Road, Codsall, Wolverhampton

Printed and bound in Great Britain by the MPG Books Group

To Jonathan

# Contents

# Templates

# Exercises

# Figures

# Preface

This book is a result of working for 28 years with the BBC, most of it with BBC Education. I have had the privilege of working with many great colleagues in the media as well as with many inspiring teachers who have contributed so much to the work. This book is for anyone teaching or studying media; I hope it helps.

# Acknowledgements

I would like to thank the following people for their help in reviewing and commenting on this work: Cas Lester, Fiona McLean, Steve Gregory, Mark Wray, Sarah Casey, Pete Wall, Andrea Peckover, Anthony Bateman and Florence and Arthur Barker.

# Part I
# Preparation and planning

# 1   How to use this book

This book is designed to take you through all the stages of producing a TV, film or radio project. The book will start right at the beginning, developing ideas and planning a project, and will take the reader through all the stages of production and finish with the delivery of the project. The book covers a number of genres; however, it concentrates on the types of production which students are most often asked to complete for exam qualifications.

The book is divided into two parts. Part I deals with research, development planning and preparation. It is intended to help you to build up a production plan. There will be various templates for you to download off the website and collate together. The aim is that having worked through Part I you will have built a comprehensive production folder, containing all your research and planning documents. These may be used to help you get the most out of your shooting and recording days.

Part II deals with recording, shooting and editing. It will give you a comprehensive guide to the practical aspects of shooting, recording and editing with helpful tips and advice.

Technical advice: There are so many different types of camera, microphones, editing packages, sound mixers that it isn't possible to offer any kind of instructional manual here. This book assumes you know how to operate whatever equipment you have and that you will be using fairly basic equipment.

TV and radio: TV and radio share some production processes, especially in the early stages of planning and research; however, clearly they differ as you get on to recording and editing techniques. Part I largely treats TV and radio together. However, in Part II there is more separation between the two media. If you are making a radio programme therefore, some of the chapters in Part II won't be relevant. However, everyone should read Part I.

The book should be used in conjunction with the website. On the website you will find printable versions of the templates and scripts illustrated in the book. Throughout the book you will be encouraged to create documents to help with your production. These are the kinds of documents you would create if you were working in a professional environment. Before you begin work on your production it may be helpful to prepare a folder and start to keep all these documents together. If you do this, by the end of the production you will have a record of the entire process. Many exam boards ask for an evaluation to be written with the project, and the records you keep will help you with some aspects of your evaluation.

On the website you will also find links to examples of different genres of radio and TV. Some of the exercises in the book will ask you to listen and critique or deconstruct the material. It will be important for you to do these exercises; the more you listen and watch, the more ideas you will start to have for your own project.

## Where to start?

When you start any project it is important to understand all the elements of the task you have to complete and the order in which you have to do them. Below is a list of the main tasks associated with making your production. To complete your production, you will need to go through all the stages below. Some stages take longer than others, but you will need to work through most of them if you are going to be successful.

This is the first document that you should print out from the website. Always have this at the front of your folder. It will be your checklist. As you complete the tasks you can tick them off; that way you won't forget anything and you'll know how far you've got to go!

## Template 1.1  List of tasks

| Tasks | What's involved | Check box |
|---|---|---|
| Ideas | This may include:<br><br>• Coming up with the ideas<br>• Discussing in your group how they might work<br>• Thinking about the style of the production. | |
| Production planning | This includes:<br><br>• Planning what you are going to do and how you are going to do it<br>• Planning who is going to do what on the project. | |
| Research/recce | This may include any or all of the following:<br><br>• Researching the topic<br>• Finding contributors<br>• Looking for locations<br>• Researching locations<br>• Getting permissions<br>• Props, costumes. | |
| Storyboards and treatments | • Storyboard. A visual drawing shot by shot of what you are going to film – used more for drama, music videos, trailers<br>• Shooting script. A rough script of what the piece will be about, with a list of what the visuals will be<br>This is used more for factual pieces. | |
| Filming/recording | • Shooting or recording the piece. | |

| Tasks | What's involved | Check box |
|---|---|---|
| First edit *(also known as rough cut or mix)* | • The first cut or mix you make of the project. This is not the finished piece and will still need work, but it should be roughly in the right shape and roughly the right length. | |
| Feedback | • The piece is shown to teacher or peers to get comments on what works and what doesn't work. | |
| **NB** | **This process of rough cut and feedback can be repeated as many times as you have time for or feel you need.** | |
| Final edit *(also known as fine cut or mix)* | • The final edit of the piece. By now it should be the right length and have the right music and all the effects. At the end of the fine cut you have the finished production. | |
| Delivery | • The production has been exported onto a drive/stick and delivered to teacher/ examiner. | |

# 2 Getting an idea

When you begin your project you may have a brief telling you what kind of film, TV or radio piece you are being asked to make. Your first task is to come up with an idea. You may have a really good idea immediately; however, a lot of groups need a little time to come up with their plans. This can be quite a daunting task if you are not used to it.

The first thing you will need to do is carry out some background research. You need to know something about the type of piece you are going to make and about the audience you are making it for, so before you start thinking about your own idea you should do more background research on your brief.

 On the website you can download some checklists (an example is illustrated below). You should keep the checklist and your notes together in your folder. The checklist will remind you of the types of questions to ask but also prompt you to think about the aims of your project.

## Research notes

When you are doing your research you should be keeping notes. There is no set way of keeping these notes; some producers tend to end up with notebooks full of scribbled notes, and others are very methodical.

You should also be clear about your objectives for your research. It's true that you may often need to do some background reading around a topic, which won't be particularly focused, but when you start the kind of research suggested in this chapter you should try to have an outcome in mind. Ask yourself:

- Why am I doing this research?
- What questions do I need to ask?
- What outcome do I need?

## Audience research

Big broadcasters have very elaborate and expensive methods of getting audience feedback and researching their audience. When you start your project it's worth thinking about your particular audience; in particular you can start to think about their behaviour when they are consuming media.

**Template 2.1 Audience research checklist**

| Who are they? | Your project may have to be in a particular genre, sci fi or romantic comedy, for example. If so, you should start to think about the audience for this type of film. |
|---|---|
| What else do they like? | What types of things interests this group of people? |
| What do they spend their time doing? | Do they have lots of leisure time? Are they busy people? |
| What other kinds of media do they consume and when? | Do they read the papers or get most of their information online? Do they read books; go to the cinema, theatre? What other TV or radio might they watch? |

The answers will be different depending on the audience you have. This type of research helps you think about the kind of approach you might take with your production. You can start to build up a picture of your audience. However, you will need to be careful about stereotyping your audience; try and canvas some opinions rather than just guess.

## Background programme research

Whatever project you have, a good thing to do is to start to look at some examples of work in the same genre. It will help you to think about your own project and give you some ideas. If you look carefully at similar types of work you will start to see how they are constructed. You will start to be able to deconstruct a piece. By deconstructing a piece and looking at its component parts you will get a better idea of how to construct your own piece. Depending on what type of piece you are making there will be different questions to ask. Try to find as many examples as you can.

Remember: keep a note of what you have looked at and where you found it. Later on it may be important to cite your sources.

## TV and film trailers

If you have been asked to do a trailer, start to look at trailers on the internet; they are very easy to find. If you know the type of film trailer you are going to make, look at three or four different trailers in the relevant genre. Try to answer the questions below for each of them. See if there are any common factors in each of the trailers.

## Template 2.2  Researching trailers

| What genre of TV/film is it | *Romance, comedy, horror?* |
|---|---|
| Who | *Who do you think is the intended audience for the piece and why?* |
| Shots | *What types of shots are used?*<br>*Wide shots, close-ups?*<br>*Are the shots moving or still?*<br>*Are the shots taken from low or high angles?* |
| V/O (Voice-over) | *How much voice-over is there?*<br>*What is the style of the voice-over: urgent, gentle, informative, does it create suspense or intrigue?* |
| Representation | *Does the film-maker use any particular characters or recognisable stereotypes?* |
| Connotation and symbolism | *Does the film-maker use symbolism or connotation to convey any meanings; if so what do they use and what are they trying to convey?* |
| Location | *Where is the piece set?* |
| Music | *How important is the music? Is it used all the time or just at certain points? How do the pictures work with the music?* |
| Structure | *What is the overall structure of the piece? How much of the story does it tell?*<br>*How does the trailer begin and end? How much of the story is revealed in the trail?* |
| Visual FX (effects) | *What else has the director used to create the film? Are there any special effects used?* |
| Editing | *What is the editing like: is it fast or slow? What is the relationship between any music and editing?* |
| Graphics | *Are there any words written up on the screen – if so what are they doing? Are there any other graphic devises used?* |

## Music videos

Again, if you know the genre of music you are going to be using, do some research into music videos using similar types of music.

### Template 2.3 Researching music videos

| | |
|---|---|
| Genre of music | *Pop, Indie, RnB. . . .* |
| Performance | *Does it feature the artists themselves or is it narrative?* |
| Who | *Who do you think is the intended audience for the piece and why?* |
| How the piece begins and ends | *What are the opening and closing shots?* |
| Representation | *Does the film-maker use any particular characters or recognisable stereotypes?* |
| Graphics/FX (effects) | *How have any of the visuals been treated; have they used graphics?* |
| Connotation and symbolism | *Does the film-maker use symbolism or connotation to convey any meanings? If so, what do they use and what are they trying to convey?* |
| Shots: | *What shots does the director use?* *Wide shots, close-ups?* *Moving shots/still shots?* *Are there lots of single shots or do the shots hang together as a sequence?* |
| Music | *How do the shots and music match?* *If it's a fast piece of music is the piece edited for lots of fast-paced cuts and vice versa?* |
| Location | *Is it all in the one place or in lots of different places? How important is the location?* |
| Structure | *Do the visuals have a story to them? Does the story match with the lyrics?* |

## Advertisements: radio and TV

Try to watch or listen to commercials from a number of different sources and channels and at different times of the day.

If you log onto the website you'll find links to lots of advertisements on the web.

## Template 2.4  Researching advertisements

| What | What type of product is being advertised? |
|---|---|
| Where | Where is it being advertised – what type of station or channel? |
| Who | Who do you think the advertisement is aimed at? |
| Style | Is it a narrative style (i.e. is there some kind of story to the ad or is it more impressionistic)? |
| Representation | Does the production use any particular characters or recognisable stereotypes? |
| Symbolism | What types of signs and symbols are the advertisers using to connect with the listener or viewer? |
| Music | What type of music is used? When is it used? |

## News reports: radio and TV

You should try to listen to or watch news reports from as wide a variety of sources as possible. If you are doing a radio piece, try to listen to reports from both commercial stations and public service stations and reports from local radio and national radio. You should try to listen to a number of very different news reports on the same day. This will give you a good idea of how different stations are approaching the same news content.

## Template 2.5  Researching news and current affairs

| Where | Think about where you are hearing the news report. What is the station or channel and who might their audience be? |
|---|---|
| What | The order of the items in the news: did this differ between the news bulletins? |
| Who | Who do you think is the intended audience for the piece and why? |

| How long | The length of the items, in particular the relative lengths: which items were given more coverage than others? |
|---|---|
| Tone | What is the tone of the news reader? Upbeat? Serious? |
| Contributors | What types of interviewees do they have, what other sounds/pictures do they use to tell the story? |
| Headlines | Listen to the headlines, and compare the headlines for the same story across the different types of coverage. |
| Balance | How balanced or objective do you think the reporting is? |
| Music | Does the bulletin use stings or music to start or end the piece? |
| News values | Compare what stories were covered by each station; did some stations give more coverage to certain items than other stations? How did the coverage differ? Were the items of local, national or international importance? |

## Factual and features radio and TV

**Factual:** A factual piece can be a short magazine item in a longer programme or it can be a long form of documentary. Since you are likely to be making a shorter piece, it's worth listening to or watching short factual items. Again it is useful to vary the types of programme you listen to, from local radio to national radio and commercial to public service. On TV it's useful to watch a range of factual items from the lighter end of factual entertainment, to the more serious types of programmes. Comparing how the different pieces work will help you to understand how they are constructed.

   **Features:** These tend to be associated more with radio than with TV, although TV has similar types of programmes. A feature will be a factual piece but would also include other material, possibly poetry, readings and music. It tends to be used for more impressionistic pieces or biographies, or slice-of-life-type stuff rather than the more current affairs end of programme-making. It is the more "artistic" end of factual programme-making.

   If you go to the website you'll find some helpful links.

| Story | What is the story that the programme-maker is trying to tell? |
|---|---|
| Contributors | Are they experts? Members of the public? |
| Who | Who do you think is the intended audience for the piece and why? |
| What | What else are they using? Pictures, sounds, music? |

| Narrative voice | *How is the story being told? Is there a presenter talking directly to the viewer or listener? If the piece is on TV is this presenter in vision?* |
|---|---|
| Music | *What type of music is used? When is it used?* |
| Authored | *How 'authored' is the piece? Does it feel like the presenter has a personal story to tell or is the narrator more objective?* |
| Linking material | *Links are the bits between the interviewees. Sometimes they can be very lengthy, sometimes short and snappy. How much linking material has been written?* |

## Creative thinking

Now that you have done a little background research, you are ready to start thinking about your own idea. One way of coming up with inspiration is to do a *creative thinking* session. In this kind of work a group of people get together to try to come up with as many ideas as possible for a project. There are lots of ways to run a session such as this; however, sitting in a group and shouting at one another isn't one of them. Although a creative thinking session is supposed to allow lots of good ideas to surface, there needs to be some sort of structure if it's going to be effective.

Creative thinking should be a collective, group activity and have a positive feel, but it's easy to get so passionate about your own idea that you stop listening to others. You may well have the best idea, but at this point you don't know that.

'**NO**' is not a good word to use during a creative thinking session. The best ideas come when everyone feels that they will be listened to with respect. If members of the group feel that they will be shouted down or embarrassed, then they won't come up with ideas and you may miss something. Try to add to an idea rather than dismiss it. As you listen to someone's idea try not to find fault with it. Ask questions and if you have further thoughts try to add to the idea.

You can download this exercise from the website if you wish.

## EXERCISE 2.1  Yes and . . .

The exercise below is to help you to get a feel for how a positive approach to creative thinking can bring out the best ideas. This is a kind of improvisation exercise. In this exercise you shouldn't be thinking about your own project; instead choose something completely unconnected with it.

---

**Part One:** Imagine that you are planning a party (*or anything else that springs to mind*). Get into pairs and choose who will start the conversation. In this part of the exercise each person will start every sentence with the words '**Yes but . . .**

For example:

- The first person makes a suggestion:
  *e.g. I think we should plan a party when the exams are over.*
- The second person responds. The first words he or she uses must be **Yes but . . .**
  Then they say whatever they want:
  *e.g. **Yes but** we don't really have a lot of time at the moment.*
- The first person responds again. The first words should be **Yes but . . .**
  *e.g **Yes but** we have to start early if we want to get a good venue.*

Carry on with this for about two minutes or until you have run out of steam, then write down how many ideas you have for your party and how far the plans have progressed.

**Part Two:** Swap partners and again choose who will start the conversation. Imagine you are having the same conversation. This time the first words of any sentence you begin will be **Yes and . . .**
  **For example**:

- The first person makes a suggestion:
  *e.g. I think we should plan a party when the exams are over.*
- The second person responds. The first words he or she uses must be **Yes and . . .**
  *e.g. **Yes and** we could make a list of all the people to invite.*
- The first person responds again:
  **Yes and** *we could find somewhere really unusual to hold it.*

Carry on with this for about two minutes, and then write down how many ideas you have for your party and how far the plans have progressed. You should find that you are considerably more advanced with your party plans after the second conversation than after the first. Some of your ideas may be a little wild but you should have found that the whole conversation was a lot more enthusiastic and enjoyable.
  Remember: listen to all the ideas, try to build on an idea rather than knock it down.

## EXERCISE 2.2 Creative thinking

OK, back to your production: the following is one way to structure a creative thinking exercise. If you want to you can download a separate sheet for this exercise from the website.

### Before you start

1  Decide how long you would like to run the session for. For the purpose of this example we will make it 30 minutes.
2  Decide who will facilitate the session. This person will be responsible for asking the questions and keeping the session to time.
3  Designate one person to write up notes. Ideally you should note down ideas on a large piece of paper or a board so that everyone can see it; if you can't do this then just get a big notepad.

4   The Creative thinking session is divided into several parts or sections which are described below. You should allocate time to each of the sessions. I have suggested one way, but you can allocate time in whatever way you wish. Once you have made a decision try to stick to it.

5   Make sure you keep your notes, however messy and scribbled; they could be an important part of any evaluation you may need to do.

Once you have all this in place as a group you should go through the sections below. Remember: the facilitator needs to keep everyone to time and remind the group which section they are considering

### Section 1 What are your parameters?                                    *3 mins*

The parameters are all the things you can't change: the restrictions or rules you know you are going to have to work with. This shouldn't take very long as everyone in the group should already know them. However, it's worth starting the session by making a checklist of what you already know about what you have to do. With a student project you will normally have been given some of these parameters. You are likely to know the genre of the piece and who it is aimed at, namely your target audience. You may have been given other parameters as well. It's worth stating what these are.

| What is it? | What type of production does your brief require? |
|---|---|
| Who is the audience? | Age, sex . . . |
| How long does it have to be? | Minimum and maximum length. |
| When does it have to be finished? | When does the final project have to be handed in? |
| How many days do I have to work it? | How much lesson time? How much time outside lessons? |
| What resources do you have? | Camera, edit facilities, people, sound? |

### Section 2 Generate ideas                                               *10 mins*

At this point anyone who wants to should suggest ideas. It doesn't matter how wild or impractical the ideas are. The main thing is to come up with as many ideas as possible. The person taking notes should start making a list of all the ideas that are mentioned.

IMPORTANT: At this point no ideas are bad. Use the Yes and . . . technique. If a member of the group comes up with an idea, however impractical, you should add it to the list. At this point in the session **no one** should be raising objections to **any** ideas; just write them all down. Let each person speak about the idea and give the rest of the group a sense of how it might work.

### *Section 3 Narrowing the ideas* *7 mins*

You should now have a list of different ideas for your project. You now need to go about the process of selecting which of the ideas is best for you. Depending on how many ideas you have you can begin by making a shortlist.

You should try to get down to a shortlist of about three ideas. If you don't have that many to start with don't worry; just go to the next stage. If you do have lots of ideas you need to find a way of narrowing them down. There are many ways of doing this but one way is to give each member of the group one or more votes on which idea they think is the best. After each person has voted, adopt the ideas with the most votes.

### *Section 4 Check your criteria* *2 mins*

You should now go back to the initial list you made yourself and check each of the ideas against the criteria you set out. How does each of the ideas match with what you already know? Does it fit your brief? Will it appeal to your target audience?

**NB:** Just because an idea doesn't fit one of the criteria, this doesn't necessarily mean you have to drop it. It may be a good idea which just needs a bit of adjustment. However, you need to know this early on so that you don't start giving yourselves impossible tasks.

### *Section 5 Final selection* *8 mins*

How you make the final decision is up to you. It may be that there is already one idea which really stands out. However, it may be that you want to work through each of the ideas a little more thoroughly. If you have three ideas on the table then as a group you should go through each one and try to come up with ways of making each of them work. Alternatively, one person could speak for each idea. Give each idea time to get a fair hearing. Once all the ideas have been discussed, you will need to come to a final decision. One idea may already have the support of most of the group or you may have to vote again. Once you have made the decision, carry out a final check against your parameters: is there anything which doesn't fit the brief? Make a note of the ways in which your idea does fulfil the brief you were given; you will find this useful later on in your evaluation.

## Conclusion

However you come to the final decision it should be the decision of the group. Although each person should have felt that their ideas had a fair hearing, once the decision has been made you all need to get behind it. You all need to support it.

At the end of this session you will have some rather messy scribbled notes with thoughts and ideas jotted down as you went along. However messy and incomprehensible they seem, hang onto them and put them into your production folder. You won't need them very much for the rest of the production but they will be useful at the end of the project.

# 3   Research

There are many different types of research. You have already done some background research into your audience and into the type of piece you are making. The type of research dealt with in this chapter is the sort of research you would do when you have your idea and are starting your project.

## Research notes

As with your background research, you should be keeping notes. This will help you during the production process as you can refer back to the notes, and it will also help with the evaluation. Just as with your audience research you should also be clear about the objectives:

*   Why am I doing this research?
*   What questions do I need to ask?
*   What outcome do I need?

## Information research

If you are making a factual piece, either a news item or a documentary piece, you will need to research the subject of your piece. You can do this in two ways:

1   Your own research from internet or books, newspapers, etc.
2   Talking to people, either experts or people who have some involvement in the piece you are making.

However you do the research, you should always be clear about what the story is you want to tell *before* you do any recordings or filming. You should already know all the main facts and you should know how you want to tell you the story. This is not to say that surprises don't happen or things don't change, but you need to do your research.

*   What are the main facts of the story?
*   Why should the listener or viewer be interested?

Remember: if you don't know the point of the story, there is no hope of a viewer or listener knowing either.

## Locations research

In any TV or radio recording you are going to need to choose where you do your filming or recordings. This kind of research is called a *recce*. You may have just one location in your production or you may have several, but you need to visit each of the places you want to use, and while you are there you will need to think about the following:

- **Look around you:** (for TV/film) What can you see, what might make a good shot? Are there different angles or spaces you can use to make it seem as if you have been to more places than you actually have? Are there any stairs, windows, balconies from which you can shoot?
- **Listen:** If you are making a radio piece, you will add a lot of colour by adding some of the sound from the location you are visiting. Think about what you can hear around you, list any sounds which might help you tell the story and add atmosphere to the piece. Is there a lot of noise? This may or may not be a problem, depending on what kind of production you are making, but it's as well to know.
- **Light:** (for TV/film) What is the light like? How light or dark is it? If it is outside, you will need to know where the sun comes from and goes to. You should also think about when there is light; if it's winter it will get darker much earlier and you will have less time to film in. Inside, where are the windows? How bright is it?
- **Permission:** Do you need permission to be in this place? Who does it belong to, and are they happy for you to work there? If you are at a location where you need permission you must find the person who can give you permission and fix a date with them when you can come back and record.
- **Story:** How can the location help you tell the story? What will help bring your story to life?

## Contributor research

If you are making a factual piece you will probably need to interview people. You need to recce people as well as places. If possible, you should go and meet the people you are going to interview. If you can't meet them, then you should at least talk to them on the phone. Interview techniques will be dealt with in more detail later on, but for the moment you should be thinking about the types of person you want to include in the piece. You need to know that they have something to say that's worth saying and that the interview will not just be a waste of time. Before you talk to anyone prepare some questions for yourself and the contributor.

Ask yourself:

- Can this person contribute to the story? If so, how do they fit into my piece?
- What kind of information do I want this person to give me? What type of interview is this: personality, factual, explanatory, witness?
- Can this person talk confidently, can they make a point succinctly or do they ramble a bit?
- Where do I want to do the interview? Do I want the person in a location associated with the topic of the piece, or should they be somewhere else?
- What is the location like? Noisy, quiet? Are there lots of people around?

The contributor:

- Make sure you know exactly who they are; it sounds stupid but it's important that you give them the right title and the right name.
- Explain to the contributor why you want to see them and what it's for.
- Tell them what you are hoping to get from them.
- Make sure they know when you want to film or record and that they are available on those dates.

## Casting

You may be doing a dramatised piece which needs a cast. Casting is an important part of the process. You should be thinking about your characters, the look, the personality, how you want them to come across. If you form a mental picture of your character you will find it easier to cast.

## Music

Often the choice of music will come later, perhaps during the edit. However, it may be that the music is an integral part of your piece and therefore you need to be thinking about it quite early on.

Unless you write the music yourself, any music recording will belong to someone; they will own the copyright to it. If you want to use music in any kind of broadcast, you will need to get permission from the person who owns the copyright. There are however a number of companies which provide mood music, sometimes referred to as background music or royalty-free music. The difference is that this music has been deliberately created for the broadcast or film industry, so programme-makers are encouraged to use this type of music. Broadcasters would usually pay a one-off fee to use the library, and critically the library is very unlikely to refuse permission since the whole point is that they are trying to sell the music. It is usually very easy to search for this type of music under genre, instrument or mood, and it is a quick and easy way of researching a large amount of music.

If you log onto the website you'll find links to some examples.

Commercial music, the type you can buy in a shop or download, will be more difficult to get permission to use. Some artists are careful about how their music is used and others simply refuse to let anyone use their music for any purpose. It is for this reason that you will probably be directed to music libraries.

## Other research

Depending on what type of programme you are making there may be other elements you need. Radio features, for instance, quite often use illustrative material such as readings, poems and archive content, even dramatised sequences. TV pieces often use still images, archive footage and sometimes dramatised sequences.

- **Stills:** There are large numbers of online image banks or libraries; some of these have rights-free images. These are quite similar to mood music libraries and you may be able to use them without any cost, but many do have costs attached.
- **Film and sound archive:** There are a number of archive houses for both footage and

sound. However, these tend to be very expensive and you are unlikely to be able to use them without incurring substantial cost. However, since the object of these pieces is for you to produce original work it's not likely that you will want to use large chunks of archive film or sound archive which after all has been made by someone else.

- **Literary material:** poems and extracts from plays are obviously fairly easy to get hold of but you need to be careful how you use them. One of the most difficult things to do is to combine literary material with factual material. You would also need to think about copyright.

## Copyright

In a professional world if you want to use this kind of material, a big part of the research process is clearing the copyright. Copyright is the legal right you have over the reproduction of your own intellectual property, whether it's something you wrote or composed, something you painted or a photograph, or indeed a film or radio piece. Copyright often lies with the person who created the piece; however, if that person is working for a company then the company may hold the rights. Rights are often bought and sold, so the person who originally made the work may no longer own the copyright but could have sold it to someone else.

Just as with music, anything you have not created yourself is likely to belong to someone, and that person or company has the right to decide whether or not to let you use the material. If they do allow you to use the material then they have the right to say how much you should pay and what kinds of rights they will sell you. In the broadcasting world you normally buy the right to use the property in a particular medium – radio, TV. You would also be restricted as to how often you could broadcast the material. The right to broadcast over the internet becomes even trickier.

There are a number of different types of copyright and they all have different rules:

- **Literary copyright:** This refers to anything which has been written. A novel, poem, a play, or any kind of non-fiction work.
- **Music copyright:** This refers to any kind of music. This will include recordings of music or sheet music, or reproducing the music yourself.
- **Stills:** Any kind of photograph which you have not taken yourself.
- **Art:** The work of art itself may be very old, but the right to **reproduce** that work of art is likely to be owned by someone, quite often the artist or, in the case of older works, by a gallery or the person who owns the work.
- **Film and sound archive:** This doesn't just mean very old recordings but anything you have not shot or recorded yourself. The rights may lie with the production company which first made the programme, or with an archive library, or with an individual.

Copyright is quite a simple concept; you want to borrow something from somebody and they tell you what they will let you do and how much they will charge you. However, the reality is that it can be very complicated to find out who owns what rights and then even more complicated to come to an agreement over what they will let you do. In big broadcast organisations whole departments are dedicated to clearing rights.

### *When do you have to pay copyright?*

Rights become an issue when a copyright item is broadcast or published, or where there is an audience for a live public performance. Thus, for instance, you can sit at home and read an extract from a play to your friends without there being any copyright issues. If you were to stand up in class and read it there is no copyright issue. However, if it was part of an amateur production to which parents and friends were invited then this is likely to be classed as a performance and there would be a copyright payment due.

Generally in a student piece the advice would be to avoid copyright material where possible but if you do include any material which is not your own you need to make sure that this is made clear and you are able to cite the source.

## Conclusion

Your programme is only as good as the research you put into it. Finding the right locations, contributors, knowing your subject will make your piece what it is. Doing good research gives you options and choices for where you want to take your piece. However, you will need to make sure that you are getting the best out of the research. You will need to have a clear idea about what you are researching, why, and what outcome you want. If you are organised and methodical about your research then it will never be wasted time.

# 4    Production planning and timelines

## Production plans

You have already started your production plan. The research notes and your creative thinking notes are your first steps. However, there are a number of other steps to help you organise yourself before you start to shoot or record anything. Writing down these steps helps you understand all the things you are going to have to do to make your production. It helps you understand how long they will take, who should be doing it, and what you will need to get it done. For many exams, marks can be given for the planning process, and it will be a part of your evaluation, so it's well worth investing a little time in this part of the project. A production plan will help you get your project in on time.

Here's the thing about plans: they very rarely work out in the way you first imagined. Almost always something will happen which will mean you have to change your plan. Sometimes it's just lots of small things which have to change, sometimes it's great big things, and sometimes it's both. But you will almost always have to change your plan as you go along.

So why bother? Why have a plan at all if it's just going to change?

Well, your plan is like a map. Imagine going on a journey: you know more or less where you are going but you don't have a map. At the first wrong turn you will get stuck and probably become more and more lost. However, if you have a map with you, then you can take as many wrong turns as you want; you will always be able to look at the map to find the way back.

A production plan will help you understand what to do when things start to go wrong (*which they almost always do*). Because you already have a list of what to do and when you need to do it by, your plan will help you make all the changes you need and still keep on schedule. When things start to get frantic, going back to your plan will make sure you don't miss anything important. So how to make one?

If you have read the previous chapters and printed out the material, then you have already started your plan. You have already come up with an idea for the piece, you've printed out a list of tasks and you've started on your research. The next thing to think about is time.

## A word about time

The funny thing about time is that at the beginning of a project it doesn't seem that important; your ideas, your creativity, the camera, the sound, we all talk about them endlessly but we never talk about time. But sometimes by the end of the project, time is really the only thing that matters. When you are up against a delivery deadline even the best ideas are lost in the general rush to get things done: *great idea, but we really don't have time* is a phrase you often hear towards the end of a production.

You need to control time; you need to be the master of time; you need a timeline.

### What is a timeline?

A timeline is a way of estimating how long things are going to take. It's an important part of your production plan. To make a timeline you will need the list of tasks from the beginning of the book. You can also get this off the website. You'll also need the blank timeline sheet which is on the website. You are going to start to put some timescales against each of the tasks so that you know how long you have to spend on each.

## EXERCISE 4.1  Planning time

Oddly, the easiest way to do this is to start at the end and work backwards. Below is an example of how you can plan your time on a project. At this point a lot of this will be guesswork. You don't really know some of these timings, but you do know what time it is now and you do know when you have to deliver. Plans don't always work out the way they started and you may need to go back and alter these timings, but at least you've got the start of a plan.

Print out the blank timeline sheet from the website. Ask yourself the following questions and start to fill in the answers; you will need the list of tasks to do this. Remember: at this stage it's a rough guide, so don't spend too long over it; it will change!

| Activity | Date | Activity | Date |
|---|---|---|---|
| When do we have to deliver the project? | | | |
| If we want to submit the final project by | | We need to finish the editing by | |
| If we want to finish our editing by | | We need the viewing/feedback by | |
| If we want to have a viewing/ feedback by | | We need to have our rough/first edit by | |
| If we want to finish rough/first edit | | We need to start our edit by | |
| If we want to start our edit by | | We need to finish shooting/ recording by | |
| If we want to finish shooting/ recording by | | We need to start shooting/ recording by | |
| If we want to start shooting/ recording by | | We need to have our script/ outline by | |
| If we want to have our script by | | We need to finish our research by | |
| If we want to finish our research by | | We need to start our research by | |
| If we want to start our research by | | We need to have chosen an idea by | |

Now go to the list of tasks and put some timings against all the tasks; you can download this template from the website.

## Template 4.1   List of tasks and times

| Tasks | What's involved | Start | Finish |
|---|---|---|---|
| Ideas | This can include:<br>• Coming up with the ideas for your film<br>• Discussing in your group how the film might work<br>• Thinking about the style of the film. | | |
| Production planning | This includes:<br>• Planning what you are going to do and how you are going to do it<br>• Planning who is going to do what on the project. | | |
| Research/ Recce | This can include any or all of the following:<br>• Researching the topic<br>• Finding contributors<br>• Looking for locations<br>• Researching locations<br>• Getting permissions<br>• Props, costumes. | | |
| Treatments | • Storyboard: a shot-by-shot drawing of what you are going to film; used more for music videos, advertisements and so on.<br>• Scripts: for a drama you will need to have a script and scene breakdown.<br>• Script outline: a rough script of what the piece will be about with a list of what the visuals will be, for each section of the story. Used more for factual pieces. | | |
| Shooting/ recording | • Shooting the film or recording the piece. | | |
| 1st edit *(also known as rough cut)* | • The first cut you make of the piece. This is not the finished production and will still need work, but it should be roughly in the right shape and roughly the right length. | | |
| Feedback | • The piece is shown to teacher or peers to get comments on what works and what doesn't work. | | |

| Tasks | What's involved | Start | Finish |
|---|---|---|---|
| **NB** | **This process of rough cut and feedback can be repeated as many times as you have time for or feel you need.** | | |
| Final edit/ mix *(also known as fine cut)* | • The final edit of the film or radio piece. By now it should be the right length and have the right music and all the effects. At the end of the fine cut you have the finished production. | | |
| Delivery | • The piece has been exported onto a drive/stick and delivered to teacher/examiner. | | |

## Conclusion

If you want to control your production process you need to be in control of your time. This may seem fiddly and irritating at the moment: you may just be desperate to get on and *do* something. However, if you were a producer on a professional shoot, this is what you would be expected to do. The more complicated the production, the more time would be spent on this aspect. Doing this now will put you in control.

# 5 Allocating tasks

## Who does what?

The next part of the plan is to decide who is going to do what. If you are working in a group on your project you will probably want to share some of the tasks. You may want more than one person to have a go at editing, shooting, recording and directing or it may be that you take responsibility for a section of the production. It's probably important that each person is involved in each stage of the production.

However, you should be able to start to think about all the jobs that will need to be done and to think about who will do them, even if you share the tasks for some of the time. Tasks in TV and radio are slightly different, so they have been split up. There are of course many other tasks in both radio and television. However, the ones listed here are the ones you are most likely to need and the ones you should think about allocating. In a professional production everyone involved will have specific tasks or jobs that they have to do. Very often they may be asked to do more than one job and combine two or more of the tasks I have outlined below. If necessary, you can print this checklist out from the website.

## Template 5.1 TV and film tasks

| Production | Setting up the shoots, organising all the cast, contributors and locations. Dealing with money and permissions, looking after the production plan and the timing. Making sure everyone knows what they are supposed to be doing and when they are supposed to do it. |
|---|---|
| Directing | This is often the same person as the producer but can be different. On the shoot itself it will involve directing the camera or actors and deciding what shots or sound to get. If it is a drama it will involve directing the actors. The director should be responsible for the storyboard, if it's used. If it's a factual programme the director should be involved in researching the project and writing the outline treatment or script. |
| Script writing | For factual programmes the producer or director, or sometimes the presenter, would normally write the script. If it's a drama or comedy you would often have a separate script writer. |

| Camera work | Operating the camera, finding the best shots, looking after any lighting, taking care of the equipment, checking the rushes, labelling the tapes correctly. |
| --- | --- |
| Sound recording | Recording sound, looking after the sound equipment to make sure it's working properly, making sure all sound is properly checked on the recording day. |
| Editing | Cutting the pictures, mixing the sound, adding music and effects. |
| Costumes/ makeup/ props | Finding all the costumes needed for the shoot. Making sure everything is in the right place at the right time and clean and tidy. Makeup artists will apply any makeup needed. They are responsible for bringing the right makeup to the shoot. Sourcing any props needed for the shoot, getting them to the shoot and having them ready at the right place at the right time. |
| Presenter | Mostly used in factual pieces, this will be the person who is voicing the piece and doing the pieces to camera. Presenters will research and do interviews and help write the script. |

## Template 5.2  Radio tasks

| Producer | Setting up the recordings and/or studios, organising all the cast, contributors and locations. Dealing with money and permissions. Looking after the production plan and the timing. Making sure everyone knows what they are supposed to be doing and when they are supposed to do it. |
| --- | --- |
| Director/ studio producer | Most of the time this is the same person as the producer but can be different. During the actual recording, whether on location or in a studio, they will be running the show. |
| Script writer | For factual programmes the producer or director, or sometimes the presenter, would normally write the script. If it's a drama or comedy, then you would often have a separate script writer. |
| Sound recordist | On location they will record all the sound. This will often be the same person as the producer/director but not always, particularly on big productions. |

| Studio engineer/ studio manager | In a studio runs the mixing desk, editing and mixing the final programme. Will mostly be the same person who did the recording, and will often be the same as the director/producer. |
|---|---|
| Spot FX | Specialised person mostly used in radio drama or entertainment programmes. They are responsible for effects (FX) needed live in the studio which can't be taken from a disc: sounds of people eating, walking, etc. In film or TV this is often called a Foley artist. |
| Radio presenter | This will be the person in the studio or on location who is voicing the piece. Presenters will research and do interviews and help write the script. |

## Why do you need to decide?

You may not want to be prescriptive from the beginning about who does what. As you are likely to be working in a group you will probably want to take turns in doing some tasks, such as directing or editing. That's great and it's a fair way to do things, but you still need to decide who is going to do what and when. Why? In any recording or shoot there are lots of tasks which need organising. Cameras need to be charged, you need to make sure all your contributors know where they are going, you need to make sure everyone has a script, etc.

Each of you will need to take responsibility for organising some of the tasks. If you know which task you are doing in any particular part of the shoot/recording then you will know what you are responsible for organising. If you are camera or sound for the day then you know what you have to think about that day and you know what sorts of things you are going to have to organise. The big bonus of course is that you don't have to think about anything else, just your task. If everyone knows what they have to organise then the whole thing becomes a lot easier.

As a group you may already know a lot about who wants to do what; if so, great: start to put names against some of the jobs. If you don't yet know who wants to do what or you all want to do the same thing then that's fine for the moment. You can allocate tasks differently for different shooting or recording days. For the moment just make a note of who wants to do what. If there are any blank tasks make sure that this isn't a task you are going to need; you don't always need costume and makeup, for example. But if you think this is a task you are going to need, then someone is going to have to be allocated to do it.

## Conclusion

Allocating tasks to people is an important part of the production planning. If it's properly done then everyone in the group should feel that they have an important part to play, and they will know what they have to do and when. In the end it will save you time and ensure that everything that needs to be done gets done.

# 6 Structure

By now you will have come up with an idea, worked out part of your production plan and done your research. This chapter is designed to help you think about the piece, to give you a structure or a way of thinking that will help you to be creative.

You don't need to read through all of the different sections if you don't want to; just find the section that deals with the type of production you are doing. However, everyone should read the first section on story structure as you will need to be familiar with these concepts to understand the rest of it. Advertising is dealt with in the next chapter, since the ways to think about advertising and the way it is structured are rather different. News and current affairs are also dealt with in a separate chapter.

 For this chapter you will need to refer to the website. On the website you will find the links to these examples of TV, film and radio, and help in deconstructing them.

## Story structure

What is meant by story structure? We are all familiar with the idea of a story, from our earliest fairy stories to complicated novels we might read or study later in life. We tend to associate the word *story* with fiction or drama. However, the word *story* is also used when making factual programmes, advertisements or music videos. Thus it is important to think about how stories are structured. There have been many theorists writing about the structure of narrative and many books written on story structure. It's outside the scope of this chapter to go into a lot of detail, so this is just to give you some pointers to think about.

Most theories on story structure break down the structure into a series of acts or stages; different theorists will have a slightly different approach, but most of them are along the lines set out in the next template.

## Template 6.1 Story structure

| | |
|---|---|
| **The situation:** | Who are the characters, where are they in life? |
| **The trigger:** | Sometimes called 'initiating or inciting incident'. Something changes in the main character's life, something that they have to deal with. |
| **The challenge:** | The character starts to deal with the problem or conflict in their life; they encounter obstacles and there is often jeopardy, a sense of danger or some kind of loss. |
| **Reversal:** | Some new problem occurs, or some new challenge which either reverses the character's first attempts to deal with the problem; it may also take the plot in a different direction. |
| **Climax:** | The situation reaches a critical point. |
| **Resolution:** | The story is resolved and finishes. |

Not all stories follow this format but the majority broadly follow these lines. Woven around this structure will be the important elements of narrative.

## Template 6.2 Narrative elements

| | |
|---|---|
| **Characters:** | Who are the main protagonists and what is their emotional journey? |
| **Themes:** | What are the underlying messages of the piece? |
| **Setting:** | Where does the action happen? |
| **Genre:** | What conventions does it fit into? |
| **Plot:** | What is actually happening? |

These elements are different in each story; there are an almost infinite number of different characters, themes, settings and genres which can be woven around the *same* basic story structure. Thus, for example, take the story of Snow White:

## *Structure*

| Situation: | Snow White is the beloved child of a king who has remarried a wicked and jealous woman, Snow White has been living under her tyranny for some time. |
|---|---|
| The trigger: | The wicked Queen consults her magic mirror which tells her that Snow White is prettier than she is. The Queen decides to kill Snow White. |
| The challenge: | Snow White has to deal with the Queen's hatred and the threat to her life. She convinces the hunter to let her go and finds herself alone in the woods. She happens upon the Seven Dwarfs and decides to make a new life for herself with them, far away from the wicked Queen. |
| The reversal: | The wicked Queen finds out that Snow White is still alive and feeds her the poisoned apple. |
| Climax: | The angry dwarfs chase after the Queen and eventually kill her. Believing Snow White to be dead, they place her in a glass coffin. |
| Resolution: | A passing prince gives Snow White a kiss and she wakes from her sleep. |

### *Narrative elements*

| Genre: | Fairy story. |
|---|---|
| Setting: | Once upon a time, far, far away! |
| Characters: | The Queen, Snow White, Dwarfs, Prince, etc. |
| Theme: | Could be said to be jealousy. |
| Plot: | A jealous stepmother seeks to destroy her beautiful stepdaughter who is saved by the kindness of some dwarfs. |

## EXERCISE 6.1  Story structure: Cinderella

Now you have a go: think of the story of Cinderella. If you wish, you can print off a blank sheet from the website Try to break it down into its component parts:

**Structure of Cinderella**

| Situation | |
|---|---|
| The trigger | |
| The challenge | |
| The reversal | |
| Climax | |
| Resolution | |

## EXERCISE 6.2  Narrative elements: Cinderella

| Genre | |
|---|---|
| Setting | |
| Characters | |
| Theme | |
| Plot | |

## Structure of trailers

The point of a film trailer is to make you want to see the film. In order to get you to watch the film, the film-makers try to convey some of the narrative elements in the film:

- A sense of the central plot and/or themes of the film
- A sense of the characters in the film
- A sense of the genre of the film.

However, in order to get this information across effectively, they will also need to use pivotal moments in the story structure so that they can convey a lot of information about the film in a short space of time:

- It will tell you something about the main character's situation.
- It will tell you something about the trigger or inciting incident.
- It will give you a taste of the types of challenge the main character is facing.

By using some of these key elements of story structure and elements of the narrative, the trailer will offer the audience a very good sense of what the film is about in a short space of time. Because film-makers concentrate on using key elements they convey a lot more than just using an extract from the film. By making sure the audience understand the genre, the trailer also ensures that the film targets the right people effectively. It's also worth noting that the trailer doesn't normally give you any information about the climax or the resolution to the film: they don't want to spoil the ending!

Before you start to make your trailer therefore, you will need to have thought about the structure and narrative elements in your story. You don't have to work it out in any great detail but you will need to think about:

## Story structure

- Situation
- Trigger
- Challenges

## Narrative elements

- Genre of your piece
- Who are your main characters
- The main points of the plot.

Unless you have some idea of this in your head you cannot use these elements to make an effective trailer.

## Structure of film trailers

Let's take the story of Snow White again. Think about the different narrative and structural elements you may want to include in the trailer.

### Snow White: narrative and structural elements

| | |
|---|---|
| **Characters:** | You would probably want to establish at least Snow White, the Queen, and possibly the dwarfs as the main characters. |
| **Genre:** | You could establish the genre of the piece; this could be done through the music, the *mise-en-scène*, etc. |
| **Plot/theme:** | You could establish the Queen as a jealous woman and you could establish that Snow White has been thrown out of the castle. |
| **Situation:** | You could establish Snow White as kind and good. You could show her living in the castle and loved by all. |
| **Trigger:** | You will need to include some reference to the mirror. |
| **Challenge:** | You could show Snow White alone in the woods or show us something of her first meeting with the dwarfs. |

Have a go yourself now and make notes on what elements you might include if you were doing a trailer for Cinderella.

## EXERCISE 6.3 Cinderella trailer

| Characters | |
|---|---|
| Genre | |
| Plot/theme | |
| Situation | |
| Trigger | |
| Challenge | |

If you log onto the website now you can see some real film trailers. There are some notes to guide you through how to deconstruct the trailer and identify the different elements.

Understanding the component parts of a story helps you to understand how film-makers strategically use the components to get across a lot of information about the film in a short space of time. When you come to make your trailer this is what you are aiming to do. It's easy to find trailers on the net so you can spend as much time as you want breaking them down; soon you won't be able to go to the cinema without deconstructing every trailer you see.

### Opening sequences

Opening sequences and opening scenes are a little like film trailers. Their job is to grab the audience and make them want to watch. They should also help to signal to the audience what kind of film they are going to be watching. If it's a comedy, this will be signalled in the opening scene. They usually also tell you something general about the *mise-en-scène*; it will mostly introduce you to the kind of environment you are in. If the opening scene is set somewhere which is totally out of character for the rest of the film it will jar slightly and set up the wrong kind of expectation.

The opening has three main functions:

1   **Grab attention from the viewer:** In broadcasting in particular the audience can be quite fickle. If they don't like the look or sound of something they switch channels pretty quickly. You will need to make sure that the opening scene grabs the audience enough to stay with you.
2   **Set up expectations in the audience:** The opening title sequence will set up expectations in the viewer in a number of respects: the genre of film, comedy, thriller, etc. It will to some extent set up expectations about the *mise-en-scène*. It may set up expectations of the character; this doesn't mean that the main characters *have* to be in the opening scene but it should somehow prepare the audience.

3  **Start the first element of narrative structure:** The opening scene will also start the first stage of the narrative structure. It will start to establish the status quo. What is the position of the main character at the start of the story, the position he or she is in before the inciting incident happens?

**Credits:** Opening title sequences often also carry some information about the film itself, the title credits. They might give you the names of the cast or director. Films vary in terms of what kind of information they give but almost invariably they tell you the name of the production company or companies at the top of the film. Even very well-established brands like the Harry Potter films start with the Warner Brothers logo. The placing of the title sequences will vary: some films open with the title sequence, others simply start with the opening scene of the film and the titles run over the opening titles, while some are a mixture of the two.

 If you log onto the website you will see a number of links to opening sequences that can be broken down into component parts. When you watch the sequences you should start to think about what the film is trying to establish in terms of narrative elements and how they are conveyed. You should also look at the ways of setting up the status quo. What are they trying to establish about the character/s which you might need to know before the inciting incident?

## Structure of factual pieces

There are a number of different types of factual programmes. They break down into four main groups:

1  **Magazine formats**: This kind of programme can cover any type of content. Typically it will have a studio presenter and then a number of filmed inserts. The insert may be on different topics or based around a theme.
2  **Specialist documentary:** This type of documentary is longer, perhaps between 30 and 60 minutes. It may or may not have a presenter but it will all be on the same topic. It could be a one-off or it could be part of a series on a particular topic. Natural history programmes are an example of this type of format.
3  **Observational:** This type of documentary sometimes doesn't have a narrator at all or the narration is very minimal. It is the kind of slice-of-life type of documentary.
4  **Factual entertainment:** Lighter types of programmes, sometimes in a 'game' format.

There are of course many other types that don't fall specifically into any of these groups.

On the surface it may not seem to you that the issues raised about story structure apply to factual pieces. Certainly the theorists tend to be talking about fiction when they are making these points. This is not meant to imply that making a factual piece is the same as making a piece of drama, but it is interesting to try to apply some of the points about story structure to a factual piece. It's quite common to hear journalists talking about their "story". But other types of factual programme-makers also think in terms of a story, from factual entertainment shows to feature-length documentaries; the film-makers always try to create a narrative for the piece.

Why should factual programmes need to have a story? Well, put simply, viewers are more engaged by stories than they are just by being given straightforward pieces of information. We also tend to remember things better. We like to hear of characters, we like a bit of tension in a story, and we like a resolution.

If you are making a factual piece then it's possible that your viewers may not know anything about the subject or indeed they may not even be that interested. Your job is to make them interested and keep them engaged, so factual programme-makers tend to use narrative devices to grab and keep our attention.

Factual programme-makers often talk about the narrative structure in a similar manner to the way writers do for fiction. Like fictional story structure there are various theories, but they all follow similar lines, some more complicated than others, but here is a basic model. If you log onto the website you will be able to see some examples.

## Template 6.3  Structure of factual pieces

| | |
|---|---|
| **Tease** | The programme-maker is trying to get the audience interested in the film. They try to tell the audience why they should stay with the film. |
| | It should set up the background and some characters in the film. |
| | It should set up some kind of anticipation, challenge, quest, puzzle or conflict that the viewer will find interesting and that will be resolved. |
| **Main piece** | This is usually the main body of the film. It sets out the argument, gives you the narrative and contains all the contributions from interviewees, etc. |
| **Conclusion** | This finishes the story and is probably some kind of recap, and answers any questions set up in the tease. |

Some film-makers will go further than this; they like to think of the body of the piece as having the same elements as a drama. They talk in terms of acts and reversal; this tends to be used for longer form documentaries As a student making a project, you are unlikely to be expected to make a long film. You are likely to be asked to make a much shorter piece, perhaps an item in a programme with a magazine format.

If you log onto the website you can see an example of this kind of factual piece and some  notes on how the item is structured.

Just as with fiction you can weave a number of different elements around this basic structure. To have a look at some of these different types of programmes you will need to refer to the website and follow the links provided.

| | | |
|---|---|---|
| **The plot and topic** | **The facts** | The actual story you are trying to tell. What kind of programme is it? |
| **Genre** | **The type of programme** | Lifestyle, consumer, investigative, arts, natural history, science. |

| Setting | Where is this happening? | This is largely determined by the story. |
|---|---|---|
| Characters: | The presenter | Will your presenter be in vision or just a voice-over? Should it be a celebrity, a journalist or an expert? Some pieces won't have a voice-over at all. Many observational documentaries use this technique. |
| | The contributors | Experts, witnesses, people affected by events, sometimes the object of an investigation. |
| The theme | Underlying message | Observational documentaries in particular tend to have an underlying theme to them. |

## Structure of a music video

Of all the forms included in this chapter, music videos have the most flexibility in their structure. In all of the above forms there is some kind of linear structure. There are of course many artists who subvert or play with conventional structures but they all tend to at least start with an understanding of what the structure is.

With a music video you are doing something slightly different. You are showcasing a piece of music. The music will be the starting place for all your decisions. However, it is possible to loosely group different types of music video. You can log onto the website if you want see some examples of the different types of music video.

## Template 6.4  Types of music video

| Performance-based video | This type of music video is based around the performance of the artist or band. |
|---|---|
| Narrative-/story-based music videos | This type of video will have a definite story in it. The story will have a beginning, middle and end. The story may be connected to the lyrics of the song but isn't necessarily. |
| Concept | The video does not use narrative, but uses an idea, impressionistic visuals and sometimes animation to carry the music. |
| Mixture | Most videos are some sort of combination of these three types of video. |

When you start to think about your music video you will more than likely begin with the music itself. You will probably start by choosing the music you want to use. The next thing you could think about is which type of music video you want to create. Do you want something which tells the story of the song or is it more impressionistic? To what extent do you want to feature the artists? This will help you anchor the basic structure of your video.

From this point you then need to start thinking about all the other elements which you might weave around the basic structure. How you do this will depend on which structure you intend to follow.

The other elements you will need to weave around it are as follows:

- **Location:** Where are you going to set the piece? If it's a narrative structure then this is obviously going to feature more prominently than if the piece has heavy graphic treatment. However, if it's a performance-based piece then location will be very important.
- **Shooting and editing style:** This will very much depend on the type of music and the type of structure you have chosen. There are examples of very simple shooting styles for a performance-based music video. Other types of video have a very much more complex shooting style. The videos use a variety of different sizes, angles and movement in the shots. Some videos use devices like high- and low-angle shots and crash zooms, and whip pans. Other videos will use a more lyrical, gentler style. A lot will depend on the type of music. The main thing is that the style of camera work you use should complement and enhance the music, not jar with it.
- **Characters:** If there is a narrative element to the video which involves more than the artists, you will need to start thinking about who the other characters in the video are.
- **Artwork:** If you are going for a more concept-based video you are going to need to spend a lot of time on the artwork. You will need to storyboard each individual shot and think about how you are going to achieve the look. It is likely to be a combination of how you shoot the piece and what effects you use afterwards in the edit. However, if you take this approach you may end up with something a little incoherent. You will need to do a number of test shoots to see how the material looks when it's treated and what you need to do to get the best effects. Putting the time in before the shoot will save you an enormous amount of headaches later.

If you log onto the website you can follow links to a number of different music videos giving you a variety of different styles.

## Conclusion

Understanding the component parts of your piece will help you construct your own material. It will help you to start thinking about how to put the piece together and you will find it much easier to get a flow into your piece. When it comes to the edit, having a strong structure in mind will be invaluable. You will have the backbone of your piece ready and the edit will start to knit together around this structure. The structure also helps you in the recording. You will know the main elements you need to tell your story. Time spent working out your structure will mean more time on the shoot, at the recording and in the edit to be creative.

# 7   Advertising

Advertising, whether on radio or TV, involves the same kinds of production techniques you would use for other types of film-making. However, advertising does involve a different kind of preparation. This chapter deals with how to approach your project if you have been tasked with making an advertisement.

## Structure of advertising

Advertising is similar to a film trail in that the film-maker is trying to persuade you to buy something and has only a short space of time in which to do it. Advertising is often studied in terms of semiotics (signs or symbols). Students often study things like target audience, and how lighting, sound, music and even typeface affect the viewer.

These are all very important aspects of advertising; however, this chapter will look at some advertisements in a slightly different way, not because the others are wrong but because this breakdown may help you think about how to structure your own work. To get the best out of this chapter you will need to use it in conjunction with the website.

## Twelve types of advertising

In 1978 advertising guru Donald Gunn created a list of different styles of advertisements. Some of these are instantly recognisable; others take a little more thinking about. However, they do cover virtually all the types of advertisement you are likely to see.

If you log onto the website you will be able to follow the links to see the different types of advertisement.

| Demo | This is probably the simplest form. The ad simply demonstrates what the product can do. |
|---|---|
| The problem | In this type of ad the viewer is shown some sort of a problem. The advertisement then goes on to show the consumer how this product solves the problem. |
| Symbolise the problem | This is the same as the last one but in this kind of ad, the problem is exaggerated or symbolised somehow. It is designed to make the point to the consumer more forcefully. |

| Symbolise the benefit | Again similar to the last type of ad but this time, instead of symbolising the problem you symbolise or exaggerate the solution. Again the idea is to make the product memorable. |
|---|---|
| Comparison | In this kind of ad one product is compared to another product. It emphasises the superiority of one over the other. |
| Exemplary story | In this ad there is a mini-story or narrative going on. The story gives the consumers an example of how the product is going to help them. |
| Benefit causes story | This is a kind of back-to-front story. You see the benefits of the product before you actually know what it is; this happens in a reveal at the end. |
| Presenter or testimonial ads | This kind of ad has someone telling us about the personal benefits they got from the product. It may be a celebrity or it may be an actor or just an ordinary punter. |
| Ongoing character or celebrity | These kinds of ads are like mini-soap operas. They are a series of ads featuring the same characters in different situations. Usually each situation is resolved by using the product that is being advertised. |
| Associated user imagery | This kind of ad features the types of people or situations with which the advertisers think the audience would like to associate themselves. There is no benefit to the product featured and no celebrity endorsement, but by associating the product with something to which they think the user will aspire, the advertisers create a positive feel about the product. |
| Unique personality property | This kind of advert describes something which is unique to this product. No other product has the same features. The types of features could be something practical, it does something no one else does, it could be aesthetic, it could be something about where the product is made, or how much you can trust the maker. |
| Parody | This type of ad parodies either some other kind of ad or some kind of TV show. |

So, what is the point of telling you all this? Looking at advertisements in this way is a little like looking at story structure in Chapter 6. Just as with a story structure you can weave an almost infinite number of plots, characters and settings around a basic structure, with an advertisement you can choose one of these structures to advertise any number of products.

## What is your product and what is the message?

Advertisers spend a lot of time and money on market research. This is to help them discover what the consumers already think about the product, what they think about other similar products, what they want from a product and a whole range of other information the agencies need to create the advertisement.

You are unlikely to have time to do this kind of research for real; however, you should give some thought as to the message you want to get across to your consumers. What are you trying to tell the consumers about your product? If you keep in mind the different types of advertisements it will help you decide. What are the benefits of the product; what is its unique selling point (USP)? Are you trying to associate the product with something aspirational; for example, being rich, being intelligent, being popular?

Unless you know the central message you are trying to get across you won't be able to create an effective advertisement.

## Target audience: who are you making the ad for?

Think about the purpose of an advertisement:

* It is meant to persuade viewers/listeners to buy a product or service.
* It is meant to associate the product or service with something positive.

Whatever type of advertisement, radio or TV, the most important thing to know is who your consumer is. Advertisements are targeted much more specifically to particular groups of people than many TV or radio programmes. At peak times in the evening, for example, a broadcaster is trying to get as many people as possible watching the channel. It therefore makes sense to go for the widest audience possible. Advertisers spend a lot of time and money finding out about their consumers and target their advertisements much more specifically.

For your project you could start by writing out a consumer profile. Who do you think is most likely to buy this product? It may be more than one type of person. However, if you have a profile like this you will start to build a mental picture of who you are aiming your product at. Some people even draw pictures of likely consumers and have them in view. It keeps everyone focused on who they are addressing. It will be useful to add this to your production folder and it will be an important part of the evaluation process.

So imagine an advertisement for a new deodorant aimed at young teenage boys. Your consumer profile might be something like this:

> *Joe is 13 years old. He enjoys sport at school but isn't a fanatic. He's into action computer games but plays mainly with his friends. He likes music and is keen to know what it's cool to like, as he tends to follow trends. Joe doesn't watch much TV but the programmes he likes he's loyal to; he's keen on teen dramas. He doesn't have a girlfriend and nor do any of his friends, but he is self-conscious about how he appears to girls and in particular about the way they think he looks. He takes quite a lot of care over his personal hygiene, but doesn't like products which would make him look feminine. His parents make most of the buying decisions but he has some influence and will use his own money to buy something he really wants.*

Here are some questions you might want to ask yourself when you create your profile for your own advertisement. You can download a blank sheet from the website. There are probably lots of other questions you could ask but these will get you started.

## Template 7.1 Consumer profile

| | | |
|---|---|---|
| **Product** | A quick reminder of what you are trying to sell. | |
| **Who are they?** | What kind of person is buying the product? | |
| **What do they do?** | You don't need to be exact – you are trying to envisage whether they are students, at school, whether they have a job and if so, what sort of level of income. | |
| **Where do they live?** | This may or may not be important. | |
| **Who do they live with?** | Again this may or may not be important but you are thinking about who makes the financial decisions. | |
| **What do they like to do?** | What kinds of social activities might they enjoy? Are they internet savvy? Again you don't have to be very specific – just ask if they like music, sport, arts, etc. Are they busy people or do they have a lot of free time? | |
| **How do they shop?** | Do they like particular brands or do they pick and mix, do they shop on the internet or go out shopping? Do they like browsing or do they only shop when they have something specific that they want? | |

Remember: You need to distinguish here between the consumers and the characters in the advertisements; they will not necessarily be the same person. You might use aspirational characters, people who you think the consumer would like to emulate.

## How are you going to tell the story?

Once you've decided *what* you want to say and *who* you want to say it to, then you need to decide *how* you are going to say it. If you look at the different types of advertising it should start to give you some ideas. However, don't be fooled into thinking that the simple ads are less effective. A strong, simple, powerful message is what you are after.

If you are advertising on radio you will only have words, music and sound. You won't have any images to convey information quickly. You may find that if you start to go for something too complicated the audience will lose the plot and your advertising will be ineffective.

You will have to start to think about who or what you are going to use to tell the story. Remember: whether in vision or just the voice-over, the character you choose to tell the story must be appealing to your target audience. It doesn't have to *be* the target audience but it has to be a character they understand and have an empathy with.

## TV advertising: copy

Your copy is the words you are going to use with the pictures. You need to be thinking about these at the same time as you are making up the story. Your copy may be a voice-over or it may be spoken by the characters in the advertisement. But whichever way, you need to be thinking about what you are going to say as well as about what you're going to see or hear.

Writing advertising copy is a very skilled task; however, one structure is the familiar persuasive writing structure:

- Open with the problem or the issue
- Explain the solution
- End with a slogan or call to action.

**Slogan:** You will need to think in particular about the last lines. Adverts often end with a slogan or memorable line that everyone associates with the product.

Good slogans are very hard to write but, just like the ads themselves. there are a number of different types. The following is a list of some of the types of slogans that are often used.

**Call to action:** Sometimes advertisements end with a **call to action**. This is where the advertisers tells the consumers what they want them to do:

- *Hurry, buy now while stocks last*
- *Offer ends Monday.*

Other calls to action are slightly less obvious:

- *Let the train take the strain.*

**USP:** Sometimes they end with the unique selling point (USP):

- *The world's only . . .*
- *Only hair gel to make it through the night. . . .*

**Benefit:** Sometimes it ends by reminding viewers of the benefit:

- *Brings the sparkle back to tired eyes. . . .*

**Rhyme alliteration:** You can use rhyme or alliteration to add punch to the ad:

*   *Tricos – The tastiest taco in town.*

**Aspirational:** Sometimes the slogan can be more aspirational and not specifically relate to the product. Nike had a slogan *Just do it.* . . . This slogan was a call to action but not directly to buy the product. It was more aspirational, associating the slogan with the power and determination of the athletes the advertisement featured.

Not all advertising copy follows this structure and it will only work for some types of advertisement; however, it offers a basic way of thinking about your copy.

## Radio advertising

Radio advertising is likely to involve the same production techniques as radio drama and you will find a lot of information in the chapter about microphones, FX and recording technique. Radio advertising, like TV, is generally very short. Thirty seconds is a common length for a radio advertisement and generally they won't be longer than 90 seconds. You therefore have to compress everything to get your message across in the time available.

A radio ad will follow the same initial processes as a TV ad. You need to know your target audience. You also need to know which radio station is the right place to advertise. Radio stations tend to have a quite specific audience, much more so than terrestrial TV and even the digital channels. So you need to be sure that the type of product you are trying to advertise will appeal to the people who are likely to be listening to that radio station.

If you log onto the website you will find some links to a large selection of radio advertise-ments. You should listen to a number of them so that you can get a sense of the types of production techniques employed.

## Writing the ad

Clearly, the wording of the ad is critical for a radio commercial; here are some tips to think about.

**Simple concepts:** You can convey a lot very quickly with pictures; on radio you are using sound only. If your idea is too complex it may well get lost in the short time you have to get the message across. Some of the complicated ideas you get in TV and film advertising aren't going to work so well on radio.

**Talk to one person:** You are talking to one person, not a big group of people. When you write the script have an image of your listener in mind.

**Keep the language simple:**

*   Keep the sentence construction simple; sentences should be short and punchy.
*   Keep active tense not passive tense.
*   Don't use complicated words or jargon.

**Name the product:** Again you have no pack shot so you need to make sure that the name of the product is clear and repeated several times during the ad.

**Call to action:** Since you don't have a pack shot in radio a clear call to action at the end of the ad or a clear slogan is essential. You need to end your ad by telling the listeners where they can buy the product, websites, any dates – *offer ends Monday* type of thing.

**Pacing:** You have only a short amount of time, so the temptation is to pace the ad very quickly; however, too much information and you will lose your listeners. If they lose track of what you are saying then they have no way of catching up and will just tune out.

## Music, effects and voice-over

- **Effects (FX):** It's perfectly possible and quite common to use music and effects in a radio commercial. However, unlike longer pieces you don't have very much time with your audience. If you are going to use music and FX then they need to be established very quickly. You cannot have complicated FX which involve the audience having to think too hard or they will miss the point of the ad.
- **Music:** Music has an immediate power; it can very quickly establish mood and genre. You just need to watch that you are not doing anything that jars with the sound of the station. You will also need to have a good idea of what kind of music the audience is listening to. If it's a station which predominantly plays easy listening, the kind of Golden-Oldie station, then there is really no point in creating an ad which uses the latest indie band. It won't meet with audience expectations and is likely to cause confusion, even create hostility to the product.
- **Voice-over:** Clearly very important in a radio ad. You need to cast the voice-over to appeal to your target consumer. The style of presentation needs to feel right for the product as well. A loud, aggressive, masculine voice is not going to be a natural fit if you are advertising mascara to a group of 14-year-old girls.

## Conclusion

Preparing your treatment for your radio or TV advertisement involves being clear about what you are selling and who you are selling it to. Advertisements tend to be targeted at a very specific group of people. Unlike film/TV/radio, advertisers tend to be as much concerned about who they are talking to as the sheer number of people they are talking to. To structure a successful ad you need to know *what* you are selling, *who* you are selling it to and *how* you want to make the pitch.

# 8 Scripts and treatments

By now you will have come up with your idea and you have done some research. If it's a factual piece, you will have spoken to people who might be in production and you have been to the places you think you might film in. If it's a music video or an advertisement you will have visited locations and thought about your cast. You have also had a good look at some examples of the types of material you are trying to make. You have started to think about how you are going to structure the piece. You should by now have a good idea of the framework for your project and what elements you are going to start to hang around the framework.

Now it's time to do a treatment. There are many different types of treatment and they will all have particular functions. Often broadcasters or film-makers prepare treatments of their script as a way of trying to pitch the idea. In this case the treatment is a kind of synopsis of the piece but it is also trying to sell the idea to someone.

Other types of treatment help you prepare for your recording or shoot and this is the type of treatment dealt with in this chapter. A treatment is the process of working out on paper exactly what you are going to film or record, and starting to gather all the information together.

The type of treatment you do will rather depend upon the type of production; different genres of productions often use different types of treatment. There are no hard and fast rules about this and you can use whatever type of treatment you feel most comfortable with, but the following will give you some guidelines.

Treatments are similar to plans. The end result is rarely exactly like the treatment. Almost all productions evolve in the process. So, why do one? Well, it will help you understand certain things about your piece:

- The structure and narrative of your piece
- The number of locations (places) you will have to visit
- How many cast members you will need
- How many interviewees/contributors
- How long the piece is going to be
- Have I got too much to do?
- Have I forgotten something?
- Is there anything I need to get permission for?
- Do I need props/costumes?

From this you will begin to understand how much time you will need to do your filming or recording and it will help you get to grips with the logistics.

The following are the different types of treatments you can employ. Not all of them are right for every project; you will need to choose the one that best suits your project.

## Treatments for drama/trailer/ads/music video

If your production is dramatised, there are two main types of treatment that will help you work out what you need to do.

1   The storyboard
2   The scene breakdown.

However, in the case of a dramatised piece, you will need to have a script before you can do either of these treatments.

## Script

Clearly, if you want a cast to act out a drama they need to know what to say. However, a script will also help you to think about other aspects of the production:

- Where is each scene to be set and how many locations are there?
- What type of action is there going to be?
- What do the cast look like and what are they wearing?
- What effects or props will I need?

### *Script layout*

Below is an example of how to lay out a drama for TV. If you log onto the website you can download a copy; you will also find lots more examples. Have a look at them to see how they are set out.

## Template 8.1  TV script

| Scene 1 |
|---|
| <u>INTERIOR:</u><br>AN EMPTY CLASSROOM. A TEENAGE BOY IS SITTING AT A DESK, READING A LETTER. HE IS NEATLY DRESSED – HIS HAIR IS SHORT. HE HAS A SLIGHTLY GEEKY LOOK TO HIM. THE DOOR OPENS AND A TEENAGE GIRL ENTERS. SHE IS STYLISHLY DRESSED AND OBVIOUSLY HAS GOOD FASHION SENSE. SHE IS ANXIOUS AND IN A HURRY. THE BOY JUMPS AND LOOKS ALARMED WHEN HE SEES THE GIRL AND HURRIEDLY TRIES TO HIDE THE LETTER. |
| <div align="center"><u>1. FLORENCE:</u><br>There you are. What are you doing?</div> |

2. JAKE:
Nothing.

3. FLORENCE:
Are you coming?

4. JAKE:
No.

FLORENCE WALKS OVER TO THE DESK AND SITS DOWN.

5. FLORENCE:
What were you reading?

6. JAKE:
Nothing.

7. FLORENCE:
Show me.

JAKE RELUCTANTLY UNCOVERS THE LETTER. FLORENCE TAKES A LOOK AT IT.

8. FLORENCE:
Oh my god! Where did you get this?

9. JAKE:
Someone sent it to me.

10. FLORENCE:
Who?

11. JAKE:
How should I know? It was just in my bag.

12. FLORENCE:
Jake, please, listen to me, you can't let this sort of thing get to you.
People who send letters like this – they are just ignorant.

13. JAKE:
But it does get to me – I can't help it – it's easy just to say to ignore it but if it was
happening to you – you wouldn't be able to ignore it.

FLORENCE SCREWS UP THE LETTER.

14. FLORENCE:
It's just crap – leave it – don't think about it.

| |
|---|
| FLORENCE STANDS UP. |
| <u>15.  FLORENCE:</u><br>Come on, let's go. |
| <u>16.  JAKE:</u><br>No – I'm going to stay here. |
| <u>17.  FLORENCE:</u><br>Suit yourself – but you're an idiot if you let this kind of thing stop you doing the things you want to do. |
| FLORENCE WALKS OUT OF THE ROOM, CLOSING THE DOOR BEHIND HER. JAKE STOOPS TO PICK UP THE CRUMPLED LETTER. |

## Template 8.2  Radio script

| Scene 1 | |
|---|---|
| | <u>FADE UP ATMOS: Empty School classroom; sounds of a football match being played outside in the distance.</u><br><br><u>Jake is reading a letter to himself under his breath.</u><br><br><u>FX Door opens.</u> |
| <u>1.  FLORENCE:</u> | OFF MIC: There you are. What are you doing? |
| <u>2.  JAKE:</u> | Nothing. |
| <u>3.  FLORENCE:</u> | APPROACHING MIC: Are you coming? |
| <u>4.  JAKE:</u> | No. |
| | FX: CHAIR SCRAPING AS FLORENCE SITS DOWN. |
| <u>5.  FLORENCE:</u> | What were you reading? |
| <u>6.  JAKE:</u> | Nothing. |
| <u>7.  FLORENCE:</u> | Show me. |
| | FX: PAPER BEING RUSTLED. |

| 8. FLORENCE: | Oh my god! Where did you get this? |
|---|---|
| 9. JAKE: | Someone sent it to me. |
| 10. FLORENCE: | Who? |
| 11. JAKE: | How should I know? it was just in my bag. |
| 12. FLORENCE: | Jake, please, listen to me, you can't let this sort of thing get to you. People who send letters like this – they are just ignorant. |
| 13. JAKE: | But it does get to me – I can't help it – it's easy just to say to ignore it but if it was happening to you – you wouldn't be able to ignore it. |
| | FX: LETTER BEING CRUMPLED UP. |
| 14. FLORENCE: | It's just crap – leave it – don't think about it. |
| | FX: CHAIR SCRAPING AS FLORENCE STANDS UP. |
| 15. FLORENCE: | Come on, let's go. |
| 16. JAKE: | No – I'm going to stay here. |
| 17. FLORENCE: | Suit yourself – but you're an idiot if you let this kind of thing stop you doing the things you want to do. MOVING OFF MIC. |
| | FX: DOOR SLAMMING. |

There are a number of things you might notice. First, each of the scenes is given a number, and sometimes each of the speeches is given a number. This is important; it helps everyone know where they are in the script. It means that if you are making notes or talking to actors or crew about a particular part of the script you can refer to the number and everyone knows exactly what you mean.

You should also notice that the writer hasn't just written the dialogue. A lot of the writing is telling you what the characters look like, what the scenery looks like and what the characters are doing. In the case of the radio script it tells you what sounds you are hearing.

## Storyboards (TV only)

Once you have a script organised, the second stage of your treatment could be a storyboard. Storyboards are most often used in music videos or advertisements. They are sometimes used in drama but they aren't very often used in factual programme-making, documentaries or news reporting, but that's not to say you can't use them for this if you want to; in fact it may be helpful.

Storyboards are very useful to help you think about what kinds of shots you are going to need and getting a sense of how the story should start to look. They will help the cameraperson understand what the director has in mind.

You can find links to some more examples of storyboards if you log onto the website. These are mostly done by professional storyboard artists. However, don't be put off if you think your drawing skills aren't up to it. You don't need to be a brilliant artist: stick men will do. Alternatively, a lot of people now use animatics to create a storyboard. Below is an example of a blank storyboard, and you can also download a blank storyboard from the website.

### Template 8.3  Blank storyboard

### STORYBOARD

Script title

### Scene:

| Action | Action | Action | Action |
|---|---|---|---|
|  |  |  |  |
| *Dialogue* | *Dialogue* | *Dialogue* | *Dialogue* |

| Shot size | Shot size | Shot size | Shot size |
|---|---|---|---|
|  |  |  |  |
| *Dialogue* | *Dialogue* | *Dialogue* | *Dialogue* |

The storyboard is just a *tool* to help you think through what you might film. Just like your plan, your finished film may not work out exactly as the storyboard said it should, and this is fine! The purpose of a storyboard is to help you think things through and get you prepared; it is not meant to be a finished work of art.

The purpose of the storyboard is so that you work out:

- What shots you are going to need
- Size of the shots
- Angle of the shots

- Moves on the shots
- Depth of field.

Like everything else, this storyboard is going to change and develop when you actually come to the shoot, but if you at least start with a good idea in your head you will have a fighting chance of getting what you need.

Below you can see an example of a blank storyboard to cover some of the script you've just seen. As you'll notice, you really don't have to be a great artist.

## Template 8.4  Completed storyboard

### Script title: The letter

### Scene 3

## Scene breakdown

The last element of your treatment you may want to think about is a scene breakdown. If there is more than one scene in your piece, this will help you decide on the order in which you are going to film the piece and who and what you will need when. You will need to think about how many locations you will need to visit and how much time you will need to allocate to each location. Remember that moving between locations can be time consuming. There is the time it takes to travel from one place to another but there is also the time involved in setting up a scene and then striking (taking everything down and packing it up). You should also allow time to do this. You will also then begin to think of the lists of costumes and props that you are going to need.

If you are planning a radio drama then the scene breakdown will help you work out all the elements you will need to bring to the studio when you mix your programme. It will also help you decide how long you will need to record the piece.

The scene breakdown becomes a sort of timetable that you can work to. So, for example, go back to the Jake and Florence story. Imagine you are going to shoot or record four scenes. A scene breakdown helps you to make the most of your time and helps everyone understand who needs to be where when and what they need to bring.

## Template 8.5  Scene breakdown

| Day | Scene numbers | Location | Cast | Props/costumes |
|-----|---------------|----------|------|----------------|
| **Day 1** Thurs 15th March | Scene 1 | Classroom | Florence and Jake | Letter |
| | Scene 3 | School grounds | Jake and Ian | iPods/mobile phones |
| **Day 2** Friday 16th March | Scene 2 | Exterior: park by gate | Florence and Annie | Jeans and T-shirt Football/kite |
| | Scene 4 | Interior: kitchen | Jake and Ian | Pyjamas Kettle/toast/butter |

## Factual programmes: outline or treatment (radio or TV)

In a factual programme the process is different. You won't have a final script until later. The final script won't appear until you are in the edit. However, you can start to create outline scripts or treatments, sometimes called shooting scripts, which are commonly used in factual programmes to help producers prepare. This time you will write down in note form what you are going to see and hear in the film, and the order in which it will appear.

You will see that the page is divided into two columns. On the left you will write down what the viewer or listener is going to hear. On the right you will write down what they are going to see. In the case of a radio recording you should write down any actuality sound. This is any sound which is not people talking but is the sounds you hear around you. Again you should divide your piece up into scenes. Pay equal attention to each of the columns. Even in factual programmes TV is a visual medium, the visuals are very powerful and you need to think about building up meaningful sequences. In radio, a piece which is just people talking can get a bit dull: you will need to think about how else you might be able to create a picture in the listeners' minds, help them to feel a part of the piece.

Just like with the storyboard, don't get too hung up on getting this exactly right. Very few finished programmes end up exactly like the outline script; they all change and develop as the process continues.

If you are making a TV programme the outline script will help you think through what kinds of pictures you are going to need to achieve; it's going to help you understand how many locations you will need to visit. It will also start to help you understand how much filming you are going to have to do, and it will start to tell you if you have taken on too much or if you have forgotten something. The same with radio: it will help you understand the number of locations you will have to visit, what kinds of sounds you are going to need to get hold of.

### What should go into an outline?

- **Structure:** The outline should reflect your story structure. It should convey a good sense of what the narrative is going to be.
- **Contributors:** It should also indicate what the main contributors are going to say. You don't need to put this down word for word, you haven't interviewed them yet. However, you should have done your research and have a good idea of what each person is going to talk about, and you should put this down even if just in note form.
- **Visuals:** In terms of the visuals, it doesn't need to be as detailed as a storyboard but it should indicate what kinds of visuals you will be looking at for each segment. Writing a treatment forces you to think about your visuals.
- **Actuality sound:** The same is true on radio for actuality sound. You should be thinking about this at the same time as the interviews. It will give a lot of colour to the piece. You should also make a note of any *must-have* sequences, shots or recordings.
- **Voice-over:** This is not the place for your polished and finished script. However, you will want to give an indication of what the voice-over is going to be saying. Don't spend too long getting every word right; just jot down a brief idea of what will be said.

An outline is not meant to be a finished script, it is not word for word what will be in the piece; as the name *outline* implies, it's a sketch of what will be in the production when it's finished. Below is an example of an outline. If you log onto the website you'll find a copy you can download.

## Template 8.6 Radio treatment

**Festival Fever**

*Each year thousands and thousands of tents are abandoned at festivals across the country as festival-goers, weary from the exertions of the parties, find the effort of packing up their tents too much to handle. The piece reports on the environmental damage caused by the vast amounts of debris left by festival-goers and the attempts of one company to make a difference. Karen Ellis reports from the Elusive Festival in Oxfordshire.*

| *SOUND FX* | *LINKS/INTERVIEWEES* |
|---|---|
| Actuality sound from the festival. Music from bands playing.<br><br>FX: sounds of crowds. | **Intro** *Voice-over will give us the details of how may festivals happen in Britain, how many people attend and what kind of environmental damage that causes. Some of the reasons why there is so much waste, the problem with mud and the difficulty of moving around.* |
| **Actuality sound:**<br>Breakfast cooking/pots and pans, etc.<br>Rolling up sleeping bags, cleaning. | **Vox pops – families, groups of teenagers**<br><br>*Describe experiences in the past. Describe how they cope with mud. Tell us how much they have to leave behind.* |
| | **Presenter link**<br>*Explains the difficulty left with organisers at the end of the festival and how they attempt to deal with the waste.* |
| **Actuality sound**<br>Interior of office, phones, computer hum, etc. | **Interview Russell Jones, Festival Manager**<br>*Explains the way in which he clears up. Litter is handpicked – it takes five weeks to clear the litter.*<br><br>*Explains how he tried to recycle but it was going to cost him too much to recycle the material.*<br><br>*Explains that the waste is taken to the recycling centre.* |

| SOUND FX | LINKS/INTERVIEWEES |
|---|---|
| **Actuality sound**<br>Festival in progress, footsteps in mud. Litter going into the bag. | **Vox pops – litter pickers**<br>*We find the litter pickers doing their job. They start cleaning well before the festival ends and carry on for five weeks. They describe what kinds of things people leave behind and what they do with it.* |
| **Actuality sound**<br>Abingdon Recycling Centre: heavy machinery crushing waste. | **Presenter link**<br>Tells us how the waste ends up at the recycling centre. Tells us what happens to material and how much can be recycled. |
| **Actuality sound**<br>Waste being loaded into the machine. | **Vox pops – recycling staff**<br>*Discuss the kinds of things they have seen thrown away.* |
| **Actuality sound**<br>Interior of office. | **Interview – Christine Adamson**<br>Abingdon Recycling.<br>*Christine explains how much of the material has to be burnt.* |
| **Actuality sound**<br>Festival in progress. | **Presenter link**<br>*Explains that attempts are being made to develop ways of dealing with the problem.* |
| **Actuality sound**<br>Alex putting up the tent. | **Interview – Alex Smith**<br>Greener Festival Lobby.<br>*Explains the way in which they are developing new types of tents which will compost.*<br>*Explains that the tents are made out of toughened seaweed.*<br>*Explains how they work and demonstrates how quickly they can break down.* |
| **Actuality sound**<br>Interior of the tent – getting beds sorted out. | **Presenter link/interview with volunteers**<br>*Invites festival attendees to try out the tent overnight. Asks the volunteers what they think of the tent. Leaves them for the night.* |

| SOUND FX | LINKS/INTERVIEWEES |
|---|---|
|  | **Interview volunteers** <br> *Volunteers tell us how they enjoyed a night in the seaweed tent.* |
| **Actuality sound** <br> Festival in progress. | **Presenter link** <br> *Sums up the story.* |

## Template 8.7  Television treatment

**Festival Fever**

*Each year thousands and thousands of tents are abandoned at festivals across the country as festival-goers, weary from the exertions of the parties, find the effort of packing up tents too much to handle. The piece reports on the environmental damage caused by the vast amounts of debris left by festival goers and the attempts of one company to make a difference. Karen Ellis reports from the Elusive Festival in Oxfordshire.*

| Visuals | VO (voice-over) |
|---|---|
| **GVs** (general views) Secret Garden Festival. Bands,different types of entertainment. <br> **WS** (wide shot) from lookout tower to show extent of the festival and the numbers of tents pan left to reveal Karen. | **Presenter voice-over** <br> *Voice over will give us the details of how many festivals happen in Britain, how many people attend and what kind of environmental damage that causes.* |
| Karen is in the middle of the festival – surrounded by tents and party-goers. | **Presenter PTC (piece to camera)** <br> *Some of the reasons why there is so much waste, the problem with mud and the difficulty of moving around.* |
| We meet the festival-goers as they are having breakfast, cleaning out tents, etc. | **Vox pops – families, groups of teenagers** <br><br> *Describe experiences in the past. Describe how they cope with mud. Tell us how much they have to leave behind.* |

| Visuals | VO (voice-over) |
|---|---|
| **GVs** of last year's festival. People packing up to go.<br><br>**WS** from tower to show the number of tents left. | **Presenter VO**<br>*Explains the difficulty left with organisers at the end of the festival and how they attempt to deal with the waste.* |
| Russell is on observation tower – in the background we can see the vast expanse of the festival behind him | **Interview – Russell Jones, Festival Manager**<br>*Explains the way in which he clears up. Litter is handpicked – takes five weeks to clear the litter.*<br>*Explains how he tried to recycle but it was going to cost him too much to recycle the material.*<br>*Explains that the waste is taken to the recycling centre.* |
| **GVs** picking litter, cleaning toilets, collecting rubbish. | **Vox pops – litter pickers**<br>*We find the litter pickers doing their job. They start cleaning well before the festival ends and carry on for five weeks.*<br>*They describe what kinds of things people leave behind and what they do with it.* |
| We find Karen by a piece of heavy crushing machinery. We see waste being loaded into the crusher – we see a line of vans waiting to unload the waste. | **Presenter PTC – Abingdon Recycling Centre**<br>*Tells us how the waste ends up at the recycling centre. Tells us what happens to material and how much can be recycled.* |
| We see recycling staff as they load material into the crusher. | **Vox pops – recycling staff**<br>*Discuss the kinds of things they have seen thrown away.* |
| We see Christine standing by the incinerator watching material being burnt. | **Interview – Christine Adamson, Abingdon Recycling**<br>*Christine explains how much of the material has to be burnt.* |

| Visuals | VO (voice-over) |
|---|---|
| GVs of festival. | **Presenter VO** *Explains that attempts are being made to develop ways of dealing with the problem.* |
| Alex is standing next to a tent he has erected in one of the outer campsites. | **Interview – Alex Eder, Greener Festival Lobby** *Explains the way in which they are developing new types of tents which will compost. Explains the tents are made out of toughened seaweed. Explains how they work and demonstrates how quickly they can break down.* |
| Karen and volunteers inside the tent. | **Presenter PTC – interview with volunteers** *Invites festival attendees to try out the tent overnight. Asks the volunteers what they think of the tent. Leaves them for the night.* |
| Inside the tent. | **Interview volunteers – Karen and volunteers the next morning** *Volunteers tell us how they enjoyed a night in the seaweed tent.* Karen standing in field after festival has ended. |
| People clearing up in the background. | **Presenter PTC** *Sums up the story.* |

## Conclusion

Treatments are an important part of the production process. Not only do they help to work out the structure of the piece but they help you prepare all the practical elements. You should know what you are planning to do before you start the shoot or recording, rather than try to work it out as you go along. The treatment allows you to think about whether you have a good strong narrative; it is also an important way of allowing you to plan for all the shooting and recording you are going to have to do and all the elements you will need to get together before you record. Treatments are an important part of your production plan.

# 9   Production schedules and safety

By now you should have had your idea, done your research, thought about the structure of your piece and done a treatment. You will have recce'd your locations and spoken to any contributors. You should now be ready to plan your actual recording.

The shooting or recording schedule, sometimes called a running order, is a detailed plan for the day. By now you may be a little impatient about the number of documents you are being asked to prepare. You are keen and eager, and ready to get going, and the thought of another document is making you irritated. It's understandable but in the professional world this is how it is done. Recording days are the most expensive part of a production and for that reason everything is prepared in order to get the best out of the time; you very rarely get a second chance. If you aren't clear about what you are trying to do you will waste time and in the end have less material to edit. Your production will suffer.

## Recording on location

Your research and your treatment should mean that you now have a good idea of how many locations you will need to visit and where they are. The most important document you are going to need to prepare before the shoot is the shooting schedule or recording schedule, sometimes referred to as a call sheet.

This document is designed so that everyone involved in the production knows where they are supposed to be, when they are supposed to be there, what they need to bring and any safety advice (see below). Depending upon what kind of recording it is, factual, news, drama, music video, you will need to include different things.

## Factual recordings

Here are three templates for a recording/shooting schedule suitable for a factual recording: a blank one and two worked examples. If you log onto the website you will be able to print off some blank copies.

# Template 9.1 Factual schedule

| *Production schedule* | | |
|---|---|---|
| **Title** | Title of the piece | |
| **Brief description** | What the piece is about and what you are intending to film | |
| **Dates** | When the recording is taking place | |
| **Production team and contacts** | Director:<br>Camera:<br>Sound: | |
| **Equipment** | What equipment you will need | |
| **Location** | Names of and directions to the locations you intend to visit | |
| **Location contact details** | Name of any person you need to contact at the location | |
| **Contributors** | Anyone you are planning to interview or feature in the shoot | |
| **Timetable** | | |
| **RV** *(rendezvous or meeting place)* | Indicate where and when the production team is to meet up | |

| Travel time | Indicate how you are going to travel to the location if you are not meeting on site | |
|---|---|---|
| Set-up | Indicate when you will arrive at the location and how long you will need to get your equipment organised | |
| Shot list | Indicate what you will be recording or shooting; you should make a list of all the shots you need to get | |
| Break/travel | You should build in some time for a break and, if you need to travel to a different location, time to travel | |
| 2nd location, shot list | Indicate what you will be recording or shooting; you should make a list of all the shots you need to get | |
| Wrap | Indicate when you plan to finish your shoot | |
| De-rig and travel | Indicate how long you think it will take to pack everything away and get back to base if necessary | |

NB: You may have only one location or you may have many. You need to plan out the time for each location.

# Template 9.2  Recording schedule

Here is a worked example of a production schedule for a radio feature.

---

**Festival Fever recording schedule**

Each year, thousands and thousands of tents are abandoned at festivals across the country as festival-goers, weary from the exertions of the parties, find the effort of packing up tents too much to handle. The piece reports on the environmental damage caused and the attempts of one company to make a difference.

| Title | FESTIVAL FEVER | | Notes |
|---|---|---|---|
| **Dates** | 11 June 2012 | | |
| **Location 1** | *Elusive Festival* | Water Down House<br>Horton<br>Oxfordshire | |
| **Location 2** | Compostable<br>Tents Ltd | 38 James Street<br>Islip<br>Oxfordshire | |
| **Location 3** | Abingdon Road<br>Recycling Centre | Abingdon Road<br>Oxford | |
| **Production team and contacts** | Production team | | |
| **Equipment** | Recording device,<br>tapes, etc. if necessary | Theo Barker to bring<br>equipment and tapes | |
| **Contributors** | Alex Eder<br>Compostable Tents Ltd<br><br>Festival Director:<br>Russell Jones<br><br>Christine Adamson<br><br>Abingdon Recycling<br>Centre<br><br>Litter pickers:<br>Elsie Taylor<br>Izzy Piggot | | |

| | |
|---|---|
| **Safety** | Please be aware that recordings will take place in a muddy field, so please bring appropriate footwear.<br><br>Recording will take place around machinery. Crews will be briefed on safety procedures on arrival at the location. |

Timetable

| Date/time | Activity | Who's involved |
|---|---|---|
| **Date** | 11 June | |
| **07:30–08:00** | RV *(rendezvous or meeting place)* : Lexworth Park School, Carterton, Oxfordshire | Producer: Arthur Howe<br>Sound: Theo Barker<br>Presenter: Karen Ellis |
| **08:00–08:30** | Travel to Water Down House, Horton, Oxfordshire | Production team will be travelling by bus. Parking available at the rear of the building. |
| **09:00–09:30** | Presenter of piece: Karen Ellis | Production team |
| **09:30–10:30** | Vox Pop with litter pickers and festival-goers | |
| **10:30–11:30** | Interview with Alex Eder, Festival Director | Production team<br>Alex Eder |
| **11:30–12:00** | Actuality sound recordings – music from festival<br>Sounds of tents loaded into vans<br>Sounds of tents being packed away<br>Sounds of rubbish collection | |
| **12:00–1:00** | Break for lunch | Production team |
| **1:00–1:30** | Travel to Abingdon Recycling Centre | Production team |
| **1:30–2:00** | Presenter of piece: Karen Ellis | Production team |

| Date/time | Activity | Who's involved |
|---|---|---|
| **2:00–2:30** | Interviewees: Christine Adamson, Manager, Abingdon Recycling Centre | Christine Adamson |
| **2:30–3:00** | Actuality sound recording, trucks arriving<br>Crushing machines | |
| **3:00–3:30** | Break | |
| **3:30–4:00** | Travel to Compostable Tents Ltd | Production team |
| **4:00–4:30** | Presenter of piece: Karen Ellis | Production team |
| **4.30–5:00** | Actuality sound machinery, production process, assembly line | |
| **5:00–5:30** | Demo of compostable tent | |
| **5:30–6:00** | Interviewee: Alex Eder | Alex Eder |
| **6:00** | Wrap | |
| **6:00–6:30** | De-rig and travel back to base | Production team |

## Template 9.3  TV shooting schedule

Here is the same story but this time for a filmed piece.

**Festival Fever TV shooting schedule**

Each year, thousands and thousands of tents are abandoned at festivals across the country as festival-goers, weary from the exertions of the parties, find the effort of packing up tents too much to handle. The piece reports on the environmental damage caused and the attempts of one company to make a difference.

| | | | |
|---|---|---|---|
| **Title** | Festival Fever | | |
| **Dates** | 11 June | | |
| **LOCATION 1** | Elusive Festival | Water Down House Horton Oxfordshire | |
| **LOCATION 2** | Compostable Tents Ltd | 38 James Street Islip Oxfordshire | |
| **LOCATION 3** | Abingdon Road Recycling Centre | Abingdon Road Oxford | |
| **PRODUCTION TEAM and CONTACTS** | Director: Arthur Howe Camera: Carolyn Sladen Sound: Theo Barker Presenter: Karen Ellis | | |
| **Equipment** | Camera, tripod, microphone, tapes | Carolyn Sladen and Theo Barker to bring equipment and tapes | |
| **Contributors** | Alex Eder Compostable Tents Ltd  Russell Jones Festival Director  Christine Adamson Abingdon Recycling Centre | | |

| Safety | Please be aware that recordings will take place in a muddy field, so please bring appropriate footwear.<br><br>Recording will take place around machinery. Crews will be briefed on safety procedures on arrival at the location. |
|---|---|

Timetable

| Date/time | Activity | Who's involved |
|---|---|---|
| **Date** | 11 June | |
| **07:30–08:00** | RV (*rendezvous or meeting place*) : Lexworth Park School, Carterton, Oxfordshire | Director: Arthur Howe<br>Camera: Carolyn Sladen<br>Sound: Theo Barker<br>Presenter: Karen Ellis |
| **08:00–08:30** | Travel to Location 1, Water Down House, Horton, Oxfordshire | Production team will be travelling by bus |
| **08:30–09:00** | Set up and rehearse for PTC (piece to camera) on terrace behind house overlooking the field | |
| **09:00–09:30** | Piece to camera (PTC): Karen Ellis | Production team |
| **09.30–10:30** | GVs (general views) of festival site. WS (wide shots) from terrace. GVs of litter pickers.<br><br>MS (mid-shots) and CUs (close-ups) from festival site of abandoned tents<br><br>General views (GVs) of people leaving the festival | |
| **10:30–11:30** | Vox Pop with litter pickers and festival-goers | |
| **11:30–12:00** | Interview with Russell Jones, Festival Director | Russell Jones<br>Production team |

| Date/time | Activity | Who's involved |
|-----------|----------|----------------|
| **12:00–12:30** | Break for lunch | |
| **12:30–1:00** | Travel to Location 2, Abingdon Recycling Centre | Production team |
| **1:00–1:30** | Set up and rehearse piece to camera (PTC) | Production team |
| **1:30–2:00** | Piece to camera (PTC): Karen Ellis | |
| **2:00–2:30** | Interview: Christine Adamson, Manager, Abingdon Recycling Centre | Christine Adamson |
| **2:30–3.00** | GVs Recycling Centre, tents being crushed, trucks arriving with old tents | |
| **3:00–3:30** | Break | |
| **3:30–4:00** | Travel to Location 3, Compostable Tents Ltd | Production team |
| **4:00–4.30** | Set up and rehearse piece to camera (PTC): Karen Ellis | Production team |
| **4.30–5:00** | General views (GVs) compostable tents, machinery, production process, assembly line | |
| **5:00–5:30** | Demo of compostable tent | |
| **5:30–6:00** | Interviewee: Alex Eder | Production team, Alex Eder |
| **6:00** | Wrap | |
| **6:00–6.30** | De-rig and travel back to base | Production team |

## Shooting schedules for drama

Drama shoots tend to be more complicated than factual shoots, since they generally involve more people. They therefore tend to have very detailed and more specialised shooting schedules. This is dealt with in more depth in Chapter 16, 'Shooting dramatsed sequences'. However, your scene breakdown will form the basis of a shooting schedule.

### Template 9.4  Shooting schedules for drama: Jake's Letter

| Title | Jake's Letter | | |
|---|---|---|---|
| Dates | 11 June | | |
| LOCATION 1 | Lexworth Park School | Lexworth Park School<br>Carterton<br>Oxfordshire | |
| LOCATION 2 | North Park | Abingdon Road<br>Oxford | |
| LOCATION 3 | 15 North Street<br>Headington<br>Oxford | | |
| PRODUCTION TEAM and CONTACTS | Director: Arthur Howe<br>Camera: Carolyn Sladen<br>Sound: Theo Barker<br>Cast: Florence James,<br>Jake Anderson,<br>Oliver Foales | | |
| Equipment | Camera, tripod,<br>microphone, tapes | Carolyn Sladen and<br>Theo Barker to bring<br>equipment and tapes | |
| Day 1<br>Thursday,<br>15 March | | Florence and Jake<br>Jake and Ian | Letter<br>iPods/mobile<br>phones |
| Scene 1<br>10:00–1:00 | Classroom | | |
| Scene 4:<br>2:00–5:00 | School grounds | | |

| Day 2<br>Friday,<br>16 March<br><br>Scene 2:<br>10:00–1:00<br><br>Scene 4 | Exterior: park by gate<br>Interior: kitchen | Florence and Annie<br>Jake and Ian | Jeans and T-shirt,<br>Football/kite<br><br>Pyjamas, kettle/<br>toast/butter |
|---|---|---|---|

## Safety and risk assessment

A second important task for the actual shoot day is a risk assessment. Safety is critical on any location recording *everyone* has a responsibility for safety.

In a professional world producers and directors are expected to manage safety on any shoot or recording, and most organisations will set out guidelines and often require staff to attend safety workshops or training. If you are working on an exam piece you are in a slightly different situation. Your school or college will have its own safety procedures. You would be expected to work within those procedures first. You should be aware of any safety requirements laid down by your college and adhere to them. This section looks at how safety would be managed on a professional shoot, but you should always refer in the first instance to your own organisation.

Everyone on the team needs to be aware of safety; however, in a professional world one person will be designated as having overall responsibility for managing safety. They have to take this responsibility very seriously. If there is some kind of accident and the person responsible is shown not to have managed events adequately then they could be held personally responsible; having said that, other people on the production team could also be held personally responsible if they behave in an unsafe way.

In professional location recordings there will be a section in the shooting schedule which deals with safety. This is usually called a risk assessment. These are fairly common documents used in many industries for different purposes.

A frequent response to being asked to do a risk assessment is that it is awkward, time consuming and unnecessary, and there is often an assumption that someone is going to try to stop you doing the things you want to do. But this should not necessarily be the case.

Risk assessment is not a list of things you are not allowed to do.

Risk assessment is:

• an assessment of what you are going to do
• what the risks might be
• how you are going to manage these risks.

Good risk assessment can increase the amount you are able to do on location rather than restrict it. The fact that there might be some risk doesn't automatically mean that you shouldn't do it, but it does mean that you have to understand the risk and take adequate precautions. The point of filling in a risk assessment form is not to create pointless paperwork but so that the person responsible for safety takes the time to think through what they are doing and what the potential problems might be. You also need to keep things under review as things change.

### How to do a risk assessment

OK, so what's involved? Producers and directors looking at safety for the first time often go to one of two extremes: they either see nothing at all to worry about and the risk assessment boils down to *I'll be really careful, honestly I will.* Or they go the other way and start to see danger in the most benign of locations, creating a whole series of inventive catastrophe fantasies. Neither approach is very helpful.

To understand risk assessment you need to understand two key phrases:

- **Hazard** – *something with the potential to cause harm (fire, electricity, things we might trip over)*
- **Risk** – *the chances of that happening and how serious the consequences might be.*

Risk assessment is about to asking yourself three questions:

*Question 1*

What is the risk?

- Are there any hazards in the environment?
- Am I bringing anything hazardous into the environment?
- Will I do anything hazardous while I am there?

*Question 2*

Who is at risk?

- Sound and/or camera crew
- Artists/contributors (anyone appearing in the production)
- The production team
- Members of the public.

*Question 3*

How do I minimise the risk?

You need to decide what measures you can put in place to keep people safe. You also need to make sure that these measures are implemented on location.

Before we go into the specifics, there are four general rules which will significantly contribute to the overall safety of the recording.

1 **Don't do it alone:** The first and most important rule is that whenever possible don't go on a location shoot or recording on your own. Always try to take someone else. Why? The main reason for this is that if you are looking down the lens of a camera or if you have headphones on, you will not be aware of everything else that is going on around you. You will become very focused on what you are hearing and/or seeing and you will start to block out everything else. This is when accidents are most likely to happen. If you have someone else with you who is not wearing headphones or looking down a camera lens, then they will notice what is going on around you. In a professional production practice varies, and it's not unknown for someone to be asked to do a shoot on their own, but not working alone is the easiest and most important safety precaution you can take. Lone working should be the exception rather than the rule.

2 **Get organised:** Sounds like an odd safety tip but it can be important. If the recording isn't properly organised it can disintegrate, with everyone shouting an opinion and no real control. It's in this kind of confusion/panic that people stop thinking clearly and that's when accidents tend to happen. An organised recording is a much safer recording.

3 **Give yourselves enough time:** Related to confusion. Recordings can be very pressurised situations and they can be made more pressurised if you don't have enough time and everyone is in a rush. When you plan your recording try to be realistic about the amount of time anything is going to take. Don't leave yourself too short of time.

4 **Think about safety early**: Most risks can be managed if you give yourself enough time, which means you can create much more challenging content.

### Who is responsible?

On a professional shoot it's usually the director/producer who does the risk assessment for a shoot or recording. If there is a particularly complicated shoot, aspects of safety will be delegated to professionals or experts; events like underwater filming or helicopter shoots, or anything of this nature would be managed by experts.

   **Remember:** when you are out and about *everyone* is responsible for safety. You should *all* have safety in mind when you in a location.

### What are the hazards?

**Are there any hazards in the environment**? You may have chosen a location where there are very obvious hazards, if you are on a building site, for example, but here are some rather more common things to think about:

* Am I beside a busy road?
* Are there any water hazards – ponds, lakes, etc.?
* Are there any drops – steep steps, etc.?
* What are conditions like? Is it slippery?
* Is it a busy environment – are there lots of people around?
* If it is an internal location – is there anything about the condition of the building that I need to think about? Are all parts of the building solid – if it's a derelict building you will need to take particular precautions.

### Am I bringing anything hazardous into the environment?

- Equipment
- Cables
- Lights
- Animals – *Animals can be unpredictable*
- Children – *Small children can be even more unpredictable.*

### Am I going to do anything hazardous?

- Use of machinery
- Use of electricity
- Stunts.

After each of these questions you should then try to think about:

- **who** is likely to be at risk
- **what** you need to do about it.

It is impossible to list all the combinations of things that you might be intending to do; however, the table opposite shows some of the most common situations you might come across.

These are just a very few examples of the kinds of things you need to think about. It's not possible to cover all the possible things you may come across but just remember three simple questions:

1   What is the hazard?
2   Who is at risk?
3   What can I do about it?

Here is a very simplified risk assessment form – you need to think about this for each of the locations you intend to visit. If you log onto the website you will be able to download this form. The following is a completed risk assessment for the production we've just scheduled.

# Is there anything hazardous in the environment?

| Hazard | Who is at risk | Precautions |
|---|---|---|
| **Hazard:** There may be obvious hazards – busy road, drops, water. | **Who is at risk:** Typically it might be the sound/cameraperson and anyone in front of the camera or being recorded. The reason is that these people are least likely to be aware of what is around them as they are focused on something else. | **Precautions:** You then need to ask yourself: What can I do to minimise the risk? The most common way of dealing with this is to select a position that reduces the risks as far as you can while meeting the production needs, and then allocating a member of the team to keep an eye on those at risk, with a particular regard to their safety. If, for example, you are recording on a busy street and moving around a lot, the designated person might stay with the cameraperson, just to make sure they don't inadvertently step back into the path of an oncoming car. Usually this is the director, as they will be with the cameraperson anyway. |
| **Hazard:** Crowds. If you are in a very crowded environment then this carries some risk. | **Who is at risk:** Possibly members of the public – if you've left bags and kit all over the place people could trip over them. If you are blocking the pavement you are forcing people to go around you, possibly out into the road. Possibly you and in particular your kit – in a big crowd it's possible for things to get stolen quite easily. | **Precautions:** Keep all your bags and stuff neatly out of the way. Appoint one team member to alert passers-by as to what is going on. That person can also make sure all the equipment is safe. |
| **Hazard:** Weather conditions. Although we don't have extremes of weather very often in this country, you should take account of the weather. | **Who is at risk:** The whole team. | **Precautions:** You can always check the weather beforehand. If it's going to be very wet, for example, the team members need to make sure they have the right clothes, particularly footwear which will grip. If it's going to be very hot, then you just need to be aware that your team will need sun block and hats, and to have access to drinks and if possible some shade. |

## Am I bringing anything hazardous into the environment?

| | |
|---|---|
| **Hazard:** Equipment, recording equipment, cameras, lights, cables, props, costume | **Who is at risk:** Most likely to be members of the public who are not aware of what you are doing. Members of the team who could trip over equipment, in particular cables. | **Precaution:** Kit will be kept together neatly, out of the way of members of the public. If cables are laid down they are positioned, taped or covered to avoid the risk of trips. |

## Will I do anything hazardous?

| | |
|---|---|
| **Hazard:** It may be that you will be operating some kind of machinery – even if it's just riding a bike. | **Who is at risk:** Usually the person operating the machinery and anyone who may be unaware of what they are doing and get in the way. | **Precaution:** Clearly you need to know that the person can actually ride a bike or whatever it is they are meant to be doing. It is extraordinary how even the simplest tasks become impossibly difficult if you know everyone is watching and filming you – make sure they are competent.<br><br>The most important thing here is to have clear lines of communication. Everyone should know what is happening all of the time.<br><br>There needs to be a clear sequence of commands so that all members of the crew understand how, when and where the action is going to take place. Anyone who doesn't need to be in the area should stay away from it. |

## Template 9.5  Blank risk assessment

| RISK ASSESSMENT FORM: Title and brief description of filming | | |
|---|---|---|
| Production | Person responsible | |
| Location | Who will be at the location | |
| **HAZARD**<br><br>What is the hazard? | Who is at risk | What precautions will I take? |
| Hazard 1 | | |
| Hazard 2 | | |
| Hazard 3 | | |

## Template 9.6  Festival Fever risk assessment

### *RISK ASSESSMENT FESTIVAL FEVER*

*Each year, thousands and thousands of tents are abandoned at festivals across the country as festival-goers, weary from the exertions of the parties, find the effort of packing up tents too much to handle. The piece reports on the environmental damage caused by the vast amounts of debris left by festival-goers and the attempts of one company to make a difference. Karen Ellis reports from the Elusive Festival in Oxfordshire.*

Description of activities:

- Filming at a music festival. GVs, interviews with members of the audience, interview with festival organisers.
- Filming at Compostable Tents factory. Filming interviews with members of staff, filming the assembly process.
- Filming at Abingdon Recycling Centre. Filming GVs plus filming interviews with staff members.

**Production**
FESTIVAL FEVER

**Person responsible for risk assessment form**
Arthur Howe

| | |
|---|---|
| **Location 1**<br>Water Down House | **Who will be at the location**<br>Director: Arthur Howe<br>Camera: Carolyn Sladen<br>Sound: Theo Barker<br>Presenter: Karen Ellis<br>Contributors: Elsie Taylor, Izzy Piggot, Russell Jones |
| **Location 2**<br>Compostable Tents Ltd<br>38 North Street<br>Islip<br>Oxfordshire | Director: Arthur Howe<br>Camera: Carolyn Sladen<br>Sound: Theo Barker<br>Presenter: Karen Ellis<br>Contributor: Alex Eder |
| **Location 3**<br>Abingdon Road Recycling Centre | Director: Arthur Howe<br>Camera: Carolyn Sladen<br>Sound: Theo Barker<br>Presenter: Karen Ellis<br>Contributor: Christine Adamson |

| What is the hazard? | Who is at risk? | What precautions will I take? |
|---|---|---|
| **Location 1**<br>**Hazard 1**<br>Filming is in a field which is likely to be muddy following heavy rain. The ground is likely to be very uneven as it has been used for a festival for the past three days. | Director: Arthur Howe<br>Camera: Carolyn Sladen<br>Sound: Theo Barker<br>Presenter: Karen Ellis | Crew advised to prepare for wet weather and bring appropriate clothing.<br><br>Camera to be handheld, no tripods.<br><br>No lighting is to be used. Lightweight cameras. |

| | | |
|---|---|---|
| **Hazard 2**<br>There will be festival-goers packing up to leave who will not have been pre-advised about filming. | Members of the public | Director will advise members of the public that filming is taking place. |
| **Location 2**<br>**Hazard 1**<br>Filming will take place close to heavy machinery. | Director: Arthur Howe<br>Camera: Carolyn Sladen<br>Sound: Theo Barker<br>Presenter: Karen Ellis | Crew will be briefed on safety procedures for this location by Company Director Alex Eder. Crew will wear protective clothing issued by the company as necessary.<br><br>Crew will be advised as to safe areas and filming positions by Alex Eder. |
| **Location 3**<br>Filming will take place in a recycling area.<br><br>Heavy machinery will be in operation.<br><br>Cars will be coming in and out of the recycling unit. | Director: Arthur Howe<br>Camera: Carolyn Sladen<br>Sound: Theo Barker<br>Presenter: Karen Ellis | Crew will remain behind safety railings at all times.<br><br>Crew will be accompanied by a member of staff from the Recycling Centre.<br><br>Crew will film from the designated walkways only. |
| **Nearest telephone**<br>Mobiles will be carried at all times. | | **Nearest 24-hour hospital and/or doctor**<br>A & E Department<br>John Radcliffe Hospital<br>Headington<br>Oxford |

**NB:** You will notice that in this risk assessment the safety briefing at the second location will be conducted by the site managers. In this situation you as the production team won't be able to properly assess the risk as you don't know enough about it: you wouldn't be expected to know exactly what goes on in a factory and what is and isn't dangerous. However, you can make sure that someone is there to advise who does understand the risks and can tell you what precautions to take.

## Conclusion

Having read the above, you may be going one of two ways. You may by now have decided that this advice is hopelessly over-protective and that a little rain never hurt anyone, and be impatient to move on. Or you may now be deep in some fantasy which ends up with the entire crew at A & E and have decided that the only safe thing to do is to stay in the school hall.

Whichever way you incline towards, just try to keep to the middle ground. A short period realistically assessing any risk and taking small, easy precautions can save you an enormous amount of time and possibly problems in the long run. That said, assessing risk can sometimes be difficult and need expert advice. If you feel unsure about something and don't know how to assess the risk adequately then you should seek help.

Even on the best planned shoots ACCIDENTS CAN AND DO HAPPEN. In these cases the priority is to take care of the injured person and then to let the right people know what has happened.

**REMEMBER:** Although this is a description of how safety is approached on a professional shoot you will need to make sure you refer to your own organisation first for safety advice.

# PART II
# Recording, shooting and editing

Part II is intended to cover the shoot, the recording and the editing: the nuts and bolts of what you are going to have to do. Part I dealt mainly with radio and TV together. A lot of the research and pre-production phases are very similar. However, Part II will deal with the two mediums separately, since there is not the same overlap. Only in the chapter on sound and the chapter on interview techniques is there a significant amount of crossover. This part of the book also assumes that you have been through all the stages of your pre-production and that you have your production folder containing all your notes. You will need to keep all this together, as you will have to refer to it and add to it as you go along.

# 10 Shot sizes, moves and framing

TV and film have their own way of describing the types of shots you can create. You will need to know some of these – not least because it's a way of describing what you are trying to do to other people. This chapter will run through some of the basics.

## Shot sizes

There are various different sizes of shot. This is not an exact science; there are no actual measurements but the following should give you an idea.

There are a number of examples here but if you log onto the website you will find a wide selection of examples.

**Wide shot (WS)/establishing shot:** This is a shot which should be big enough to show you all the action in a scene. It should help the viewer with the geography of where everything is. You will usually need to get wide shots for every location you visit. Generally, people tend to try to get the wide shot first. If you are using lighting, wide shots tend to be the most time-consuming shots to light. The wide shot also establishes the 'line of action' or the '180-degree rule', which will be discussed later.

*Figure 10.1a* Example of a wide shot

*Figure 10.1b* Example of a wide shot

**Long shot (LS):** This tends to be used when talking about people and means you would have the whole body in the frame.

*Figure 10.2*
Two examples of a
long shot

**Mid-shot (MS):** This shows a smaller area than the long shot but still contains quite a lot of information. If there are people in the scene then you would tend to have their head and torso, perhaps down to the waist.

*Figure 10.3
Two examples
of a mid-shot*

**Medium close-up (MCU):** Somewhere between a MS and a CU; if you are looking at a person then it would tend to be a head-and-shoulder shot.

*Figure 10.4* Two examples of a medium close-up shot

**Close-up:** You are looking in detail at something in the scene. If it is a person then it would be just the head or hand, or some other specific part of the body. If it's an object, it's likely to be some kind of detail.

*Figure 10.5* Two examples of a close-up shot

**Big close-up (BCU), sometimes called extreme close-up:** This would show some very small detail you want to feature.

*Figure 10.6*
Two examples
of a big close-up
shot

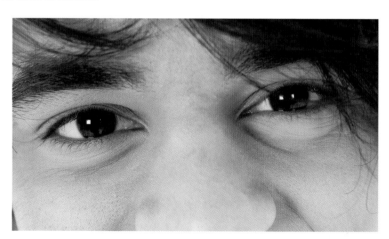

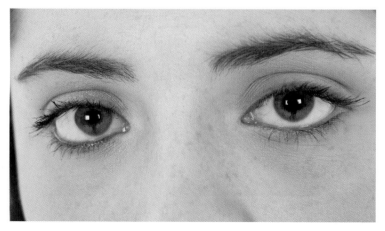

## Singles and two shots

Sometimes directors will refer to the shots by the number of people in it. This is usually when they are shooting a scene with a number of people and then want to have closer shots on just one or two. Normally this is just confined to shots with either one or two people in it. A shot with just one person is referred to as a single. A shot with two people is referred to as a two shot.

*Figure 10.7*
An example
of a wide shot

*Figure 10.8*
An example
of a two shot

*Figure 10.9*
An example
of a single shot

## Changing shot sizes

When you come to take a sequence of shots on the same subject, it will be very important to change the camera angle each time you change shot size. If you don't do this your shots won't cut very well. The general rule is that you should change the camera angle by at least 30 degrees between two shots on the same subject if you want them to cut together.

*Figure 10.10*
Changing shot
sizes, wide shot

*Figure 10.11*
Changing shot
sizes, mid-shot

*Figure 10.12*
Changing shot
sizes, single

Understanding the names of shot sizes is very important; however, that said, there is no fixed rule for what should be in any size shot. They tend to be relative to one another. If, for example, your wide shot is taken to show a busy high street and shows the whole length of the high street, a CU of the same scene could actually be one person picked out from the crowd. You might be showing the whole person but relative to the size of the WS it's quite a close shot.

**Point of view (POV):** This type of shot makes the viewer think that they are seeing what the character or presenter is seeing. You are taking a shot from the point of view of a person or object. You may have seen whole films made as a point-of-view shot. For example, *Cloverfield* Director Matt Reeves (2008) was seen from the point of view of one of the characters supposedly shooting home footage.

*Figure 10.13*
Three examples of
a point-of-view shot

**Over-the-shoulder shot:** Similar to a point-of-view shot but in this type of shot you will also see a small part of the person: for example, a bit of the shoulder or head. This is to orientate the viewer as to whose point of view they are looking from.

*Figure 10.14* An example of an over-the-shoulder shot

## High and low angle shots

Shots can also be taken from different heights; any of the above shots can be taken from a number of different angles. The effect can be fairly extreme or it can be quite subtle. Using different heights creates variety.

**Low angle:** This type of shot gives the viewer the impression they are looking up at something (Figure 10.15).

**Eye level:** In this type of shot the viewer is on the same level as the person or object in the shot (Figure 10.16).

**High angle:** In this type of shot it's as if the viewer were sitting above the scene and looking down on it (Figure 10.17).

**Bird's eye:** This gives the impression that the viewer is right on top of the action looking down on it, like a bird hovering overhead (Figure 10.18).

**Oblique angles:** This is also known as a Dutch tilt or canted angle. In this type of shot the camera itself is tilted to one side. This gives the viewer a sense of instability; it is sometimes used to create a sense of fun and anarchy in a piece (Figure 10.19).

*Figure 10.15*
Three examples
of a low-angle shot

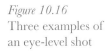

*Figure 10.16*
Three examples of
an eye-level shot

*Figure 10.17* Three examples of a high-angle shot

*Figure 10.18* An example of a bird's eye shot

*Figure 10.19* An example of an oblique (canted or Dutch) angle

## When to use which shot

There are no hard-and-fast rules as to when you should use which shot. If you watch different programmes you will see a huge variety of different shots. However, there are some conventions which you may start to notice, although these are by no means 'rules'.

- **Wide shots/establishing shots:** These are often used at the beginning or the end of a scene. As the name suggests, the shot establishes in the minds of the viewers where they are. If you stay on wide shots for too long the viewer may start to feel a bit disconnected with what's going on and lose interest.
- **Mid-shots/medium close-ups:** These tend to be one of the more common types of shot. You will see them used a lot in both drama and factual programmes. They also offer a way to get to the close-ups. Cutting from a wide shot to a close-up can sometimes be a little disorientating for the viewers and they are not sure which bit of the wide shot they are looking at, so directors often put in a mid-shot to help viewers know where they are going.
- **Close-ups/big close-ups:** This kind of shot is used for two main purposes. If you want to draw the viewer's attention to something in particular then you can use a close-up. It tells the viewers that this is something important that they should pay attention to. If you use the shot in this way you will need to be sure that you have a reason for drawing the viewer's attention. The reason doesn't necessarily have to be given in the commentary or dialogue but there must be a point to it. The second reason is to give the piece a more intimate feel. If you are interviewing someone you might use a close-up if the speaker is talking about something rather personal or important to them. In a drama, close-ups are used in the same sort of way for more sensitive points in the script.
- **Point-of-view shots:** As the name suggests, you should use this shot when you want to show action from the point of view of a character or contributor. It's often used in drama to tell us what the character is seeing or looking at. In a factual piece, you may

want to see something from the point of view of one of the contributors. For example, if you were making a piece about costumes for a theatre show and you were filming someone actually making some costumes and doing some kind of intricate work, you might want to show that as if you were the person doing the sewing.

- **Over-the-shoulder shots:** These are not dissimilar in some ways to the point-of-view shot; however, they are a little more distancing and a little more formal.
- **High and low angle shots:** These may be used for a number of purposes. They can be a type of point-of-view shot. Thus, for example, if you had two characters in a drama, one standing and one sitting, then in order to get the point of view of the characters you would need to use an angled shot. So if you wanted a shot of the character who was standing from the point of view of the character who was sitting down, you would need a low angled shot looking up and vice versa. They can also be used as a kind of stylistic device to add variation to a scene. You sometimes see presenters shot from a low or high angle to add interest to a shot. They can also be used to suggest power. A shot looking down on someone can make them look less powerful than a shot looking up at them. Be aware though that a low angle shot isn't usually very flattering to the person in frame.
- **Oblique angles:** These tend to be used largely as a stylistic device. They can add fun and interest to a piece, and can be almost playful. If you are using this type of shot you will need to be sure that they fit with the style of your piece and are used consistently. Just the odd one or two thrown in can appear a little strange.

## Camera moves

There are also a number of camera moves you can make. Some of these involve swivelling the camera on the tripod, or using the zoom; in other types of shot the camera itself moves; in some the camera needs to be handheld and in others you have to have special equipment such as tracks, jibs and cranes. This chapter assumes that you are not going to be able to access this type of equipment so will touch only briefly on them.

- **Pan:** The camera remains on the same spot but swivels either from left to right or vice versa. It should have a definite start and finish.
- **Whip pan:** A very quick move from right to left or vice versa.
- **Tilt:** The camera remains on the same spot but tilts up and down. It should have a definite start and finish.
- **Zoom:** The camera zooms in from a wide shot to a closer shot or vice versa.
- **Crash zoom:** A very quick move towards or away from an object.
- **Tracking/dolly shot:** This can only be achieved with special equipment. Tracks are similar to small railway tracks. They are laid down on the ground; the camera is mounted on a dolly, a kind of tripod on wheels, which then moves along the tracks. It's often used in drama; you see it particularly when characters are walking and talking, and you the viewer are moving along with them; they are not getting any further away.

    In a tracking shot the direction of the movement could be at right angles to the direction of the camera lens (see Figure 10.20) or it could be travelling in the same direction. Alternatively, or it can move towards the object or away from it (see Figure 10.21).

    Without this equipment to hand you can try to reproduce this move by holding the camera in your hand and walking beside the character. However, you need a fairly steady walk to pull this off. You will also need someone to walk beside you to make sure

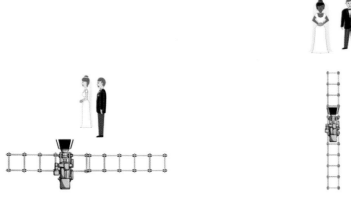

*Figure 10.20* Tracking at 45-degree angle      *Figure 10.21* Tracking in front of subject

you don't bump into things. Sometimes people mount the camera on bikes/pushchairs and move the camera that way. It's worth a try, but any bumps in the ground will show up on the camera move, so you will need a fairly smooth surface.

• **Cranes/jibs:** These are specialist pieces of equipment which allow the camera greater movement up and down; however, you are unlikely to have access to this type of kit.

### When to use which move

Just as with shot sizes, there is no hard-and-fast rule as to when you should be using moves.

• **Pans and tilts:** These can be similar to an establishing shot; they let the viewers discover what they are looking at. Sometimes they can be used to visually describe something. They can be used to show the viewers something in particular that they need to see in detail but that you can't show in just one shot. Pans are often used in drama to follow a character.
• **Zoom:** This is sometimes used instead of a straight cut. You have started on a wide shot to establish where the viewer is and then you want to draw their attention to something or you want to move in to a closer shot on a presenter or a contributor. Zooms tend not to be used so much these days.
• **Whip pans and crash zooms**: These are more stylistic. Similar to oblique angles to a shot they can add a sense of fun to a piece. Again they need to be used consistently and only where appropriate. If you use a crash zoom in on a contributor who is talking about a difficult episode in their childhood, for example, it will look rather insensitive and as if you are making fun of them.
• **Tracking shots:** These are used when you want to move the viewer with the presenter or character. Unlike a pan or a zoom where you start on one shot and end on another, with a tracking shot the size and framing on the presenter or character can be the same; it's just that the presenter has moved and you have moved with them.

### Be afraid!

Moves should be handled carefully. There is a temptation to move the camera all the time – up and down, side to side, to try to cover everything. This is often called 'hose-piping' and is generally regarded as a poor filming technique. It is next to impossible to edit and the viewer will start to feel rather sick. If you are going to use a move it should have a definite start and a definite end, and you should know why you are doing it. You should also leave a handle on both ends of the move. A handle is about five seconds at the beginning and end of a shot where the camera does not move. You will find this useful when you come to the edit. Some types of programmes of course do have this technique of moving the camera all the time. However, it's a very particular approach and, unless you have deliberately chosen to use this style, stay clear of hose-piping.

## Tripod or handheld

You will also need to think about whether you want your camera to be mounted on a tripod or handheld. Again, there is no right or wrong answer to this; it's a creative decision you have to make.

- **Tripod:** Gives a smooth effect. The pictures are held steady and the moves are much smoother. It is easier to rehearse shots and the material is likely to be easier to edit. The disadvantage is that it takes time to set up and may feel a little static.
- **Handheld**: Taking the camera off the tripod and either holding it in your hands or, if the camera is big enough, putting it on your shoulder. The advantage is that you can move quickly and easily. It can give the piece quite a lively, immediate effect. The disadvantage is that shots are likely to be unsteady and more difficult to edit. If poorly done it looks terrible and your viewer will quickly tire of it.

If you are taking a handheld shot it is best to use two hands. The first hand will go through the strap and hold the camera. The second hand will cradle the bottom of the camera. You should use the first hand to operate all the switches; the second hand is just there to keep the camera level and steady (Figure 10.22). Handheld shots are not an excuse for hose-piping. You need to know what your shot is before you record it.

*Figure 10.22* Holding the camera for handheld shots

## Framing a shot

Framing a shot well is quite an art form; it is complex and ultimately subjective. However, framing a shot on video is not unlike framing a shot in photography; there are some basic rules which will help you to take a better shot.

### *Looking room*

If you have a person in shot, whether a presenter, interviewee or character, you need to frame the shot so as to give the person enough 'looking room' (Figures 10.23 and 10.24). If they are looking to the right then you need to leave some space between the end of the character's nose and the edge of the right-hand frame. If you don't do this it looks as if the character is bumped up against a wall.

*Figure 10.23* Two examples of a correct looking room shot

*Figure 10.24* Two examples of a poor looking room shot

In Figure 10.23 both the girl and boy have quite a lot of looking room. There is quite a lot of space between the end of the nose and the edge of the frame. Figure 10.24 shows what they look like if the shot is framed without looking room. It's a slightly odd effect and makes you think they are about to bump into something. Stills photographers tend to play around with this a great deal, but in filming when a character or contributor is talking it looks quite odd not to give them some looking room.

## *Headroom*

Similarly, you will want to position your characters and contributors to give them enough headroom. You want to avoid cutting off too much of their head or make it look as if their chin is resting on the bottom of the frame. Generally speaking, if you have to choose between one of the two it's better to cut off a bit of the top of the head than to have the chin resting on the bottom of the frame, but it should be possible to frame so that neither happens.

*Figure 10.25* Two examples of a poor headroom shot

*Figure 10.26* Two examples of a correct headroom shot

*Figure 10.27* Two examples of a poor headroom shot

### Rule of thirds

If you have studied photography you will be familiar with the term 'Rule of thirds'. It's an easy way of helping you frame your shots. It applies both to stills photography and video filming.

Imagine your frame, then draw three imaginary horizontal lines dividing the frame into three, and then imagine and draw three vertical lines also dividing the frame into three. The four spots where the lines intersect are the best spots where you want the viewer to focus on. The reason for this is that it's thought that when you look at a picture the intersection of those four lines is the place your eye most naturally looks at. If you put the things of most interest in these spots your brain will feel comfortable with that position.

Nobody is arguing that you have to frame every shot in this way; your programme would start to look very odd and boring if you did. But it's a tip well worth knowing.

*Figure 10.28* Rules of thirds

### Depth of field

Depending on what camera you are using you may or may not want to think about depth of field. In order to play with the depth of field you will have to be able to perform two things with the camera. You will need to be able to control the amount of light coming into the camera, so you will need to control the aperture. You will need to change the focal length; that is to say, you will need to be able to zoom in and out. If you can do either or both of these things on the camera you will be able to play with the depth of field.

*Figure 10.29* An example of a long depth of field shot

*Figure 10.30* An example of a short depth of field shot

What is depth of field? When you take a shot with any camera you focus on a particular subject within the frame. Depth of field is the distance behind and in front of the main subject which is also in focus. If there is a shallow depth of field it means that the area in the foreground and behind the object on which you have focused will be blurry or soft. If you have a long depth of field it means that much more of the foreground and background will be in sharp focus.

Look at Figures 10.29 and 10.30 on the previous page. In the first image everyone in the shot is in focus and it has a long depth of field, but in the second image the person in front is in focus but the peoples behind have gone soft, even though the image is a similar size: it has a shorter depth of field.

There are two ways to alter the depth of field. The first way is to alter the aperture or iris. If you want to get a shallow depth of field and have more of the picture looking blurry, then you need to open the aperture. The more you open it, the shorter the depth of field and more of the picture will look blurry. If you want everything to stay in sharp focus then you need to close the aperture. The smaller the aperture, the more of the picture will stay in sharp focus.

However, opening and closing the aperture to this extent may not always be possible. If you are outside on a very sunny day and you open the aperture right up, there will be too much light coming into the camera and it will burn out; that is to say, it will just look all white. If there isn't very much light naturally and you have no artificial lights then you won't have enough light coming into the camera and it will look too dark.

The second way to alter the appearance of the depth of field is to move the camera and use the zoom lens. If you physically move the camera further away from the object on which you want to focus and use the zoom to create the same size of shot, then you will get a short depth of field. You will need to use a tripod if you are going to zoom in a long way. Any camera movement is exaggerated when you are on a long lens and a handheld shot will look very shaky. If you want more of the picture to stay sharp (longer depth of field) then you need to physically move the camera closer to the object you want to focus on and zoom out.

With a combination of changing the focal length (the amount you zoom in or out) and altering the aperture you will be able to change the depth of field on most video cameras.

Why alter the depth of field? There are no set rules; it is down to your own creative sense. However, the effect of having a shallow depth of field is to give more contrasts in the shot; it also makes the viewer concentrate on the object you want them to focus on. It makes the subject of the frame stand out more. It creates a softer, slightly more dreamy image. However, this may not be appropriate to what you want. A journalist reporting on a situation going on around them might want everything to stay in focus. That kind of dreamy look may not be something you feel is right for the piece.

## EXERCISE 10.1   Depth of field

Line up seven books on a table, one behind the other but slightly staggered so that you can see them all. Make the middle book the focus of your shot. Frame up the shot so that you have all the books in the shot filling most of the frame, but make the middle book the focus of the framing.

Take the shot twice. The first time put the camera as close to the books as possible and zoom out so you get all the books in the shot on wide angle. The second time keep the camera at the same level but stand further back and use the zoom to create the same size shot. Stand as far back as you can and still have the same framing.

If you have easy access to an edit suite then record these two bits of commentary below and lay the pictures on top of them. If you don't have easy access to an edit suite you can just play back each of the two versions of the shot and read the commentary over it. It should be fairly easy to see which shot best matches which piece of commentary.

## *COMMENTARY*

1   On the table were a range of books but only one of those books really captured the imagination of the children.
2   On the table were a range of books from the school library. The books covered a variety of different topics.

## Conclusion

There are no hard-and-fast rules for film grammar and for what shot to use when and where. This is up to you and your own creativity. However, it is worth knowing what's available to you. The more you know about the effect which different shots have then the more creative you can be about how you use them. The more you play and practise with material before you do your shoot the more confident you will be about trying different things when it comes to the shoot.

# 11 Crossing the line or the 180-degree rule

You hear the phrase 'crossing the line' talked about a lot and you'll hear a lot of people seeming to be quite anxious about it. This is largely because it's quite difficult to explain. However, the good news is that it's very easy to know when you've done it; the bad news is you may discover it too late. That's why you have to get your head around it.

Crossing the line is more important in some situations than in others. It is important to understand the term if you are shooting dramas or action sequences. It is also important in factual programmes if you have two people talking to one another or if you have some kind of action sequence with people moving in and out of frame.

So what is it and why do we need to know about it? Well, it's important to keep the geography of a sequence making sense in the mind of the viewer. If you have established a scene in a wide shot, you will probably want to use some closer shots as well. A viewer will form a map in their mind of where people are in the frame, even if they can't see them. If they appear in an unexpected place then it will confuse the viewer and they will stop watching the piece and start wondering why everyone is jumping around.

The easiest way to think about it is to imagine that there are two people in the scene. Then draw an imaginary line between the two objects. That line is called the '180-degree line' or sometimes the 'line of action'. Then draw a circle using the line as the diameter of the circle. Look at Figure 11.1: if you start by taking a wide shot from the right half of the circle, all the other shots should be taken from the same side of this line. They can be taken from any position or angle within the 180 degrees of the semicircle, but once you cross that line into the left half of the circle the shots will start to become confusing to the viewer.

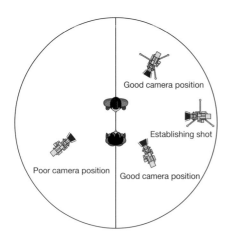

Good camera position

Establishing shot

Poor camera position

Good camera position

*Figure 11.1* Crossing the line

Look at the image in Figure 11.2. The camera is in front of the table at which the couple are sitting. The vertical line on the floor represents the line of action. If the camera stays in front of the table and then cuts to a close-up of each of them individually the girl will be looking towards the right and the boy towards the left (Figure 11.3). This is consistent with what the viewer has seen in the wide shot and they will not get confused.

*Figure 11.2*
Establishing
the line of
action

*Figure 11.3*
Two examples
of a single from
correct side

However, if you take the wide shot from one side of the table and then move the camera around to the other side of the vertical line and take the close-ups from the opposite side, it would have the disorientating effect of making it look to the viewer as if they had swapped positions (Figures 11.4 and 11.5). This will confuse your viewer and they will stop watching the film and start trying to make sense of the geography. You can easily try this yourself; even a sequence of shots from a stills camera will demonstrate the effect.

*Figure 11.4*
Re-establishing
the line of
action

*Figure 11.5*
Two examples of
a single from
wrong side

## EXERCISE 11.1  Crossing the line

You can have a go at this yourself if you wish. You will need to have a camera and access to edit facilities if you want to try this out. Below is a short script. There's also a list of shots and a diagram of where to take the shots from. If you take these shots and try to edit them together as a piece then you will immediately understand the 180-degree rule.

You can download the script from the website.

***Scene interior:*** *A teenage girl and boy are relaxing in the social area of the college. They are sitting on opposite sides of a coffee table.*

|  |  |
|---|---|
| 1.  GIRL | How's it going then? |
| 2.  BOY | OK I suppose. |
| 3.  GIRL | Have you told her yet? |
| 4.  BOY | No . . . but I'm going to. |
| 5.  GIRL | You said that yesterday – why are you so scared? She isn't going to mind. |
| 6.  BOY | I will – I just haven't had a chance. |
| 7.  GIRL | Not had a chance! You were with her all of yesterday, of course you had a chance. |
| 8.  BOY | I'm just waiting for the right moment. |
| 9.  GIRL | Rubbish! You just haven't got the bottle – I'm telling you she's not going to care one way or the other but you need to tell her. |
| 10.  BOY | OK, OK, don't go on. I'm seeing her this dinnertime – I'll tell her then. |

SHOT LIST

1. 1 x wide shot of the whole scene

2. 1 x close-up of boy *Speech 4–10*

3. 1 x close-up of girl *Speech 3–10*

**CROSS THE LINE and then take**

4. 1 x close-up of boy *Speech 4–10*

5. 1 x close-up of girl *Speech 3–10*

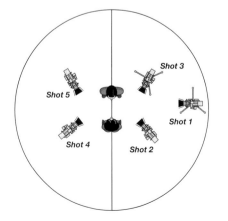

*Figure 11.6* Crossing the line

Once you have shot the piece, start to edit it together: you can use any combination of shots you want. However, it should become immediately obvious that only certain combinations of shots will make sense.

## Moving the 180-degree line

So far so good. However, people rarely stay still for long, and in dramas they tend to get up and move around. In this case the 180-degree line will move with them. Look at the two pictures in Figures 11.7 and 11.8. As the boy gets up and moves, the red line representing the line of action moves with him. So long as you stay on the right side of the line, you won't have a problem with the geography of the scene and you will find your edit much easier.

If you go onto the website you will see a number of examples of how the 180-degree line moves with the action in a shot.

*Figure 11.7* Moving the line, establishing shot

*Figure 11.8* Line of action moved

## When can you cross the line?

Directors can and do cross the line all the time. You can, for example, create a second wide shot from a different angle. This will reorientate the viewer and they will now accept the change. However, once you have established this new line of action you will need to stay with it.

However, if you want to do this, you will need to know what you are doing and you should approach it with caution.

If you log onto the website you can see some examples of how directors play with crossing  the line.

*Figure 11.9*
An example of a
re-establishing shot

*Figure 11.10*
Two examples of a
single shot

## Conclusion

Crossing the line or the 180-degree rule is a helpful guideline. Directors do ignore it on certain occasions; however, unless you are trying to deliberately confuse the viewer you should try to keep the geography of a scene clear and it's probably best to stick to the 180-degree rule and stay on the right side of the line.

# 12 Lighting

Lighting is obviously a key component of a video shoot. Huge amounts of time and money can be spent on lighting. Good lighting is very complex and skilful, and to get good at it you would need a lot more tuition than this book can provide.

Lighting may not be a component of your project over which you have much control. You may not have access to any lights. The good news is that modern cameras are much better at lower lighting levels, so there is less need for lighting now than there was in the past. But you will still need to give some sort of basic thought to lighting.

The lighting set-ups covered in this chapter will only be helpful when you are shooting fairly close up. They will work for presenters or interviewees, or close-ups on objects. They are not going to be helpful when you are shooting very wide shots or shots with a lot of action in them. This kind of lighting is very complicated and demands a lot of special equipment, and therefore is outside the scope of this book.

## Things to remember

A camera is not nearly as sophisticated as your eye. Your eye is an amazingly sophisticated instrument. The pupil regulates the amount of light coming into your eye but your eye can also deal effectively with contrasting amounts of light. So, for example, if you are in a room looking out of the window on a sunny day, the amount of light outside is quite different to the amount of light inside, and yet your brain allows you to see both perfectly happily. If you are outside and sitting in the shade looking at a sunny spot, you can see things happening in the sunshine just as easily as things happening in the shade, providing it's not too dark. A camera is not nearly as good at this.

To be technical for a moment: whereas the range of contrast your eye can deal with is 1000:1 a standard camera of the type you are likely to be using can only deal with about 100:1. You are ten times better than a camera at dealing with contrasting light conditions. This is the main issue you are going to need to be aware of when you are shooting.

This chapter is split into two. The first part deals with how to make the most of available lighting. This will assume that you have no special lights and are making do with the sun, or with lighting that is already available. The second part will go through some of the basics of lighting assuming you have a small lighting kit.

### Shooting in available light

It's highly likely that you are going to be making a video without the help of any lighting kit. In some senses this is good: one less thing to worry about! However, you will still need to understand some of the basics if you are going to get the best out of the light you do have. Since you don't have any lights to even out the contrasts, you need to think about shooting so that you minimise the problem.

### *Shooting against a window*

If you shoot against a window or against another bright light, you will come up against the problem of contrast. Except for the dullest of days or at night, the light outside the window will be brighter than the light in the room. This means that if you place an object in front of the window you will need to do one of two things. You can adjust the exposure so that you can see the object in the room. If you do this then you will get burn-out effect in the window; it will look as if there is a blinding white light outside the room. The other option is to close down the iris to accommodate the amount of light outside the window, but then anything in the room will look very dark; it might almost appear as a silhouette. Sometimes this can create a nice effect but if you use it for an interview it will look as if you are trying to disguise the interviewee! Figures 12.1, 12.2 and 12.3 give you an idea of the effect.

Since you have no lights to balance out the amount of light for the camera, your only option is to not shoot into a window or light; if for some reason you have to do this, you should choose the time of day when there is least light: late afternoon, evening or, less likely, early morning. You would then need to make a judgement as to how much flare or burn-out you can tolerate in the shot. This is also true of any other bright light source – the sun, lamps, candles will all create this issue of contrast.

*Figure 12.1*
Poor
camera
position

*Figure 12.2*
Exposure
set for
exterior
light

*Figure 12.3*
Exposure
set for
interior
light

### Three-point lighting

Even if you are not using any kit it is helpful to understand the basics of lighting. The most basic lighting set-up is called three-point lighting. There are three types of lights in this set-up.

1   **Key light:** This is your most important light source; without kit you can use natural light as your key light. In an interior it could be a window; outside it is going to be the sun. A key light will be quite strong and may cast shadows. You should never shoot directly into a key light.
2   **Filler:** This is a secondary light source. It will come from the opposite side to the key light. It will fill in the bits that the key light can't reach and may soften shadows. You'll be lucky to find any natural filler lights and you will need to be a little inventive.
3   **Backlight:** This light goes behind the object you are filming. It helps to give the shot some depth and distinguishes the object from the background.

The three types of lighting follow this order. If there is only one light source then it's the key light. If you have two light sources then it should be the key light and filler. The backlight is the last one.

### Shooting interiors

If you are shooting inside during the day, the most likely key light is the window. In this instance if you are shooting something close up such as a person or an object you should avoid shooting directly into the window but you can put your subject to one side so that the window becomes your key light (Figures 12.4 and 12.5).

*Figure 12.4* Correct camera position

*Figure 12.5* Camera position for shooting near windows

Window

However, sometimes there isn't quite enough light or you may want to light the other side of the person or object. You may want to add some light. If you don't have any kit there are a couple of ways you can do it (Figures 12.6 and 12.7).

*Figure 12.6* Camera and fill positions

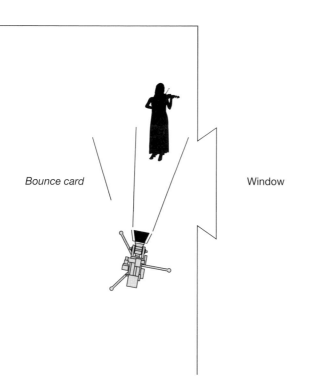

*Figure 12.7* Camera and bounce

Bounce card

Window

First, you can use the available sunlight from the window but reflect it back onto the other side of the person or object. In effect you are creating filler light. For this you will need a large piece of white card or paper – even a piece of polystyrene, the bigger the better. You can position your person/object to one side of the window as before. A third person needs to stand in front of the window, but out of frame and angling the card so that it reflects or bounces the light coming in from the window onto the person being interviewed. The reflected light is acting as your filler and will help with any shadows or dark spots (Figures 12.8 and 12.9).

*Figure 12.8* Without the fill

*Figure 12.9* With the fill

A second option is to use the lighting that already exists in the room as an alternative key light. It's likely that table lamps or standing lamps will be more effective than overhead lighting, particularly if you are lighting people. Overhead lighting directs the light to the top of someone's head. This is not necessarily the part of the body you most want to light for video; usually you want to light the face and in particular the eyes. To do this a table lamp is going to be the best, ideally something like an angle-poise lamp which you can direct.

You should have the lamp positioned at the just above the height of the person being interviewed. It should be positioned just to the left or right of the camera and directed towards the face. However, if it is making your person squint it's not positioned right; just alter the angle slightly.

**Warning:** If you are going to be using lamps in this way it needs to be thought about in your Risk Assessment. Once you start having stuff plugged into sockets, you create risk in that you need to make sure that:

• The equipment is in good order – no frayed leads, etc.
• The electricity supply is safe to use.
• Cables do not become a trip hazard. Cables need to be stuck down with gaffer tape or if you can't do that put a mat or coat over them to warn people and to stop them tripping. Never have cables stretched tight.

This may sound like an over-protective fuss; after all, you use electricity all the time and you turn lamps on and off all the time. However, remember that when you are looking down the lens of a camera or concentrating on shots you will not be thinking about anything else and therefore you are much more likely to trip over something. Often there are lots of people moving about in a small space and again this will make you much more likely to trip up.

### Shooting exteriors

Without expensive lighting equipment it's not really possible to add any lighting when you are shooting outside. However, there are a couple of things that can improve the lighting.

#### Contrast

The same applies to contrast outside as it does inside. Obviously the weather affects this and the issue of contrast is much greater on a sunny day than it is when it is cloudy.

Shooting directly into the sun will have the same effect as shooting into a window. You will get a kind of blinding white light around the object you are shooting or you will get it in silhouette. Equally, if you are shooting an interview or piece to camera it may not be a good idea to shoot with your back to the sun. It will mean that the person in front of the camera is likely to be looking directly into the light and will start to squint and become uncomfortable. It is best to shoot at an angle to the sun (Figure 12.10, overleaf).

Just as you did with the window, you can use a piece of card or polystyrene to bounce some light from the sun onto the other side of the person's face. On a bright day you may find that the person has a shadow cast across one side of the face; bouncing some sunlight back can eliminate the shadow.

*Figure 12.10*
Camera position for
sunny conditions

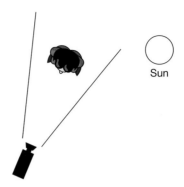

Sun

*Shadows*

On a sunny day you will find that there are lots of shadows around. Again this will create the issue of contrast. If half of your shot is in sunshine and the other half in shadow the camera will not cope with this contrast nearly as well as your eye. On a wide shot this is fine: you can't and shouldn't eliminate the shadows; but if you are filming a close-up or piece to camera, interview, etc., you will need to make a decision as to whether you are going to be in shadow or in sunshine. Half and half is no good.

If you find yourself in a situation where you have to film in part shade and part sun, you have two options – use an umbrella or something similar to create some shade. Alternatively, just wait, and the shadow will move as the sun crosses the sky.

**Remember:** The position of the sun moves, so you will need to think about where the sun is in the sky. You may find that a particular shot is fine in the morning but by late afternoon is not possible because the sun is now directly in your shot. When you do your recce you should be thinking about where the sun is and plan your shooting around this. Again this will be particularly important if you are filming in spring and summer on bright, sunny days.

## Using lights

If you are lucky enough to have access to some lighting kit then you have a little more flexibility. However, unless you are in a professional world you are really only likely to have a basic kit which can provide light when you are filming close up. You are very unlikely to have the huge lights you would need to illuminate a big space, so I wouldn't worry about this.

Lighting effectively is an extremely skilful and creative aspect to film-making, but learning lighting techniques takes a lot of practice and all but the most basic set-ups are really outside the scope of this book. This chapter covers the most basic lighting set-up. However, practice varies widely and most cameramen and women develop their own preferred styles, and there is no real right and wrong.

Basic lighting can affect three aspects of your shot.

1   **Highlight:** It can highlight some part of the shot. If you are filming a person or an interview you will probably want to highlight the face, but it could be something else.
2   **Mood:** Lighting can create a mood to the piece. Lower levels of lighting create a more sombre mood; brighter lights convey a more upbeat mood.
3   **Depth:** Good lighting can create a sense of depth in the room. It can give the piece a less two-dimensional feel to it and bring in a more three-dimensional feel.

### *Three-point lighting with kit*

Just as with natural light, there are the same three important lights (Figure 12.11).

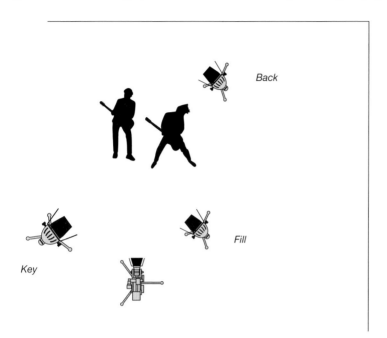

*Figure 12.11*
Camera and
lighting
positions for
three-point
lighting

*Key light*

The main source. It is usually a hard light which will create shadows. It is usually placed just above the height of the person or object and to the left or right of the camera. This means it will create light on one side of the object and create a shadow on the other side. If there is a visible light source in the shot (e.g. a window), then the key light should come from the same side. This will give the impression that the light is coming from the visible source.

*Filler light*

The job of the filler light is to disperse the shadows caused by the key light and to light the part of the person or object that the key light cannot reach. It should be placed on the opposite side of the camera to the key light. This should be a softer, more diffuse light. You can achieve this by moving the light further away from the subject or opening the doors to the light so that it floods over a wider area. Sometimes camera operators use trace across the lights. This is a special kind of tracing paper that softens and diffuses the light. Be careful though: putting ordinary paper in front of a hot light may just end up with a lot of burnt tracing paper and a fire hazard. There are many other ways of diffusing, and endless amounts of kit you can buy, but I'll just assume for the moment that you don't have access to this.

*Backlight*

The job of the backlight is to help the object stand out from the background. It gives the shot a greater sense of depth and a slightly more three-dimensional feel. It should be placed to one side of the object rather than directly behind the object. It is usually a hard light; if you place it directly behind the object the light would be shining straight into the camera.

*Which light to use*

Of course you may not have three lights, in which case:

*   One light     Use the key light
*   Two lights    Use the key light and filler
*   Three lights  Use the key light, filler and backlight.

If you look at the images shown in Figures 12.12 to 12.17 it will give you a good idea of how each of the lights affects the look of the shot.

*Figure 12.12*  Positions key, fill and backlights

*Figure 12.13*
Effects with
three lights

*Figure 12.14* Position key light and fill

*Figure 12.15* Effects with key light and fill

*Figure 12.16* Position with key light only

*Figure 12.17* Effect with key light only

## EXERCISE 12.1  Lighting

To do this exercise you will need to have a basic lighting kit. You will need to set up in a fairly darkened room. You should have at least two of you doing the exercise, or more if you want. Choose a person or object to film and then find a shot you like; don't make it a very wide shot. Arrange the lights as you have them in Figure 12.11. Don't put your object next to a wall. Make sure there is some distance between the object and the wall behind, and if possible try to put something in the background. Take the shot in the following ways:

* no lights
* key light only
* key light and filler
* key light, filler and backlight
* filler only
* filler and backlight
* backlight only
* backlight and key light.

Take the shots in any order; don't stick to the one I have given you. Once you have all the shots you can start to compare the effect that each light has on the shot. If you log onto the website you can find links to sites which allow you to play with this type of lighting.

## White balance

Different light sources give a different overall colour. Daylight has a slightly bluer or cooler light. Ordinary light bulbs have a more orange or warmer light. Fluorescent lights tend to be a bit cooler or bluer than ordinary light bulbs. Our eyes will automatically make an adjustment and, if you look at something white in daylight, it will still look white if you bring it inside and look at it under a normal light bulb. The camera needs more help. The images shown in Figures 12.18 to 12.20 (overleaf) show you the type of effect achieved if you don't white balance. The first image has the kind of blue effect you get with daylight. The second shows the kind of effect you get using light bulbs. The third image gives a better colour balance.

### *How to white balance*

As with contrast, our eyes are much better at white balancing than a camera. We just do it automatically and don't have to think about it, but a camera won't be able to do this. Not all cameras will come with a manual white balance but a lot of them do. If you have a camera with a white balance then it's worth playing around with it to find out what it does.

Some cameras have an automatic white balance. The camera will automatically try to adjust for the type of lighting you are in and will attempt to guess at what will be the best setting. However, if you want to make it more accurate or if you just want to have a go and see what happens, you will need to adjust it manually.

The way to do this is to get something white, usually a piece of paper or card. Point the camera at the white card and zoom in so that about 80 per cent of the frame is covered. Make sure you have the right focus and the right exposure. Adjust the white balance: there is likely to be a *set white balance* option; allow it to adjust so that the camera knows what colour white is. It should indicate to you when the white balance has been achieved. The rest of the colours will adjust themselves to the new setting. If you do this you will need to remember to do it again for every new location. If you don't do this, all your other shots will come out very orange or very blue depending on where you have moved from and to.

*Figure 12.18*  Too much blue

*Figure 12.19*  Too much orange

*Figure 12.20*  Correct white balance

*Figure 12.21*
Camera
positioning
for white
balancing

## EXERCISE 12.2  White balance

You will need a camera which allows manual white balance. Take an object or a person and frame a shot. You should take exactly the same size and angle of shot in four different ways:

1   Set up an interior shot with the lights on, do a white balance and then take the shot.
2   Go outside and take the same shot. Do not alter the white balance.
3   Take the same shot outside but do a white balance first.
4   Go inside and take the first shot again, but don't alter the white balance from the previous shot.

You should find that your first shot looks OK but the second shot looks very blue. The third shot will look OK but the fourth shot will look very orange.

## Conclusion

Getting good at lighting takes a lot of practice and getting lighting right can be hugely time consuming. Even on quite simple shoots it can take up to an hour to get the lighting right for a quite straightforward shot and on big drama sets it can take much longer. You need to know in advance what kind of mood you are going for with your lighting. Is it bright, naturalistic, or are you looking for a more moody, stylised look? If you are going to be using lighting kit then it's a good idea to practise as much as possible before you put yourself under time pressure for your actual shoot. If you are using lighting then always build lighting time into your shooting schedule, a minimum of 30 minutes for lighting any one set-up.

**Remember**: Lights use electricity, they are hot and they can fall over easily. You will need to think about this in your Risk Assessment.

# 13 Recording sound

When you are working in radio obviously sound is the medium, and you need to be able to understand how to get the best sound from the equipment you have available.

When you are on a shoot it is just as important to think about the sound as it is to think about the pictures. More footage is wasted in the edit because of bad sound than because of bad framing. The best interview, best piece to camera or most interesting shots can be rendered useless because not enough attention has been paid to the sound.

If you are recording on location you will need to be aware of what sounds are going on around you. Sound is slightly odd; the ear can tolerate and accept some sounds much more easily than others. A continuous sound in the background, even if it's quite loud, may not be that detrimental but a single noise – a crash or something similar – can be much more annoying.

The real issue with sound comes when you start to edit. If, for example, you are interviewing someone and a car passes in the distance, this in itself is not going to be particularly disturbing, particularly if you have already established that the interviewee is close to a road. However, when you come to do your edit you may want to stop the interview or make a cut while the noise of the car is in the distance. If you do this you will get a sudden drop or jump in the sound, and it can be disrupting and annoying for the listener. Bizarrely in this situation you often end up adding some traffic noise over the edit, just to smooth out the jump. For some reason are eyes are perfectly happy to accept shots which jump around all over the place; however, our ears don't like it much when the sound does the same thing, particularly on radio, if you don't know the source of the sound. The ear likes those transitions to be fairly smooth.

## Wild track

If you are recording in any location it won't be possible to cut out all the noise. You will have to deal with some of the noise around you. Therefore, because the ear seems to be fussier than the eye, it's very important to get some wild track when you are on location. Wild track is simply a minute or so in which you just record the ambient sound – that is to say just the sounds around you. It should have no talking on it at all. You should do this even if you are recording in a quiet room. You will be surprised that a quiet room isn't that quiet and even if it is you should still record the silence. The reason for this is that when you come to the edit you can use your wild track to smooth over any sharp sound edits. You will need to do this for every different location you use. Wild track is something that can get overlooked while you are recording or shooting, but it's very important that you get into the habit of taking wild tracks. If there is a particular person in the group with responsibility for sound then they should be the person nagging the others not to forget the wild track.

## Microphones, direction and range

You may not have that much choice in the type of microphone you are going to be using; however, it's worth knowing about them so that you can make the best of the ones you have. The following is a list of microphones that are commonly used. Even if you don't have much choice over the type of microphone you use, if you know something about them, then at least you can understand the issues a particular microphone might pose.

   The first thing to understand about microphones is the direction from which they will pick up sound. They are not all the same. Imagine that the microphone is in the middle of a circle. Some microphones will pick up sound from all the directions around the circle; others will only pick up sound from a small portion of the circle. Different microphones tend to be used in different circumstances.

### *Omnidirectional microphones*

This type of microphone picks up sound all around it (Figure 13.1). Think of a microphone positioned in the middle of a circle: an omnidirectional microphone will pick up sound from every direction. This may be useful if certain situations, for example, if you are trying to achieve a lot of ambient sound. However, it's less useful for dialogue, interviews or for presenters, as it is harder to distinguish one sound from another.

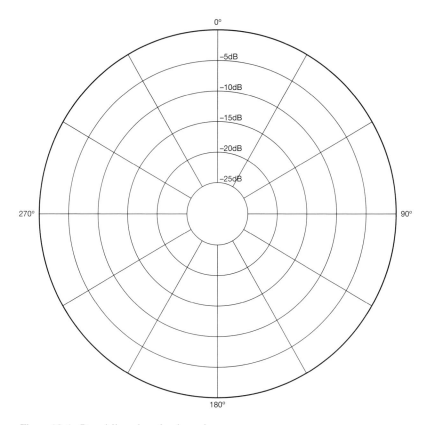

*Figure 13.1* Omnidirectional microphone

## Directional microphones

Directional microphones allow you to prioritise a sound source. A directional microphone will record sound coming from one direction. It won't completely cut out all the other sounds but it will make one sound source much stronger. These types of microphones are much more useful on location when you have dialogue or are interviewing someone. It means that if you direct the microphone towards the person talking it will pick up much more of what they are saying than anything else and the words will stand out from the background noise. There are several different types of directional microphones; they differ according to the pattern in which they pick up sound.

## Figure-of-eight microphones

A figure-of-eight microphone will pick up sound from two opposite directions but not from the side. The area defined by the hard black line in the diagram below is the area from which the microphone will pick up the sound. It's a useful microphone in a handheld situation where you might have a presenter in vision talking to an interviewee and you want to record both people.

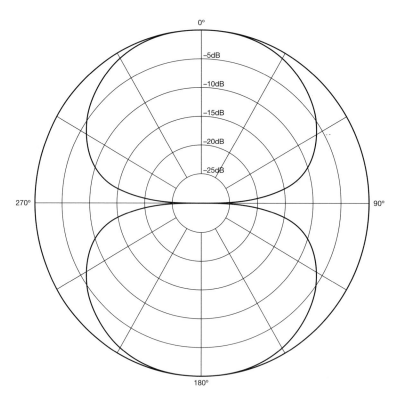

Figure 13.2
Figure-of-eight microphone

## Cardioid microphones

A cardioid microphone will pick up sound from in front of the microphone and to the side, but it won't pick up any sound to the rear (Figure 13.3, opposite). These microphones are useful if you are recording dialogue or an interview. However, you will need to be careful,

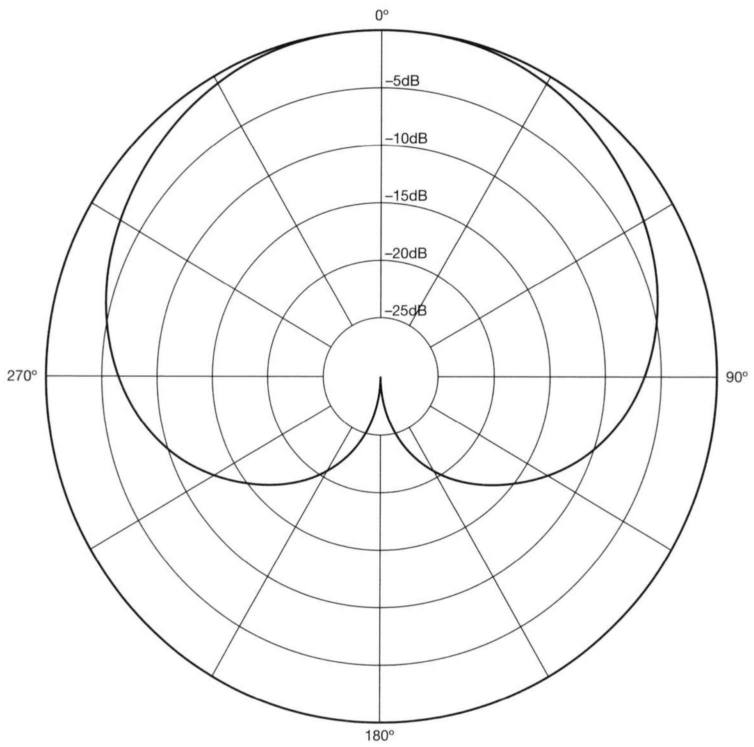

*Figure 13.3*
A cardioid
microphone

as they are more prone to being distorted by wind noise and popping. Popping is a distortion which happens when someone is speaking into the microphone, often when you use words beginning with P or B – where you exhale breath. It causes a nasty distortion. You also tend to get more handling noise, the sort of rustling noise which comes from the microphone itself moving.

### Hyper-cardioid microphones

A hyper-cardioid microphone will pick up sound to the front and some sound to the side, but not quite as much as a cardioid microphone, it will pick up some sound from the rear but not a lot (Figure 13.4, overleaf). It will have the same issues around wind noise and popping as the cardioid.

### Shotgun microphones

A shotgun microphone is an even more directional microphone (Figure 13.5, overleaf). The areas which will pick up sound are much smaller. It would be a good microphone to use if you were in a very noisy situation and wanting to pick up one person talking. However, it's quite easy to get it horribly wrong and end up picking up completely the wrong bit of sound unless you are monitoring it quite closely. The other disadvantage of using a very directional microphone is that it can start to sound a little unnatural. It's as if the voice has become disembodied from its surroundings. It is largely a matter of balance. You want a little bit of the sound of the room so that you get the atmosphere, but not so much that it becomes difficult to listen to.

*Figure 13.4*
A hyper-cardioid
microphone

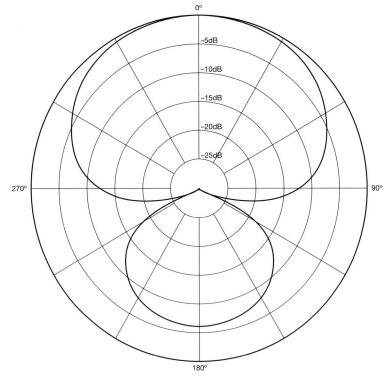

*Figure 13.5*
A shotgun
microphone

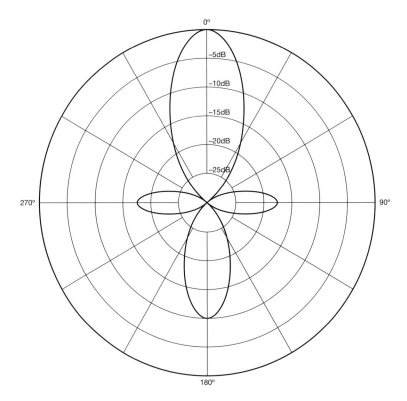

Even if you don't have any choice over what kind of microphone you have, you should check what sort of microphone you are using. This is fairly easy to do if there is no indication on the microphone itself. Start recording and clap or click your fingers in different positions around the microphone. If you have sound-level meters you can watch what happens; if you don't, then just use headphones and your ears to check when the sound is loudest.

## Types of microphone

As well as differing in range and direction, microphones also differ in terms of size and how they are mounted. The following are some of the most common types of microphone you are likely to come across.

### Camera microphones

These are the microphones that are built into the camera: sometimes it's just a small microphone that you cannot see, while some cameras have a microphone mounted on the top of the camera. While these are suitable for home movies, they are really the least effective type of microphone, and if at all possible you should try to avoid using them in most circumstances. The problem is that while they may be fine for recording ambient sound (the sounds around you) they won't be much good for recording interviews or dialogue. The reason is that the microphone can't get close enough to the person to record sound in such a way that it becomes distinct from the ambient sound. Some microphones are directional and some are not; however, what you will get is dialogue/interview and ambient sound all mixed together at the same level, and it will sound very indistinct. Most cameras have an input for some kind of microphone, and if at all possible you should try to use an additional micro-phone if you want to record dialogue/interviews.

*Figure 13.6* An example of a camera mounted microphone

### Handheld microphones

You often see reporters or presenters using this kind of microphone. The reporter holds the microphone and speaks into it. It will be connected by a cable either directly to the recording device or camera or via a mixer. These tend to be directional microphones. If you use a handheld microphone you will need to learn how to hold it properly to avoid getting noise from the cable and connections. Figure 13.7 (overleaf) shows the best way to hold the micro-phone. Usually the best position to hold the microphone is below chin height. You should try to talk across the top of the microphone rather than directly into it; this will cut out distortion and popping. When you move the microphone to the interviewee try not to shove it in their face; just hold it below the chin so they can talk over it. You should also try to hold it in such a way as to stop any cable movement at the connection. Loop the cable and grasp it in the hand holding the microphone. This means that most of the cable can move, but the point where the cable is connected to the microphone is not moving (Figures 13.7 and 13.8).

*Figure 13.7* An example of the correct way to hold a microphone

*Figure 13.8* An example of a poor way to hold a microphone

*Lapel microphones*

These are also called lavaliers or neck microphones. They are clipped onto a person's clothing, and sometimes they are on view and at other times they are hidden. They are also attached to the mixer or camera with wires. They can achieve a good sound but a problem will arise if they aren't attached very carefully so that every time the person moves the microphone will pick up the sound of their clothes rustling and sometimes even the heart beating! Unless you are recording a drama it's best to attach the microphone to the outside of their clothing; this will cause less rustling. Sometimes you can position the microphones facing downwards; this gets rid of the popping sound on words beginning with P or D. Remind the person that they are connected to the camera so that they don't suddenly get up and walk away. If you want to hide the microphone you will need to be able to tape the wires firmly so that you get as little movement as possible.

*Radio microphones*

These are similar to lapel microphones but they are wireless. They are good if the person has to do a lot of walking around. The disadvantage is that they are quite expensive and you are unlikely to have access to them; also they can get some distortion if the wireless isn't working properly. They will have the same issues as lapel microphones with regard to noise from clothes.

## Mounts

There are a number of different ways of holding a microphone. The lapel microphones and radio microphones just clip on to clothing; the other types of microphone can be held in different ways.

*Table mounts*

This is in the form of a mini-tripod that can sit on a table. It is best used on radio when your interviewee is sitting down. It's not normally used on TV these days.

*Large stands*

These are similar to the table mounts but much bigger. You can adjust the height and angle of the microphone – they are very versatile but not easy to use outside as they are easily knocked over.

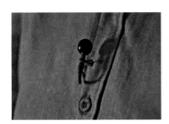

*Figure 13.9* An example of a lapel microphone

*Figure 13.10* An example of a table stand

*Figure 13.11* An example of a large stand

*Boom*

This is a type of stand or pole which is held by the sound operator. Usually it will be a directional microphone. This type of microphone avoids the problem of hearing clothes rustling. It also means that the interviewee isn't connected to the camera or mixer with wires. It is quite a useful way of recording several people talking, as you can easily move the microphone slightly to favour the person speaking. However, if it's mounted on a pole it really needs a separate person to hold it. It's quite difficult to hold a boom and operate the camera or mixing desk at the same time. It can also be quite tiring if it is used for a long period. If you are filming, because

*Figure 13.12* A boom

it's not usually shown in the shot, you have to be careful of shadows cast by the microphone, which can look a little odd. You also have to be careful when you change shot size that the microphone isn't suddenly in the frame. If you are filming you should try to get the microphone as close to the person as possible without getting into the shot.

## Setting up your microphones and the sound levels

There is no exact science to this; it's more of an art. There are things that you definitely want to avoid, such as distortion or wind noise, or clothes rustling. However, the balance of the sound is more subjective.

If you are recording a voice or perhaps an instrument or some other specific sound, you are trying to balance what you are recording with the acoustic or ambient sound. If you are recording on a location then there will always be some kind of ambient sound. The aim really is to balance the sound so that you can clearly hear what is being recorded but haven't completely lost the ambient sound, as this contributes to the listener's sense of place.

The critical thing is to get the distance between the microphone and the item you are recording right. There is no set formula for this: you will just have to try it and then listen. However, as a general rule you will want to get the microphone as close to the object as possible without getting any distortion and at the same time keeping a balance between the item you are recording and the background sounds.

### *Checking your levels*

You will need to check the sound in the same way as you check camera shots. Before you record any sound you will need to check the levels. If you are recording a voice you will need to ask the contributor to say a few words for level. You should ask them to speak in their normal voice and to sit or stand in the position they feel comfortable in. You should then move the microphone around them; don't ask them to move for the microphone. If you move them out of the position they feel comfortable in then, as the interview progresses, they will start to move back to their most comfortable position without really noticing what they are doing, and then your sound levels will start to change.

Once you have the person in position and speaking in their normal voice you will need to check your sound levels. If you are using a mixer it will have a sound level gauge on it. Some recording device and some cameras also have meters for sound levels. You should be watching the gauge. The sound levels should be peaking just below the red line. As people speak, their voices will get louder and softer, and the beginnings of words will tend to be louder than the ends. You will notice that the gauge usually lights up or a needle goes up and down. The highest level the needle hits is called the peak. If the highest level is in the red zone you are in danger of getting distortion and you will need to either move the microphone or reduce the volume. If the highest level is peaking significantly below the red zone it may be too low and you will lose some of the words, so you should move the microphone closer or increase the volume.

## Wind

If you are recording outside then wind can be an issue. The wind can blow across the microphone and cause a nasty sound. This is particularly a problem with handheld and boom microphones but can also be an issue with lapel microphones. One option is to find a more sheltered spot to do the filming, but this may not be possible from the point of view of the pictures. If this is the case you will need a wind sock. These range from fairly inexpensive pieces of foam that go over the end of the microphone, right up to the much more expensive big, hairy-looking things you may have seen. However, that said, even with the most expensive windsock it can be difficult to get good sound in very windy conditions, so if you are out in a howling gale it's best to find a sheltered spot.

## Headphones

It's vital to listen to the recording wearing headphones, often referred to as 'cans'. What you hear naturally is not what the microphone is picking up. It could be more or less but it will be different. If you want to monitor sound you will need to be wearing headphones; it's much more difficult to monitor sound without them.

## Background noise

Before you start recording, listen again to all the background noise. Is there anything you can eliminate? Sometimes there may be music or the radio playing in the background; you should ask for them to be turned off. Sometimes there is machinery which is making a noise; it may be possible to get this turned off. You should also unplug any phones if possible and obviously ask for all mobile phones to be switched off.

*Figure 13.13*
Two examples of a windshield

### Monitoring sound during a recording

Depending on how many people you have in your group you may have allocated someone exclusively to do the sound, or you may be combining it with another role. However, it's very important that when you are recording, someone is monitoring the sound. If you are shooting it's very difficult to operate the camera and monitor the sound at the same time. If there is a camera and director, then it's better for the director to monitor the sound rather than the camera.

What are you listening for?

#### Levels

The first thing you should check is that the level of the recording is correct. If for some reason the person has moved, the recording levels will have changed. You may either be getting distortion from a higher level or losing sound because the level is too low. If this happens you need to alert the rest of the team. If you are doing an interview, wait until the end of the answer the person is giving and then alert the camera, or director. If it's a piece of dialogue, wait for a pause, or if it's a short piece wait until the end of the piece. You will then need to adjust the microphone to the new position. Again, it's better to change the microphone than to ask the person to move. They will probably move back to their former position unconsciously. Check your levels again and then restart the recording.

#### Background noise

The main thing to listen for is changes in background levels. If you are on location there will always be some level of background noise. The way you set the microphones will have helped to balance the person talking with the background noise. However, the levels of background noise can change. For example, you may be in an office where there is the hum of a computer. It will have been impractical to turn off all the computers and you have decided that the level of the computer hum is fairly low and consistent, and so is not a problem. If, however, during the interview for some reason the computers all turn off and the humming stops, then the background noise level will change. The problem is that when the programme is edited the change from computer hum to no computer hum will sound a little odd to the ear. In this case the thing to do is to redo the section where the computer went from hum to no hum. However, it's worth remembering that during the edit it will be difficult to cut between the sections with the hum and sections without the hum, so it may mean redoing some more to cover yourself. This will be a particular problem if you are recording a drama, as you will not be recording in sequence.

#### Intermittent noise

The other thing you need to listen for is intermittent noise. This could be a door banging, a plane going overhead, or a particularly loud car horn. Is it something that drowns out the person speaking or something which is likely to distract the person listening? Again this is something of a judgement call. If, for example, you are interviewing someone in a park and there is a dog barking in the background, so long as the bark isn't too loud it may not be a problem. If the listener or viewer knows the person is in a park and expects there to be children and dogs there, then they probably won't be disturbed by the noise. However, if you were in the office environment and you heard the sound of a dog, perhaps coming through an open window, the listener or viewer is likely to be much more distracted by this as they are unlikely to associate dogs with offices or other quiet environments, and will start to wonder where the noise is coming from. While they are wondering they will stop listening to your speaker. If the piece is a drama then the intermittent noises are likely to be quite problematic unless they can be accommodated within the scene.

*Speak up!*

Don't be afraid to speak up. If you are monitoring the sound then it's your responsibility to speak up if you think there is a problem. Under pressure there is a natural urgency to keep going and sometimes it's difficult to stop the flow of events. However, if the sound is poor there won't be very much you can do about it during the edit, particularly if you are using basic editing packages. It is much better to get the sound right there and then. There may be times when you need to make compromises but at least you should be aware that you are making them.

Lastly, **wild track**: Don't forget it – you'll need it in the end!

## Conclusion

The technical aspects of recording sound need planning and thought. The choice of microphone, the choice of mounting and where you record will dramatically affect the piece. You may not have the luxury of choice, but at least if you understand what the issues are you will be able to make allowances. Do not be fooled into thinking that sound is easier than pictures; it isn't. Remember: more things tend to go wrong with the sound than with the pictures, so plan your sound.

# 14  Taking a shot

Before you start shooting for film or TV it's worth thinking about the process of actually taking a shot. Filming should not be just a sequence of unplanned and random shots. Each shot that you take needs to be planned and thought about. Once you have found the shot you want to take, you may need to rehearse it. This is particularly true if it is a piece to camera or if there is some action in the shot. Your shot may include some kind of movement, pans, and tilts; again it's useful just to rehearse this before you actually take the shot. You will want to know where your shot begins and ends and get a sense of how long the shot is going to take, and how interesting it is. There is no point having a long, slow pan which mostly just shows sky or grass. You need to have a good reason to use these kinds of moves. You should rehearse your shots a couple of times, just to get a good sense of what you are trying to achieve.

## Handles or top and tailing a shot

When you record a shot you will need to take more than you need. You will need to hold the shot at the beginning and the end. This will make things easier when you come to the edit. The bits at the beginning and end are often referred to as a handle or top and tail. When you go to take a shot, after the camera starts running, count to five before you say, 'action'. At the end of the shot, count to five before you say, 'cut'. That way you will always have a handle. This is particularly important if there is going to be a move on the shot. It is very difficult to cut into a moving shot. You need to hold the camera steady for five seconds before starting any move and leave the camera steady at the end of the move. You won't use all these bits but you will need some of them.

## Camera left, camera right

At times you will need to think about where to put objects or people in frame. You will also need to direct the eye line or to direct action, and you will need to tell people to move or look left or right. This can get confusing, since when you are behind the camera you are often facing the opposite way to the people you are filming. The convention for this is to talk about 'camera left' or 'camera right'. You always describe the position from the point of view of the camera. If you are behind the camera it will also be your left and your right.

## Running a shot

When you take a shot there is a set sequence of commands which everyone tends to follow. It can sound a little militaristic but the reason for this is so that everyone is ready and knows what they are supposed to be doing and when. It saves a whole lot of confusion. The actual words you use can vary but whatever you choose to say it should follow the same sort of pattern. Imagine for the moment that you are going to do a piece to camera. The person in front of the camera has rehearsed the lines and you have rehearsed the shot. You now want to get everyone ready to take the shot.

You can download this sheet from the website.

## Template 14.1 Taking a shot

| | | |
|---|---|---|
| Director says: | We are going to take a shot of. . . | *Describes briefly the shot you are going to take.* |
| Director says: | Everyone get set please | *This means everyone goes to their places. If you are not involved in the shot then you need to make sure the camera can't see you. The safest place is behind the camera, particularly if it is a wide shot. For close-ups it's not quite so important.* |
| Director says: | Everyone ready? | *If there are any problems other team members say so.* |
| Director says: | Stand by, quiet please | *Everyone knows the shot is about to happen.* |
| Director says: | Cue camera | *The camera operator starts running up the shot.* |
| Camera says: | Camera running | *This means the camera is happy that the camera is working and running the shot.* |
| Director says: | Action | *This means any action can start from the presenter and the camera can start making any moves.* <br><br> *Anybody else involved in the team should remain quiet and still until the shot is finished.* |
| Director says: | Cut, thank you | *Camera stops running, and everyone else can start talking or moving again.* |
| Director says: | Everyone happy? | *If there were any problems on the shot or noises, or anything that means you need to take the shot again, then the camera and sound should say so. The presenter may also want to go for another take; other members of the team should contribute any thoughts or make suggestions.* |

| If another take is necessary the Director says: | We need to take that shot again (explain why): can everyone get set please | *If for some reason you want to take the shot again then you should repeat all the above steps. However, you will need to tell everyone why you want to repeat it. Otherwise whatever it is you didn't like will just happen again.* |
|---|---|---|
| If happy with the shot the Director says: | Thanks everyone – we are happy with that; let's move on to . . . | *The Director tells everyone what the next shot will be and they start to set up for this.* |

Not every director in the world slavishly follows this script but they will go through something similar. This whole approach may feel a little unequal, particularly when you are used to working together and making joint decisions about everything. It may also feel a little uncomfortable for the person in the role of director to be barking orders at everyone; other people tend to take to it fairly easily.

The reason for this approach is to keep things moving and not to get bogged down in endless discussions. It also means that less time is wasted retaking shots because someone wasn't paying attention or didn't know what they were supposed to be doing.

If you are sharing the role of director then everyone can have a go at running the show for a while. But it's a good idea to give each person a section of shots to be responsible for rather than everyone trying to be responsible for every shot. You'll find you get a lot more done that way.

## EXERCISE 14.1  Taking a shot

If you want to get a feel for taking shots in this way you can set up a fairly simple shoot and set yourselves a time limit to get your shots.

For example, here is a short scene with three people involved: a presenter and two contributors. The presenter is standing with a contributor on each side. She or he is going to introduce the two characters and ask them both two questions. You will need two props: a pair of boots or shoes and a small mat. You will need to be in a team of at least five people: 1 x presenter, 2 x contributors, 1 x director, 1 x camera; you could add others if you have enough people.

Here is the script; you can download this from the website if you wish.

| 1 | Presenter: | Hello and welcome to this week's edition of Festival, the magazine programme that reports on the best of the festival season. |
|---|---|---|
| | | This week's edition is concentrating on the problem of mud. Each year manufacturers produce new products to help fans deal with the problem of mud and today we are going to test two of the products. I have with me two willing volunteers. |

| | | First Alex . . . Alex: how experienced are you with festival mud? |
|---|---|---|
| 2 | Alex | Well, I've been coming to festivals for about four years now and mud is a constant problem; it stops me moving around, getting where I want to go and it causes chaos in the tents. |
| 3 | Presenter | So what are you testing for us today? |
| 4 | Alex | I'm going to be testing these self-cleaning boots; they have been specially coated with a new substance that means mud can't stick to the boots – making it much easier to walk. |
| 5 | Presenter | Great, thanks Alex, now over here I have Samantha; now Samantha, you are new to festivals? |
| 6 | Samantha | Yes that's right, this is my first time, I'm not quite sure what to expect. |
| 7 | Presenter | And what are you testing for us today? |
| 8 | Samantha | I'm testing a tent doormat; the idea is that you place the mat in front of the tent and if it detects mud it will let off an alarm so the person knows to get rid of the mud before coming into the tent. |
| 10 | Presenter | Great, thanks, we'll be finding out how they got along later in the show, so good luck to you both. |

For the purposes of this exercise I want you to shoot the following:

1   A WS of the whole script showing the presenter and both of the contributors.
2   A MS of the whole script showing just the presenter; she or he should turn to the person she or he is talking to at the appropriate time.
3   A MS of speeches 1–4 showing the presenter and Alex.
4   A MS of speeches 2–4 showing just Alex and the boots.
5   A CU of the boots.
6   A MS of speeches 5–9 showing the presenter and Samantha.
7   A MS of speeches 5–9 showing just Samantha and the mat.
8   A CU on the mat.

This means that you are trying to get eight shots of this particular scene. You don't need to go to lots of trouble finding the right location or lighting. Anywhere will do. If you can't find a mat, just use a large piece of paper or a scarf. For the purposes of this exercise you are trying to get the feel of setting up for different shots on an action sequence or piece to camera. The aim is just to get the shots efficiently.

Here is what you need to think about:

- The order in which you are going to take the shots.
- The composition of the shot.
- The 180-degree rule.
- Move the camera each time so that you get a different angle on the shot.
- Go through the sequence of commands I have described when you are actually taking the shot.

You can take turns at what task you are doing but once you have got your task you should stick with it. If you stick with the processes described you should get through it fairly quickly; if you don't you will take much longer.

## Conclusion

Running a shoot can be pressurised and hard work. Lots of things can go wrong and lots will go wrong. However, having a firm control of the shooting process will help you keep things moving and making sure that you make the most of your time. There will be less confusion and more productivity.

# 15 Shooting factual

Shooting for factual programmes and shooting for drama involve slightly different techniques. There are aspects which overlap but there are also aspects which are completely different. This chapter will talk you through some of the main techniques you'll need for factual programmes. The first thing is to think through the main tasks in a factual programme and who does what. Any shoot can be a pressurised situation; the more everyone is aware of what they are supposed to be doing the better. The shoot will run more smoothly and you will have more time to think creatively. There are usually far fewer people involved in a factual shoot than a drama and often the same person will do several tasks. How you decide to allocate the tasks is up to you but you just need to make sure that someone is doing it.

## What does the director do?

Directors and producers are often the same people in factual. As director/producer you will be in charge of the shoot. You are not just creatively in charge but also logistically. You need to keep the whole thing going, keep the show on the road, and make sure everyone knows what they are doing when. This is really hard to do at the same time as being very creative, but that was why you did all those forms and schedules, so that you had that side sorted out.

From the research, planning and recce you should now have a good idea of the kind of shots you want. However, as with all the other plans this can change slightly when you are on the ground. Shots which seemed a very good idea in theory turn out to be not quite so good in practice. This is fine; so long as you know the kinds of shots you will have to do to make the piece work then it's fine to embellish. Once you are looking through a camera, many more ideas will come to you and you can start to be quite creative. You may see two or three alternatives, and if you've got time you can always do it more than one way. However, you should keep referring back to your treatment to make sure that you are not missing anything vital.

### Starting the shoot

One of the most daunting moments of a shoot is when you first start. So what do you do first? What do you do when you arrive on location? Here are a few steps to get you into it.

1   Remind everyone what they are doing and the order in which they are doing it.
2   If there are people who don't know each other make sure that you introduce everyone; you should know all your production team but there may be contributors who don't know everyone. If they don't know, you should also explain each person's role (e.g. *Hi,*

*this is Steve, he's on camera today and this is Jane, she's doing sound, this is Alex Cox, the company manager, and he is going to be talking to us today).*

3    Tell everyone what the first shot is going to be and give some indication of how long you want to spend on it (e.g. *We are going to start with Karen's piece to camera from the terrace. I think this will take about half an hour and then I'd like to go down into the field and get some GVs*).

You may feel a bit stupid saying this to people you've been working with and know well, and who have drawn up the shooting script with you, but it will help you to feel in control of the situation. You can then hope that people will start to spring into action, since they all know what they are doing for each section and when they should start doing it. If they are staring at you blankly then remind them what they have to do (e.g. *Emma, can you make sure Karen gets some makeup on and help her get ready? Steve, shall we go to the terrace and have a look at some shots?*).

## What does the cameraperson do?

Camera and director can sometimes be rolled into one, in which case you will only be discussing things with yourself, but if you have different people doing these jobs you will need to be in constant discussion with them.

Once the camera is in position it's the job of the director and camera to find the shots. The director should have an idea of what kind of shot they want and the cameraperson will look for it but also offer up suggestions. They are the people looking through the lens and usually they have a lot of experience, so directors would be foolish to ignore their suggestions.

The cameraperson is responsible for thinking about the best framing for the shot, the best angles, depth of field, etc. They can discuss this with the director but they are the people looking down the lens, so they should also be coming up with ideas.

Importantly the cameraperson is responsible for the lighting. Whether or not you have a lighting kit, it's the cameraperson's job to think about the best lighting for the shot. If you are outside, they should also be thinking about where the sun is and where it is going to; that way you can help make decisions about the order of shots.

They should also take responsibility for the safekeeping of all the rushes. They should also make sure all the rushes are properly labelled. For some reason people find this quite an irritating job although it's perfectly simple; however, you will regret it if you don't, as you will spend hours looking at irrelevant rushes find the shot you want.

## What does the sound recordist do?

You need to start thinking about the sound around you. You will need to start thinking about background noise and how much this is affecting any interviews. Remember: a constant background noise is much less disturbing than an intermittent one, particularly if the viewer already knows the source of the noise. If you are doing an interview, it is the sound person who is responsible for making sure that the levels are correct and you have the right balance between the interviewee or presenter and the ambient sound.

If done by different people, sound, camera and director need to constantly talk to each other. Sound should be advising on what he or she can hear and whether it's acceptable or likely to be a problem. At the end of a take the sound should let the camera and director know if there were any sound problems on the take; if there were they can take the shot again.

## Other tasks

### Contributors

In a factual recording these are likely to be the interviewees, although they may not be part of your group. You should make sure that any contributors are kept informed of what is going on. There is nothing more dispiriting to a contributor than to watch a group of people running around like headless chickens and to have no idea when they are going to be needed, or indeed what they are going to be asked to do. If there are delays then that's fine, but make sure the contributors know about it and know when they are likely to be needed. When you come to shoot, explain to them what they are going to have to do, and if you are likely to have to ask them to repeat some action then explain this to them in advance. You should also remember to thank them at the end of the contribution. If you need them to do something again, thank them first and then ask if you could repeat the action but be very clear why you want to repeat it; that way they won't do the same thing again.

### Production assistants / runners

These are not often used on factual programmes which tend to have small budgets. However, if you do have one, the role can cover the following:

*   **Shot listing:** Making a list of all the shots which have been taken. You should also note the best takes.
*   **Fail safe:** Making sure that the director and camera are getting all the shots on the shot list. In the confusion it's easy to forget something but having someone referring back to the shot list and jogging your memory is always a good thing.
*   **Scouting:** It may be that you haven't had time to do proper recces, so staying one step ahead of the shooting and looking for a good position for the next shot can be very helpful.
*   **Communication:** Making sure everyone knows what's happening. If the director isn't being very good at communicating what's happening then you can help out.

## Different types of sequences in factual programmes

On a factual programme there are a number of different types of shooting you are going to have to do. It's worth getting clear in your mind what you have to think about in each case.

### Shooting pieces to camera (PTCs)

A piece to camera is generally done by the presenter of the programme. It differs from an interview in that the person is generally scripted; they have written the piece first. They are also talking directly to the viewer, so they should be looking directly at the camera. If you are planning a piece to camera you need to think about the size of shot you are looking for. You also need to think about the location, particularly if it is a wide shot. The choice of location should help tell the story. You should plan any moves. Is the camera going to tilt or pan? Is the presenter going to walk and talk or just talk? If you are planning moves then there should be a good reason. Is there anything they can refer to, perhaps with a gesture or turn of the head? Are they using any props? What is the feel of the piece? Is it reflective or is it energised?

This can depend on what part of the piece you are in; pieces to camera tend to be more energised at the beginning and more reflective at the end. Think about the performance. This will depend to some extent on your target audience and the nature of the piece you are doing. Journalists tend to give a fairly straightforward performance as they want to foreground the story. However, if it's more of an entertainment piece then obviously the performance of the presenter is very important.

### Length

Think about the length of pieces to camera. Long pieces to camera rarely work well; they tend to end up sounding like a lecture and an inexperienced presenter finds it very difficult to hold a performance for very long. Thirty seconds or about 90 words is probably about right and anything longer than a minute (180 words) may start to sound laborious.

### Presenter eye line

A presenter needs to look directly at the camera (Figures 15.1, 15.2 and 15.3, opposite). They also need to stay looking at the camera all the time and not let their eyes wander. The moment they do they will start to look shifty or as if they don't know what they are doing; it's not a good look.

### Angles

You should also think about the angle of your shot. Do you want the presenter at eye level or would you want to look up or down on them? This mostly depends on the style and the subject matter of your piece; just remember: you can vary the angles, but beware of making the piece start to look a bit comical with too many different shots.

## Shooting interviews

Lots of factual programmes include interviews. These can vary in length and type from a quick vox pop to a lengthy interview with an expert. They may also include eyewitnesses or they can be characters in your piece who may not be experts but who have the kind of experience which will illuminate your subject.

When you are shooting an interview there are a number of things you need to consider. Interview technique is very important and is dealt with in a later chapter. For the moment just think about how you might set up an interview.

### Location

The first thing to consider is where do you want to do the interview? This will depend a little on who you are interviewing and what they are going to be talking about. However, if possible you will want to put your interviewee in a situation that is interesting to the audience. An office isn't a particularly interesting location, although for some types of interviews it is appropriate. Ideally, however, you would choose a location which relates to the subject. This is not only more interesting for the viewer but it is likely to stimulate a better answer as he or she is closer to the subject.

*Figure 15.1* An example of a correct eye line shot

*Figure 15.2*
Two examples
of a poor eye
line shot

### Shot sizes

Typically interviews start with a mid-shot. This helps the viewer understand where the interviewee is, particularly if he is on location somewhere. A head shot doesn't tell the viewer very much. However, you may want a slightly more intimate shot as well, particularly if the interviewee is recounting something personal. A closer shot tells the viewer a lot more about the emotional content of the answer; it will help the audience connect. A combination of wider shots moving into closer shots tends to work well.

### Moves

One thing to avoid is moving your shot during the interview. You should avoid zooms and pans. During the edit you will find it difficult to cut on a move and you will be left with a long, rambling answer. If you want to change shot sizes you should do it between answers, not during them.

### Framing

You should also check your framing on a shot. Remember to think about looking room and head room. Don't cut off the interviewee's chin or have their nose tight up against the edge of frame.

### Eye lines

Eye lines are important during an interview. Unless there is a particular reason you want a low or high angle shot, generally you want the interviewee's eye line to be the same as the interviewer's. So if the interviewee is sitting, the interviewer should be sitting and if the interviewee is standing so should the interviewer. If there is a discrepancy in height between the two you might need to compensate a little (Figures 15.3, 15.4 and 15.5a, opposite).

   The interviewee should never be looking at the camera; this will give the impression that they are the presenter. However, they should not be looking too far either to the left or to the right of camera; you should avoid profile shots, and you should make sure that you can always see the whole face and both eyes. If the interviewer is not in shot then the way to deal with this is to make sure the interviewer sits or stands as close to the camera as possible and asks the interviewee to look at them and not at the camera. That way the eye line will be either just to the left or to the right of the camera which is where it should be. If they are looking too far to the right or left viewers will start to feel disconnected (Figures 15.5b, 15.6 and 15.7, see page 148).

*Figure 15.3*
Eye line too
high

*Figure 15.4*
Eye line too low

*Figure 15.5a*
An example of
a correct eye
line shot

*Figure 15.5b*
An example
of a correct
eye line shot

*Figure 15.6*
Eye line to
camera shot

*Figure 15.7*
Eye line too
much in profile

When you are framing a number of interviews for the same piece then it's a good idea to alternate which side of the camera the interviewer sits or stands between interviews. Thus if you have four interviewees, two of them will be shot with the interviewer standing to the left of the camera and the other two will be shot with them standing to the right of the camera. When you come to the edit, the shots will start to have a more varied feel (Figures 15.8 and 15.9).

*Figure 15.8* Interviewee looks camera right

*Figure 15.9* Interviewee looks camera left

### Interviewer in vision

If you want to have the interviewer in shot there are two options. You can go for an over-the-shoulder shot (Figure 15.10, overleaf). In this type of shot the interviewer should stand immediately in front of the camera and slightly to the left or right. The camera person then widens the angle slightly so that part of the head and one shoulder of the interview is in frame. However, this is not a very comfortable shot and you would not want the whole interview to be conducted in this way. You might just use it to establish the interviewer and then move to a closer shot.

*Figure 15.10* Over-the-shoulder shot

The other option is a two shot where you have both the interviewer and the interviewee in shot (Figure 15.11). This type of shot tends to be used in pieces which have presenters. The presenter is a kind of constant presence and you don't want to lose them from the interview. In this case you should have the interviewee and interviewer standing next to each other and slightly angled towards one another. Again you should angle them so that you can see as much of the face as possible.

*Figure 15.11* Two shot, presenter and interviewee

Again you can change the shot sizes. A wide shot tends to be used to introduce the piece or if there is something in the surroundings that the interviewee is likely to refer to. You might choose to move to closer shots or even single shots for the rest of the interview (Figures 15.12 and 15.13).

*Figure 15.12*
Single of
interviewee

*Figure 15.13*
Single of
presenter

## Matching shots

If you are doing a two-shot interview but have chosen to move into closer singles, you may want to have singles on both the interviewee and the interviewer. In this case you should try to match the shot sizes. It will feel very odd if you have an MCU on the interviewer asking the question and then cut to a CU on the interviewee for the answer. You should try to shoot both in the same size shot (Figures 15.14 and 15.15, overleaf).

## Changing shot size

Just as with a presenter you should avoid moving in and out of shot sizes too much. If you have been using single closer shots then coming back out to a wide shot will signal something to a viewer. It will either signal that you are coming to the end of the interview or that you are going to talk about something which they can see around them.

*Figure 15.14*  Two examples of matching shot sizes

*Figure 15.15*  Two examples of non-matching shot sizes

### *Finishing an interview in a two shot*

Conventionally, if a presenter is in shot then they might end the piece by thanking the interviewee and then perhaps moving on to another piece to camera. When you are thanking the interviewee you can have both people in the shot. You may then choose to come to a closer shot for the piece to camera if you are moving on to a completely different subject.

### *More than two people*

If you are shooting an interview with more than one interviewee then the same sorts of rules apply. If the interviewer is in shot you should place them in such a way as to have them slightly turned towards the interviewees but not so much that you lose their full face. They can either be in the centre or to one side. You should use a wide shot as your opening shot so that the viewer knows who is there and then perhaps cut to closer shots. However, when the interviewer moves from talking to one interviewee to a different one it's a good idea to come out to a wide shot so that the viewer gets the geography of who is talking next.

*Figure 15.16* Presenter plus two interviewees

*Figure 15.17*
Two examples
of a two shot

## Angles

You will also need to decide on the angle of the shot. This is really up to you and how you want the piece to look stylistically. Conventionally, interviews tend to be done with the camera at eye level. If you were interviewing for a news report you would try to keep the camera at eye level.

- **Low angles:** If you use a low angle shot for an interview or for a piece to camera it has the effect of making the interviewee seem powerful, as if they were looking down on you. You might stylistically want to go for a different angle; just be aware that this is not the most flattering angle for most people. If you are going for an extreme angle you will probably want to keep the pieces quite short. Those kinds of angles can be fun but people get tired of them quite quickly and they soon start to look laboured.
- **High angles:** These have the effect of making the viewer feel more powerful in relation to the interviewee or presenter. Again, for stylistic reasons you may want to take this angle but again be aware it won't sustain very long interviews or pieces to camera.

## When to use which shot

There are no fixed rules about when to use what shot. Directors will tend to mix them up all the time. It will only really become clear when you start to edit. However, there is a tendency to use a wide shot or establishing shot early on in the scene so that the viewer gets a sense of where they are and the geography is established. This is not a hard-and-fast rule by any means but it's something to consider. You should avoid moving in and out all the time for no particular reason. When you are shooting a sequence you could start with a WS, move into to MS and then to a CU. However, it will start to look a little odd if you begin with a WS, go straight to a CU and then out to MS, then BCU and then back to a WS. You will discover more about this when you start to edit, but when you are shooting just try to remember to get as many shot sizes and angles as you can to give yourself as much flexibility in the edit as possible.

## Shooting action

Shooting action is filming things that are happening, or filming someone doing something. It may be action that is already happening or it may be something you deliberately set up. It might be that you are just trying to give the viewer a sense of where they are. However, when you shoot action you need to start to think in sequences rather than single shots. You should be thinking about shooting a number of shots which can all be edited together to make an interesting sequence. Shots are rarely much good on their own; one shot only of lots of different things will be worse than useless in your edit. There are several types of action sequences you might have to shoot for a factual programme:

### Close action

This is small-scale action which doesn't involve people moving around too much or moving in or out of shot a lot. You may need to shoot something that someone is doing. It might be some kind of process.

   In order to be able to do this effectively the action will need to be repeated a number of times. As you only have one camera, which can only take one shot at a time, if you want different sizes of shots on the same action you will need to repeat the action.

Typically, a static shot tends to become quite boring after about five seconds; the conventions of film lead us to expect the shot to change. Of course that's not a rule. Many people use much shorter shots and there will be directors who like to hold shots for much longer. But if you imagine a piece of action which takes one minute, you are likely to change shots about 15 times. This does not mean to say that you have to have 15 different shots; you can come back to the same shot a number of times but you do need enough different shots to give the piece some variety.

Some people talk about a five-shot rule. That is to say you should take at least five shots for any sequence. Here are some of the shots you might think about getting:

- A wide shot – sometimes called a master shot.
- Mid-shot: you should try to get at least two of these from different angles.
- Either of the above shots but from the reverse angle.
- Close-ups or cutaways: these are there to show particular parts of the action.
- POVs: point-of-view or over-the-shoulder shots.

### Wide shot

The wide shot should if possible show the complete actions. If something is continuous or you can't do it that many times then this may not be possible. The shot needs to be wide enough to show all the action at the same time. It is sometimes also called a master shot, that's because when you come to the edit, you can always return to this shot if you don't have anything else. However, you will need more than just the wide shot, first because just one shot will be very boring, and second, you can't see anything in detail.

### Moves on a wide shot

Since this is your master shot then depending on the feel of your piece you may not want to have too many moves on it. Possibly you may want to move onto the action at the beginning

*Figure 15.18* Shooting action, wide shot

or off the action at the end but be wary of too many moves in between; you will give your-selves a lot of problems during the edit. However, there are certain styles of programme that use moving shots a lot; they have a high-energy feel to them and the camera is rarely still. They give a sense of urgency and action and of things happening. If this is your style then fine, but you really need to make a decision about that to start with; you can't really mix and match: you have to commit to it!

*Mid-shots*

This will help you get into the action. Going from a wide shot straight to a close-up can leave the viewer feeling a little disorientated, so you will often need to go to a mid-shot first. You should try to get several mid-shots from different angles and you should definitely get one from a different angle to the wide shot. When you come to edit it will feel awkward to cut from a wide shot to a mid-shot at the same angle. This is called a jump cut and can look quite ugly. Again, some directors like to use this kind of shot as a stylistic device but it's difficult to use effectively.

*Figure 15.19*
Shooting
action,
mid-shot/
two shot

*Figure 15.20*
Shooting
action,
mid-shot/
two shot

*Over-the-shoulder or point-of-view shot*

This gives the viewer the feeling that they are watching what the character is seeing. Obviously this only works if you have a person in the shot. It's sometimes helpful to be able to see part of the person's head or shoulder (Figure 15.21).

*Figure 15.21* Shooting action, over the shoulder

*High and low angle shots*

These give a different perspective and will add variety to your finished piece. You can do this dramatically by having a very high or low angle, or something a bit more subtle by changing the height of the tripod or standing on something if you are handholding the camera (Figure 15.22).

*Figure 15.22* Shooting action, low angle

*Close-ups – cutaways*

These need to have a purpose. Random cutaways may not be that useful in the end. You may want to show some particular part of the action. There may be some detail that's important (Figures 15.23 and 15.24). It's often a good thing to have a close shot of the person's face; this would be quite a versatile shot when you come to the edit. Again you need to vary the angle from which you take the close-ups; this will give your piece a feeling of movement and be much more interesting (Figure 15.25, opposite).

*Figure 15.23* Shooting action, close-up

*Figure 15.24* Shooting action, close-up

*Figure 15.25* Two examples of shooting action single shots

Depending on how long the action is, you may not want to shoot all the action in close-up as well as a wide shot, but you should shoot enough to give you a good variety of shots.

*Continuity*

If you are shooting action you need to think about continuity. This means that the action is repeated in the same way each time. When you cut the piece together the viewer is not going to be aware that you have shot this piece of action several times. It needs to feel as if it's the same piece of action you are watching. You therefore need to make sure that the action is repeated in the same way. For example, if the person has to pick up an object, the object should be in the same place to start with each time and they should use the same hand to pick up the object.

*Handles, or top and tailing a shot*

Remember to put handles on the beginnings and ends of all your shots.

## Bigger action

Close action is one type of sequence; you may however need to shoot some action which is much bigger. It could be someone entering a shop and buying something. What you shoot will depend on what you are trying to achieve, but the same basic rules apply. Just as with close action you will need to shoot the same action several times.

*Wide shots*

These need to be big enough to tell the viewer where they are. You may want to take a couple from different angles to give yourself some variety.

*Moving in and out of shots*

Your subject could be in position when you come to the shot or he or she could walk into view. It's also often a good idea to let the subject walk out of shot as well. This is particularly true if the next time you see them they will be somewhere else. Thus if you are looking at the example of someone walking down the street and going into a shop then you may want to start with the subject walking down the street but finish the shot either with him walking out of the frame or walking into the shop. By the end of the shot you will no longer see the subject.

This means that when you find the subject again the viewer won't feel confused. They know he has gone somewhere and are perfectly happy to accept that he is now in a shop. However, if you cut from a picture of a person walking down the street while they are still in frame and then the next shot shows the same person in a shop, it tends to confuse the viewer; they wonder how they got from the street into the shop.

*Mid-shots and close-ups*

If the action is quite long, you may want to spend some time time with the subject walking down the street; in this case you can get some MS and CU as well. Again there should be a purpose to it. If you cut to a close-up the viewer will think you are trying to tell them something. If you aren't purposeful about these shots you will confuse the viewer; they will wonder why you suddenly cut to a close-up of the buttons on his shirt: what are you trying to tell them? While they are trying to work this out they are not watching the rest of the film. Remember too that if you are taking more than one size shot on the same piece of action you will need to change the angle of the camera between shots.

However many close-ups and mid-shots you do like this, make sure that you have all the action in wide shot, particularly the beginnings and ends of the shot, as these will be important in the edit. As with close action you need to remember:

- **Handles:** Again, remember to put handles on the beginnings and ends of the shots.
- **Camera moves:** Be careful of camera moves, pans, tilts etc., and make sure they have a purpose: no hose-piping. You will find it very difficult to edit otherwise.
- **Change the angle:** Make sure you get a good variety of different angles on your shots.

### Following action

Sometimes it's not possible to repeat an action several times. For example, if you were filming a carnival parade you can't ask the floats to come past three or four times to get your shots. In a big drama this is probably what would happen or they would have lots of cameras, but since this is factual you won't be able to do this. In this case the type of filming you do is called 'following action'. Basically this means that the camera has to follow what is happening rather than direct it.

However, even if you are adopting this approach, you should be thinking in sequences and thinking about a variety of shots. It does mean thinking a bit on your feet, so the more you know up front about what you are going to film the better.

With this kind of shooting it's very much down to the cameraperson. You can't set up shots in the ways described earlier; no one is going to stop the parade while you get ready and shout 'Action!' In order to get the best out of this type of filming you need to be aware of the type of story you are trying to tell. So the cameraperson needs to be briefed on the types of shots they are trying to get. If the story is about the fabulous costumes, they need to be focusing on this. If the piece is about potential trouble, they are more likely to be concentrating on the crowd. If it's about the economic benefits of a town having a carnival, they will need to be looking for shots of people buying things, and so on.

### Wide shots

Invariably you are going to need a wide shot. This will tell the viewer where they are and what they are looking at. If you have done a recce, you will have chosen a spot from which you can do a wide shot. If you haven't been able to do so, this is probably the first shot you need to find. This will establish the action and from there you can move into closer shots However, if it's possible it's a good idea to get a wide shot from different angles; again this will give you flexibility in the edit. It will help establish the geography of the scene in the mind of the viewer.

Lots of moving shots won't be a good idea here. You should also try to keep the camera still. A lot of action in front of the camera with lots of action from the camera itself can leave the viewer feeling a little seasick. Don't forget the handles on either end of the shot.

### Mid-shots

As discussed earlier, the success of this type of shooting depends on the cameraperson knowing the subject of the piece and looking for the right shots. They may not have much time, so they will really need to be clear about what they are looking for. Again a lot of movement in the shots here may end up being confusing and difficult to edit. Movements need to be smooth and purposeful rather than random. For the most part keep the camera still and you can let the action happen in front of you.

You will need to move around quite a lot to get different types of shots, and again you should vary the shot size and angle as much as possible to give as much variety as possible.

Finally, you could help the viewer orient themselves by creating some kind of fixed point in the shot. This very much depends on where you are, but in the carnival, for example, there may be some kind of distinctive building or other fixed object. If this is in the wide shot it could also be included in some of the mid-shots. It needn't be the focus of the shot; it can just be in the background, and even though it may be quite subtle it will help the viewer feel orientated.

### Close-ups

As with the mid-shots you will need to understand what you are trying to say in the story before you can shoot any close-ups successfully. Like the mid-shot, a steady camera will probably be more helpful and easier to edit than one with lots of movement in it. Again, if you do use a move you need to put handles on either end of the shot.

Sometimes this kind of shooting is used to create a feeling of *veritas* (truthfulness). Some documentary film-makers like to document rather than direct what is happening. These tend to be personal stories rather than science or history programmes. Remember:

• let the action happen in front of the camera
• take several master shots
• know the story
• vary the angles and sizes of the close-ups and mid-shots
• you can always use more shots; take as much as you feel you can in the time.

The advantage of this type of shooting is that it has quite an energetic feel to it; it's lively and if done well can make the viewer feel very much part of the action.

### General views (GVs)

GVs are sometimes referred to as wallpaper shots, a slightly disparaging term! The name refers to the types of shots you get on location which show the viewer something about the story. You may, for example, be filming a piece which follows a group of teenagers on their first foreign holiday. The GVs would be the shots of the airport, the resort they were staying at, the local shops, beaches, and anything else that will give the viewer a flavour of the location and add colour and variety to your piece. GVs have a number of purposes.

### Establishing shots

These can help the viewer understand where they are and give them a flavour of what is going on. GVs give you an opportunity to film what is going on around the story.

### Help commentary

For the most part you want to try to get your pictures to tell the story; however, you may sometimes need some commentary. Your GVs will help you when you have a commentary section. However, there will be times when you will need to give a bit of commentary and you will need some pictures.

*Introduce contributors*

When you write the commentary you may need to introduce one of your contributors; some GVs of this person going about their business can help with this. You need to be a little careful about doing this; it can easily start to feel extremely clunky. If you introduce contributors in this way make sure they are doing something meaningful; shots of people walking down a street or walking into a building can look very staged and rather dull.

GVs should not simply be a collection of rather random shots. You should still think in terms of sequences, wide shots followed by mid-shots and close-ups on a particular scene. The sequence of shots should be trying to tell the viewer something. Nor are GVs a place to start hose-piping or taking long, meaningless pans. The same kind of thought needs to go into the shots. Use moves sparingly and for a good purpose, and as always make sure that you leave handles on either end of the shot. While you should think carefully about them, you should also get lots of them. They will add an enormous amount to your film.

## Conclusion

Filming for documentaries or other factual programmes involves a number of different techniques. You won't always need all of these techniques; however, it's worth having them at your disposal so that you can bring them out if necessary. When you are doing your planning it's worth thinking about which technique you are going to have to use and when.

# 16 Shooting dramatised sequences

This chapter assumes that you that you are shooting single camera. This means that you are only shooting with one camera rather than with several cameras. In TV, dramas can be shot single camera but can also be shot in a studio with multiple cameras at the same time. A lot of sit coms are shot this way. There will be a number of cameras positioned around the studio space. The director may be on the studio floor but may also sit in a separate gallery and watch the shots on a bank of screens; sometimes they will split their time; they will block the action from the floor but then go into the gallery to rehearse and record. The shots are all rehearsed and chosen in advance. As the scene is played, a vision mixer will change the shots which are being recorded and at the end of the shoot the piece will emerge more or less edited. This method saves time because there are several cameras getting all the different shots at the same time.

However, since you are unlikely to have access to this kind of technology this chapter is going to deal with single camera dramas. Here, since you will only have one camera, you will need to shoot the same scene a number of times to get all the shots you need, WS, CU, etc. While this can be more time consuming these days it's a more popular way of shooting a drama, since it gives you a lot more freedom as you are not tied to a studio set-up. It allows for much more variety in the types of shots and the lighting.

Shooting for factual and shooting for drama is similar in many ways but also differs in others. This chapter looks at some of the processes involved in shooting for drama. If you have read the chapter on shooting for factual some of this will be repetitious, but there's no harm in going over it again.

## Tasks

One of the biggest differences between factual and drama is the number of people involved. Drama shoots tend to involve many more people. There will of course be your cast, but there will also be costumes and props to think about. You will also need to think carefully about how to organise the shooting days to get the most out of the time you have available.

Just as with any other shoot, good team work is essential. It's very important that everyone understands what they are responsible for. Just as with factual, this will vary according to the size of the production and you may be combining tasks, but even if this is the case it's worth remembering what the tasks are.

## *Producer*

It's much more common on a drama shoot to have a producer and a director. This is partly because the tasks are very different and partly because there is more to do generally and you need more people. In a professional shoot the producer would hire the director, be responsible for the money and the logistics, and make sure the piece is delivered. They will also attend shoots and edits. If you do choose to have a separate producer role on the shoot itself, this person could take charge of keeping the shoot moving. They should take charge of the shooting schedule, make sure people know what they are doing when, and help with trouble-shooting and communication.

## *Director*

The director is in charge of the creative vision. They should be the person responsible for interpreting the storyboard and choosing the shots. They are also responsible for communicating with the actors, letting them know what they want out of a scene and how to interpret the script. They need to think about how the shots are going to edit and making sure that they have all the shots they need. They also need to work with the sound and camera to get the right material. On the shoot itself it is the director's job to let everyone know what is going on and who is supposed to do what and when. Just as with a factual shoot this can be hard to do at the same time as thinking about all the shots. Again the preparation work you have done will help here. If you have a good storyboard and a good shooting schedule it gives you the framework for the day. As with the factual it's important to start the day by:

- Reminding everyone what they are doing and the order they are doing it in.
- Introducing everyone – you will probably know each other but if you have new people on the team let them know who everyone is and what they are doing.
- Tell everyone what the first set-up will be and how long you want to spend on it. You will need to keep this kind of communication going all through the day.

If you start this way you will feel more in control of what's happening. Everyone should have a shooting schedule which will tell them where they are supposed to be and what they need when they get there. However, you may need to remind them. If you are new to drama then a good shooting schedule will be important. You will need to work out what time you have available and how much time you can realistically spend on any one scene. Your shooting schedule should remind everyone how long you have got.

## *Camera*

You may have combined this with another job, which is fine, but the camera operator's job is to work with the director to find the best shots. The storyboard will have given you some ideas as to which shots you are looking for but things can change when you are actually looking down the lens of a camera, so you should be constantly offering up suggestions and thoughts if you think there are better ways to achieve a good shot. Most of your communication will be with the director and sound; however, you may also be talking to the cast as to the best positions or moves for the camera. You should be thinking about the best framing for the shots. The camera is also responsible for lighting the shot: you may be using some basic lighting kit and if so it is the cameraperson's job to make sure the lighting is there and in working order, and to light each individual shot. If you are shooting outside you should also be conscious of the sun, which may affect the framing of a shot or indeed the order in which shots are taken. You will be watching out for things like reflections in windows and mirrors; sometimes these reflections show the camera and crew, which rather destroys the illusion you are trying to create. You are also responsible for the safekeeping and labelling of the rushes. It's going to be very important that all the rushes are clearly labelled so that when you come to an edit you won't waste time playing endless rushes to find the shot you want.

### Sound

You will need to think about the dialogue coming from the actors but also any background noises which may be affecting the dialogue. If you've read the chapter on sound you will be familiar with the types of things you will need to consider. Sound, camera and director need to constantly talk to each other. You should be thinking about the continuity of sound. You can't intercut sound taken from a microphone close-up with a microphone 20 metres away. You should not be afraid to alert everyone if you think there is a problem with the sound. At the end of a take you should be clear whether you think the sound was OK or whether there was a problem and you may need to retake. They may get irritated at the time but they will thank you later.

### Props / costumes

You will need to know both the script and the shooting schedule. It will be your job to have the right costumes and props ready at the right time. You will also need to think about extra props; for example, if you want someone to open a can of beer, you will need more than one can. Remember: in a single camera shoot you will be doing the same shot several times. While one scene is being shot you will need to start thinking about the next one so that you can have everything prepared. If you are looking after costumes it's always useful to have a needle and thread to hand, just in case. Also keep spares of anything that can get easily torn; tights, for example. During the shoot you will need to be watching the costumes to make sure that nothing is torn, dirty (unless it's supposed to be), and hanging right.

### Makeup

If you decide to make up your actors you will need to allow time for them to get made up. As the person in charge of makeup you should be looking at the production schedule to see who is in which scene and getting them ready in time. You will need to be on set early as the first thing that normally happens is that people get made up. Proper makeup is quite a complex task and outside the scope of this book. However, when you are actually shooting, especially if it is hot, you may notice people starting to get a little sweaty or shiny. If so, you will need to dab a bit of powder on them, and if you only have one item in the makeup bag it should be powder. You should also be watching for running mascara and that sort of thing; it becomes quite exaggerated when there is a close-up shot.

### Continuity

You will need to have someone watching for continuity. When you shoot a drama you will probably not shoot in sequence. Therefore you need someone keeping an eye on the script and watching that all the scenes will eventually run smoothly together and that the action will make sense. You will probably shoot a number of takes of different scenes and the continuity person will need to make sure that the action is the same each time. If, for example, you are taking a wide shot of someone picking up a glass, when you come to do the same thing in a mid-shot you will need to make sure that the actor picks up the glass with the same hand and holds it in the same way; otherwise editing becomes very difficult. The continuity person is there to keep a note and alert the team if something is different. Continuity can also make sure you don't miss out any shots: easier to do than you might think.

### *Shot listing*

Make a list of all the shots which have been taken and where they are, since this can be helpful in the edit. It will also be useful if you have a lot of retakes. Sometimes there is a long scene and someone forgets their lines right near the end. You may not want to run the whole scene again but just take the part where the person forgot the lines. It's useful if someone is keeping a note of all the different retakes you did.

You may not have enough people in your group for all these tasks to be done by different people. However, even if you combine or share the tasks you should be allocating them to someone. Once you have been allocated the task you should be aware of what you are going to be doing and when.

### *Locations*

You are likely to be fairly limited in the type of location you can film in. Without lots of money you aren't going to be able to hire anywhere and it will be difficult for you to do any complicated shooting in a public place, as you are likely to block footpaths, etc. So you are not likely to have a lot of choice. However, you should try to make the most of the locations to which you do have access. What might seem to you at first to be just one location may in point of fact serve as several locations. Most action will take place in quite a small area, and with careful camera angles and positioning of the camera you can get quite a lot out of some locations.

## Rehearsing

Your project is about creating a film; you are not expected to get Oscar-winning performances from your classmates. The examiners will be looking at many aspects of your piece other than the performance of the cast. However, there are a few simple ways of getting better performances from your cast which will help to give your piece a more polished feel. Since you are likely to be new to directing and your cast new to acting, here are some of the things you might want to think about.

### *Rehearsing lines*

Before you start filming anything you should rehearse your lines. This is a chance for the actors and directors to get an idea of how the script actually sounds rather than how it reads on the page. It is also a chance for the actors and director to think about the delivery of the script and their performance. If you are just rehearsing the lines rather than the moves, then it's not quite so important to be at the actual location; you can just find an available room and rehearse the lines sitting down. Depending on what you have chosen to do, you may want to rewrite a little. If there are some sections which are hard, you can rewrite to make them simpler. However, you should not spend too long on this. One session is enough. The piece will only really come to life when you start blocking and moving the scene.

### Character profiles

Before you start rehearsing, you should know the piece well. You should have a short character profile for each part in the play. You should have something of the characters' backstory, their history up until this point. This may have been provided by the writer or you may have to envisage it for yourself; however you do it, it's probably worth running through these character profiles and backstories before you start rehearsing.

### Characters' relationships

You will also need to think about the characters' relationships with each other. How well do they know each other? Are there any pre-existing tensions between them? What kinds of emotions are they each bringing to the scene?

### Purpose of the scene

What is the purpose of the scene? Is there something that the characters want from each other? Do any of the characters in the scene have particular goals? Is there some plot device contained in the scene?

### What comes before and after?

It's useful to remind actors what has happened during the scene they were in immediately before this one (i.e. in what mood were they when they left that scene?). When you shoot out of sequence it's easy to lose track of the emotional threads which build across a drama.

### Listen

Another good tip for new actors is to tell them to listen and try to respond with their lines, rather than just say them.

### Don't overlap

You should tell your actors to let the person finish speaking before the other starts; it's hard to edit if two people are talking at the same time, unless this is your intention.

### After rehearsing lines

The normal process after rehearsals is for the director to give notes. While the rehearsal is taking place the director should be noting on the script any points he or she would like to give to the actors about the performance. These might be general points about the character or performance or they might be quite detailed notes on specific lines. Directors vary enormously as to the kinds of notes they give, from the very general to the most specific. Actors tend to vary as to how much notice they take of the notes and the extent to which they will discuss them with the director. If you are rehearsing lines without cameras or moves then it's probably best to stick to quite general notes. If possible, use positive feedback – *I really liked the way you did . . . I think perhaps we could do more of that or I think the scene was working well when . . . I think we should try and develop that. . . .* The main point is to give everyone a feel for what the piece is about.

Even the best actors struggle to remember lines, actions, etc. Don't make it too difficult; directors often have to keep it simpler to make it better. The best directors try to make it easier for actors; they may ask, 'Where is this difficult and how can I make this easier?'

Since in this instance you are working as a group, it's probably a good idea to let everyone have a say about what they liked and what they feel could be developed. Try not to let this become an endless and rambling discussion, just give each person a chance to comment on the scene or try something a bit different if they wish. **Remember:** rehearsing lines is an important part of the process but it shouldn't go on for too long. Rehearsals are rather like creative thinking sessions. They are a time when you want as many ideas as possible to surface but at the same time they shouldn't disintegrate into a free-for-all, with everyone shouting out their ideas at the same time.

If you are the director, it's worth using this time as an opportunity to give some more thought to the shots as well as the performance. You should think about the size and angle of the shot and whether you want any moves. You should have already given some thought to this when you prepare your storyboard, but this may change as you start to hear the line actually spoken. Hearing something out loud can significantly change your thoughts.

## Blocking a scene

Before you start any drama shoot you will need to block the scene. This means you will need to decide where, when and how the actors are going to move. You will also have to decide on any business. Business refers to any actions an actor needs to perform other than saying the lines. It may be simply picking up a book and reading, or some very complicated actions. You need to rehearse the blocking in the same way as you rehearse the lines. This is important whether it's a stage or screen drama, but for TV or film drama the way you block the piece will have a significant impact on how you choose your shots. If an actor is performing an important piece of business with his or her hands then there is no point showing just a close-up of his face; you will need to choose a shot which shows the action. Blocking the scene will also help you to decide on the different camera positions you are going to need for each shot as well as the height angle and framing.

It's obviously going to be easier to block a scene if you are in the location in which you are filming, and if at all possible this is what you should try to do. If it isn't possible and you are using a different space, then you will need to be very aware of the layout of the location in which you are going to film so that you can replicate the actual location as closely as possible.

## Choosing your shots

There are no hard-and-fast rules about how you should shoot a scene; if you gave a piece to ten directors they would probably come up with ten different ways of shooting it. Have another look at the piece of script from the chapter on treatments, and start thinking about the types of shot you might choose. There are several points which it will be useful to remember:

- **Establishing the location:** If this is the beginning of the scene the viewer will normally need some way of establishing where they are. You will therefore need an establishing shot or wide shot fairly early on in the scene. It doesn't have to be the first shot but you will probably want to establish the location fairly early on in the scene.
- **MS:** Generally the closer you get the more involved the viewer will become in the scene. However, jumping straight from a wide shot to a closeup might be too big a jump; it may not look very smooth. Often directors will use a mid-shot to bring the viewer into the action. You will need to remember to change the angle of the shots so that you do not have an uncomfortable cut.
- **Close-ups:** These add intimacy and intensity to a scene; you should think about the point in the scene where there is most drama and tension.
- **Point-of-view shots:** You may want to take shots from the point of view of the characters. Remember: the angle will change depending on the point of view. If, for example, you want to take a shot of Florence at the door from the point of view of Jake sitting down, you will need a slightly low angle shot because Jake is sitting down and Florence is standing up. To get a sense of the point of view you would need to have the camera at the height of Jake and angled up slightly. The reverse is true if you were to take a shot of Jake from Florence's point of view. You may also want a point-of-view shot of the letter. Again this would need to be taken from the point of view of the character, so a shot of the letter taken from over the shoulder of the character who is reading the letter would normally work.
- **Moving shots:** Think about these. Moving shots are normally most effective if there is a reason for the move. You may want the camera to follow Florence as she moves across the room to the desk. This camera move is motivated by the fact that the character is moving. However, simply panning between Florence and Jake while they are standing may look a little odd unless there is some motivation in the script for the camera move.
- **Camera angle:** Think about the angle you are using. Remember: if your camera is flat onto the scene it doesn't give the picture much depth. If you are shooting the two characters at the desk you may want to try using a slight angle to the left or right which will give the picture a lot more depth and make it look a little more interesting.
- **High and low angles:** Be careful with high and low angles. In the viewer's mind they tend to be associated with a point of view. So if you suddenly decide to shoot a low angle shot of Florence the viewer will tend to assume that Jake has somehow got down onto the floor and is looking up at her or some other unlikely scenario, which would account for your choice of camera angle. If you use a high angle the viewer might assume that one of the characters has stood up. If two people are sitting next to one another then you would usually opt for a camera at eye line. Again there are no hard-and-fast rules, and when you watch films you will see directors using all kinds of angles. The main thing is to be aware of the effect that this might have and use them for a purpose rather than for the sake of it.
- **Depth of field:** You can alter the depth of field by positioning the camera and using the zoom lens. However, you will need to think about when and why you want to use a long or shallow depth of field. Remember: a shallow depth of field directs the attention of the viewer onto the main focus of the scene. Anything in front or behind the main focus will be a little soft or blurry.
- **Matching shots:** Often when there is a piece of dialogue between two characters the camera will switch between close-ups of the two characters as they speak. It's a good idea to get matching shots, so that if you do a close-up of Jake's dialogue you should also do

a close-up of Florence's dialogue. This will help a smooth edit. You should make sure that the shots match and that the two characters are the same size in frame.

- **Shooting close action:** If you are shooting a piece of close action, for example Jake taking the letter out of his pocket, to help with the editing you should film the complete action. So, in this instance you would start with a shot of the pocket with no hand in vision, film the action of the hand coming in and taking the letter, and then let the hand and the letter go out of frame. You may not end up using the whole shot but it will give you maximum flexibility in the edit.
- **180-degree rule or crossing the line:** Remember the rule on crossing the line. Stay on the right side of the line for your shots and that way the viewer won't get muddled about the geography.

## Storyboards and shot lists

At this point you will probably need to start to revise your storyboard. The rehearsal and blocking process should mean that you will want to make some changes or additions to any storyboard you have sketched out so far at the treatment stage.

However, not everyone finds storyboards that easy; an alternative is simply to describe the shot in words rather than draw an actual picture. The key point is that before you start shooting you will need to have either a detailed storyboard or a detailed description of each shot. For each shot you should describe:

- The size of the shot.
- The angle of the shot.
- The depth of field. *Remember:* moving the camera closer to the action and closing the aperture will mean a longer depth of field (less of it will be blurry) and vice versa.
- Camera moves. If there is a camera move you would normally draw or describe the beginning and the end of the shot.
- Any action from the actor.

## EXERCISE 16.1  Blocking and storyboarding drama

Here is the piece of the script from the earlier chapter on treatments; you can download this from the website. Read it through and try to work out how you would block it, and then start to think about your storyboard or shot list. Either describe or draw the shot on each piece of action or dialogue. Indicate the size, angle, framing and any moves you want.

Think about:

- Where and how you are going to establish the location.
- How would you cover the move as the girl walks from the door to the table?
- What kinds of size shots you would use.
- What kind of angle would you use?
- How would you handle the depth of field?
- Remember the 180-degree rule or crossing the line.

| Scene 1 | |
|---|---|
| Interior<br>AN EMPTY CLASSROOM. A TEENAGE BOY IS SITTING AT A DESK, READING A LETTER. THE DOOR OPENS AND A TEENAGE GIRL ENTERS. SHE IS ANXIOUS AND IN A HURRY. THE BOY JUMPS AND LOOKS ALARMED WHEN HE SEES THE GIRL AND HURRIEDLY TRIES TO HIDE THE LETTER. | |
| 1. FLORENCE<br>There you are. What are you doing? | |
| 2. JAKE<br>Nothing. | |
| 3. FLORENCE<br>Are you coming? | |
| JAKE<br>No | |
| FLORENCE WALKS OVER TO THE DESK AND SITS DOWN. | |
| 4. FLORENCE What were you reading? | |
| 5. JAKE Nothing. | |
| 6. FLORENCE Show me. | |
| JAKE RELUCTANTLY UNCOVERS THE LETTER. FLORENCE TAKES A LOOK AT IT. | |
| 7. FLORENCE<br>Oh my god! Where did you get this? | |
| 8. JAKE<br>Someone sent it to me. | |
| 9. FLORENCE<br>Who? | |

| | |
|---|---|
| 10.  JAKE<br>How should I know? It was just<br>in my bag. | |
| 11.  FLORENCE<br>Jake, please, listen to me; you can't let<br>this sort of thing get to you. People who<br>send letters like this – they are just<br>ignorant. | |
| 12.  JAKE:<br>But it does get to me – I can't help it –<br>it's easy just to say to ignore it but if it<br>was happening to you you wouldn't be<br>able to ignore it. | |
| FLORENCE CRUMPLES UP THE<br>LETTER. | |
| 13.  FLORENCE<br>It's just crap – leave it – don't think<br>about it. | |
| FLORENCE STANDS UP. | |
| 14.  FLORENCE<br>Come on, let's go. | |
| 15.  JAKE<br>No – I'm going to stay here. | |
| 16.  FLORENCE<br>Suit yourself – but you're an idiot if you<br>let this kind of thing stop you doing the<br>things you want to do. | |
| FLORENCE WALKS OUT OF THE<br>ROOM, CLOSING THE DOOR BEHIND<br>HER. THEN JAKE STARTS TO PICK UP<br>THE PIECES OF CRUMPLED PAPER.<br>SCENE ENDS. | |

## How much to shoot

Your storyboard is a sequence of shots. It is a sketched-out example of how your piece will look once it's edited. However, when you actually come to shoot the piece it is best to shoot more than just the shots in your storyboard or shot list. You will find the performances rather jerky if you film only one shot at a time.

A drama director will run whole sections of a scene in one shot and then run the whole section again in a second and third shot if necessary. This gives the actors a chance to achieve a better performance and it gives you a bit more choice in the edit. Thus, for example, in the preceding script there is a section at the table from Speeches 4–13. The director is likely to shoot the whole of this section three ways: once in a close-up on Jake, once in a close-up on Florence and once on an MS on the two characters. Although not all of this will be used in the edit, it will give you more flexibility.

However, if you try and film the whole of every scene in every conceivable shot size just to give yourself flexibility you will soon find yourself running out of time. You will need to find a balance between getting a good performance and enough coverage and leaving yourself enough time to get the essential shots.

You can simply write down a list of the shots that you want to get, but the example below gives you a slightly different way of doing it, which makes it very clear how much you intend to shoot. The different colours show the different types of shot and how much of the dialogue or action is going to be covered in which shot. You will notice that much more of the action and dialogue is covered in each type of shot than will be used in the final piece.

You can download this from the website.

## Template 16.1 Tramlines script

| DIALOGUE AND ACTION | W/S | MS JAKE at table | MS FLORENCE at table | CU letter on floor | POV JAKE reading letter | CU JAKE |
|---|---|---|---|---|---|---|
| INTERIOR; AN EMPTY CLASSROOM. A TEENAGE JAKE IS SITTING AT A DESK, READING A LETTER. THE DOOR OPENS AND A TEENAGE FLORENCE ENTERS. SHE IS ANXIOUS AND IN A HURRY. JAKE JUMPS AND LOOKS ALARMED WHEN HE SEES FLORENCE AND HURRIEDLY TRIES TO HIDE THE LETTER. | | | | | | |
| FLORENCE There you are. What are you doing? | | | | | | |
| JAKE Nothing. | | | | | | |
| FLORENCE Are you coming? | | | | | | |

| DIALOGUE AND ACTION | W/S | MS JAKE at table | MS FLORENCE at table | CU letter on floor | POV JAKE reading letter | CU JAKE |
|---|---|---|---|---|---|---|
| JAKE No. | ▓ | | | | | |
| FLORENCE WALKS OVER TO THE DESK AND SITS DOWN. | ▓ | | | | | |
| FLORENCE What were you reading? | ▓ | ▓ | ▓ | | | |
| JAKE Nothing. | ▓ | ▓ | ▓ | | | |
| FLORENCE Show me? | ▓ | ▓ | ▓ | | | |
| JAKE RELUCTANTLY UNCOVERS THE LETTER. FLORENCE TAKES A LOOK AT IT. | ▓ | ▓ | ▓ | | | |
| FLORENCE Oh my god! Where did you get this? | ▓ | ▓ | ▓ | | | |
| JAKE Someone sent it to me. | ▓ | ▓ | ▓ | | | |
| FLORENCE Who? | ▓ | ▓ | ▓ | | | |
| JAKE: How should I know? It was just in my bag. | ▓ | ▓ | ▓ | | | |
| FLORENCE Jake, please, listen to me, you can't let this sort of thing get to you. | ▓ | ▓ | ▓ | | | ▓ |
| People who send letters like this – they are just ignorant. | ▓ | ▓ | ▓ | | | ▓ |
| JAKE But it does get to me – I can't help it – it's easy just to say to ignore it but if it was happening to you you wouldn't be able to ignore it. | ▓ | ▓ | ▓ | | | ▓ |
| FLORENCE TEARS UP LETTER. | ▓ | ▓ | ▓ | | | ▓ |
| FLORENCE: It's just crap. Leave it – don't think about it. | ▓ | ▓ | ▓ | | | ▓ |
| FLORENCE STANDS UP. | ▓ | ▓ | ▓ | | | |
| FLORENCE Come on, let's go. | ▓ | | | | | |

| DIALOGUE AND ACTION | W/S | MS JAKE at table | MS FLORENCE at table | CU letter on floor | POV JAKE reading letter | CU JAKE |
|---|---|---|---|---|---|---|
| JAKE No – I'm going to stay here. | | | | | | |
| FLORENCE Suit yourself – but you're an idiot if you let this kind of thing stop you doing the things you want to do. | | | | | | |
| FLORENCE WALKS OUT OF THE ROOM, CLOSING THE DOOR BEHIND HER. JAKE STARTS TO PICK UP THE PIECES OF THE LETTER. SCENE ENDS. | | | | | | |

You will notice that working out your shots in this way tells you two things:

1   It tells you what shots will cover which pieces of dialogue; it also tells you how many times you are going to have to run the same pieces of dialogue. This should start to give you an idea of how long it's going to take.
2   It also tells you the order of importance. The most important shot is on the left and the least important on the right. This way you know in which order to shoot them so that if you do run short of time you will have the most important shots.

## What to shoot when

Generally, when you start shooting a scene like this you would start with the wide shots. When you have lights the wide shots will usually take the most time to light. The lighting for the wide shot also forms the basis of the rest of the lighting. This is the most time-efficient order to shoot in. Even if you aren't using lights the wide shot is probably the one to start with. You will need to think about the sound here. If you have a choice, what kind of microphone will you use? If it's a boom, how close can you get for the sound?

In a short scene like this you could record the whole thing in a wide shot. You are unlikely to use many of the wide shots after the beginning up until the end but it gives you options. It doesn't really take that much more time to record the whole thing than to record specific lines.

You will then need to prioritise which are the most important shots. You should do the most important shots next; that way, if you run out of time you will have enough to cover the rest of the scene. In your shooting schedule you will need to indicate the most important shots.

•   **Singles:** When you come to shoot the singles, again you can run as much of the scene as you could conceivably use in that size shot. You should run all the dialogue from both characters and not just the one you are filming. First, this gives you options to use reaction shots (the shots of the person reacting to what the other one is saying). Second, it will feel smoother and the performance will be better. Third, it will give you the opportunity for L-shaped editing, which will be discussed later.

- **Reverses:** If you shoot a character from one shot size and angle, you should also shoot the reverse shot on the second character at the same size and corresponding angle. Again this will give you the opportunity and flexibility in the edit to choose between shots.

- **Retakes:** Identify why the shot has gone wrong and solve that problem before you shoot again; don't just keep shooting in the hope that it will be all right this time. For example, are you expecting your actors to remember too much in one go, is the blocking too complicated, are you expecting them to remember lots of tricky continuity? Does the camera operator not have enough time to move? If you think about why the shot has gone wrong then you may be able to change something to make it simpler.

- **Remember:** Filming takes a lot longer than you think. It can take several goes to get just one shot right. There are lots of things to go wrong – sound, actors, camera – and they don't always go wrong together. They can each go wrong separately and then you will have four takes just to get one usable shot. Inexperienced directors tend to massively underestimate the amount of time it's going to take. A good storyboard and shot list will help you identify which are the most important shots that you must have and which are good options.

## Continuity

By now you should be able to see why it's important to think about continuity. You are shooting the scene in lots of different ways over quite a long time span, but when it's edited together the viewer will need to feel that the whole thing has happened in a matter of minutes or seconds.

- **Continuity of costume and props:** If there are a lot of props around, it's quite easy for things to be moved without anyone noticing. But you need to make sure that if a prop is visible in a mid-shot or close-up it's in the same position as it was in the wide shot, unless of course some part of the action meant that it was moved. Props which pop up and disappear like magic can be a little disconcerting to the viewer. The same is true of costumes. All members of your cast need to keep the same costume for wide shots and close-ups in any given scene. You will need to think about how they were wearing the clothes (e.g. if the character was wearing a coat and carrying a bag and a holdall, was the coat done up, which shoulder did they have the bag over, what hand were they carrying the holdall in?). Sometimes the costume person will take a photo of the characters just to remind them how they were dressed. This is particularly important if you aren't shooting the scene all in one go.

- **Continuity of action:** This can be hard to remember which is why someone needs to be looking out for it. But, for example, if you see Jake putting the letter in his left-hand pocket in the wide shot, then, when he comes to take the letter out of his pocket later in the scene, he needs to take it out of the same pocket or else the action will feel odd. If Florence is holding the letter in her right hand as she reads it in the wide shot, then she needs to hold it in the same hand when you take the closer shots. As you can imagine, the more action, the more complicated the continuity becomes.

- **Continuity of weather:** The weather is notoriously changeable; it can be dull and grey one day and then the next very bright and sunny. For this reason, if you are shooting outside you should try and film a particular scene all in one go. Try not to film over two days. If you do and the weather has changed then the piece will be impossible to cut together.

- **Continuity on location:** If you are shooting in a public place where life is going on around you, it's going to be very difficult to control the continuity. You can't control what members of the public do and where they go. You may, for example, have two people standing in the street talking, with a bus in the background. However, by the time you get to do the close-up or mid-shot the bus is likely to have disappeared and the shots will look odd when you cut them together. If you have a multi-million-pound budget you can close the street off and control what's happening; however, in your case I would think carefully about your location and try to choose one where the continuity problems won't overwhelm you.

## Moving from one scene to the next

As well as thinking about the continuity within a scene itself you will need to give some thought about the continuity between different scenes. Our brain gets bothered by some things but then completely unbothered by others. The trickiest situation is if you have a character at the end of one scene and then the same character appears at the beginning of the next scene but in a different location. If the same character appears in the last shot of one scene and the first shot of the next scene, our brain becomes confused and doesn't understand how that character jumped from one place to the next.

There are several ways of dealing with this:

- **Establish the new location:** Careful choice of shots to begin and end scenes. You may want to start on something other than the character, namely a cutaway – this will give our brains enough time to adjust; however, you will need to make this a part of the action, as every shot in a drama has to tell a part of the story. Thus, in the example above, if Florence leaves the classroom and the next scene has her sitting in a café, you might use an MS of the person serving behind the counter in the café to establish the new location. The question for the director is not 'How do I bridge between shots of my main character in different locations?' but what shot are you going to use to show the viewer you have moved to a new location? Cutting to an irrelevant cutaway may confuse the viewer more, since they will assume you're showing them something that they need to see.
- **Change the size of shot:** A dramatic change of shot size is often enough to establish a change of scene. If you end one scene with a CU or MS of a character, then a VWS on the same character to start the next scene will help the viewer. So in our example, if your last shot was a CU of Florence as she leaves the room, the next shot could be a VWS of Florence walking down a street; this will make the cut appear smooth.
- **Find the character:** Make the first shot a move that starts on something which establishes the location and then moves to reveal the character. So at the end of the first scene have the character walk out of the frame. When you start the next shot make sure you don't start on the character but use a move to 'find' or 'reveal' the character.

# Music

Music in drama is usually added during the edit rather than during the shoot. This is true not just for the incidental or non-diegetic music but also for most diegetic music. If, for example, your characters are meant to be listening to some music, you would lay this music during the edit rather than have them listening to it while they are talking. The reason is that editing music is very difficult to get right and if you get it wrong it's very obvious. Since you will be cutting together lots of different takes, it will be impossible to cut any music running behind it if you record the music and dialogue at the same time, and you will end up with lots of ugly sound edits. You should record the dialogue with no music, even if it is part of the action, and then lay the music later during the edit.

## Music videos

Shooting a music video is a very similar process to shooting a drama. You would use the same techniques of blocking and storyboarding your shots. The real difference is that your music and lyrics are your script. You will need to think about how your shots develop over the song.

Music videos have the advantage that they don't necessarily have to create the same kind of reality as might a drama. There is in one way a lot more freedom. However, this is rather two-edged. Too much freedom without a lot of thought and your music video will end up a bit of a mess. Lots of shots coming at you but not a lot of cohesion, and the viewer will soon tire of watching it.

You should use the same techniques of storyboarding your music video and then produce a shot list in the same way.

- **Performance-based videos:** In this type of video you will obviously want to think about the location. Are you going to show the video in a venue with an audience or will you film somewhere else? You will also need to think about the sequence of shots. Which musicians will you feature, which instruments will you feature? To do this effectively you will need to know your music. There's not much point featuring the drummer during a solo by the bass guitarist. You will need to think about camera angles and moves, and how these might best complement the music. You have a lot more freedom in the edit with this type of music video but you don't want to end up with a confusing mess.
- **Narrative-based videos:** Here you are going to use the same techniques as I described for drama; however, instead of a script you will have your music and possibly the lyrics.
- **Concept-based videos:** This is likely to be a combination of specially shot material and then graphic or video effects laid on top. You should have a good idea of the types of video effects you want to use before you edit and have experimented with some material. This will also tell you if there is anything you will need to watch out for. For example, some effects may not work well if the shot is too dark or, if the shot is moving, you need to know this kind of thing before you start shooting.
- **Music:** You will need to be able to play the music on the shoot. You will need some kind of playback device so that the artists can hear the music. However, you won't use the sound from the shoot except in exceptional circumstances. Just as with a drama, if you are shooting things lots of times and in many different ways you are going to have to edit the shots together. If you use the sound on location you will also have to edit the sound together. This is very difficult, as editing music is much harder than editing speech. It is

much better to lay the music once all the shots have been put together. This does create the problem that if there are sung lyrics you will have to make sure that it is 'sync'd'. This means that the music has to fit the movements of the singer's lips. This is why you need to have the music at the shoot so that you know everyone is singing at the right speed. Because there is generally no dialogue in a music video you don't have the same problem as with a drama. When you get to the edit you wouldn't use the location sound but just lay the clean music track at the edit.

## Conclusion

As you can see, even a very simple set-up involves quite a lot of thought; the more people and the more action, the more complicated it becomes and the more carefully you have to think about each individual shot and how to cover the action and dialogue effectively. It is very difficult to get all these elements right, particularly if you are not experienced. That is why thorough preparation is absolutely essential. If you have done a good storyboard or shot list then you don't need to worry about having to remember what shots you will need. If you have done a good running order for the day then you won't need to spend time reminding people about what they are supposed to be doing next and answering lots of questions. If you have allocated tasks properly you will find that fewer things are forgotten.

All this preparation will leave you free on the day to look at the things you will need to think about: getting the best framing for the shots, getting the most interesting shot, getting the best performance from the cast. If you've done your prep then you will have more head space for the things that should be done on the day.

# 17 Interview techniques

Before reading this chapter you may find it useful to download the treatment for a factual programme from Chapter 8.

   If you are doing an interview for either radio or television there are a number of tips which can help you to get the best out of the interview. In previous chapters we talked about the technical aspects of setting up an interview: the location, the shot composition, the ambient noise, the type of microphone, etc. This chapter deals with how you talk and relate to your contributor. The tips relate both to television and to radio; however, it's worth remembering that radio is a very much more intimate medium. When you listen to the radio you feel much closer to the contributor than you do if you are watching a television programme.

## Purpose of the interview

There are a number of different reasons why you might want to interview someone. A lot depends on the kind of programme you are making. If you understand the purpose of your interview it will help you to prepare the questions properly.

*   **Factual:** You are asking the person to give you information or to demonstrate something.
*   **Explanation:** You and the audience already know the facts but you would like to have them explained or elaborated.
*   **Opinion and controversy:** You may be covering an issue over which there is some kind of debate and you are asking the interviewee to comment on one side or the other.
*   **Witness/experiential:** Your interviewee may be a witness to or participant in an event. They may have some kind of personal experience which is relevant to your piece. In this case you might be looking to them to provide you with some kind of colourful description; this may also involve some sort of emotion, particularly if you are dealing with a sensitive subject.
*   **Celebrity interviews:** You may be lucky enough to find a willing celebrity to interview. Some of these may be a vehicle for the celebrity to promote their latest work, or they may be involved in some kind of issue.

It is perfectly possible that the same person could give you different types of interviews or combine some of the above elements in the same interview. The main thing you need to be clear about is what you are looking for in the interview.

## Preparation

- **Preparing yourself:** You should have a list of things you want to talk about and you should brief the interviewee on what the interview will be about. Above all you will need to know why you are doing this interview, the main points you want the interviewee to cover and how it fits into your piece. You should write these points down so that you can refer to them and make sure they are covered.
- **Know about the subject**: The more you know about the subject itself the better your interview is likely to be, so you should be well prepared. If the interview is part of a discussion or debate or where there is some sort of controversy, you should know both sides of the argument before you start the interview, and not find out all about it from the interviewee. You should also know any relevant facts about the subject. You can prepare briefing notes for yourself, making a list of the relevant points. Finally, you will need to know the name and position of the person you are interviewing. Sounds odd but it's not unknown for the name of an interviewee to go flying out of your head the moment you meet them, so make sure you have their name and position written down. When you first meet, you should check with the interviewee that you have the right name and pronunciation and that any title is correct.
- **Prepare the interviewee:** You should have given the interviewee a briefing during the research and preparation stage, but it won't do any harm to remind them what the interview is for, what kinds of areas you want to cover and how long you think the interview will take. It may also be useful for the interviewee to know who else you are interviewing.
- **Prepare areas for discussion:** You may want to make a list of questions for yourself. However, you will need to use this list carefully and selectively. You shouldn't feel that you have to slavishly stick to the questions you have written, in the order you have written them. The interview will become rather wooden if you do this. If you can, it is much better to make a note of the areas that you want to cover, rather than a list of specific questions; it will sound much more natural if you can do this rather than read a scripted question, and it well put your interviewee more at ease. You should always be prepared for a follow-up question which should come out of the last answer you heard.

## Questions

### *Listen to the answer*

Oddly, the most important piece of advice when you are interviewing someone is to listen to what they are saying. This sounds fairly obvious; however, when you have got microphones, cameras to worry about and fretting about the sun or background noises you start to get distracted. Added to this you may start to get worried about what you are going to ask next and whether the next question is still relevant or whether it will sound stupid now. Perhaps the interviewee has answered the second question at the same time as the first, and now you can't remember the third question; again you will start to get distracted and stop listening to the interview. If you stop listening to the interview you won't be able to ask follow-up questions. You will simply have to read off your list. The interviewee will pick up on the fact that you are distracted and start to feel a little uncomfortable; they may feel that they aren't doing a very good job. Your aim is to get a relaxed feel to the interview. Look at the treatment from Chapter 8 and think about the opening interview.

## Opening question

Some interviewees may feel a bit nervous or take a little time to get into their stride. You may find it useful to ask some sort of general question to start with; it should be on the subject but should be a bit of a warm-up question. Sometimes it's useful to repeat the opening question at the end of the interview; once the interviewee has warmed up a bit they will probably give you a better answer.

## Follow-up questions

A follow-up question is one which arises out of the answer the interviewee has just given. You may want them to elaborate a little or there may a supplementary question you need to ask. It helps put the interviewee at their ease if you pick up on something they said in the interview as a starting point for the next question. For example:

> *I was interested in the point you just made about litter – can you tell me . . .*

> *You just touched on something there which I'd like to ask you a bit more about.*

The interviewee will automatically feel a little more relaxed as he or she realises you have been listening, and encouraged that you have picked up on something and want to know more.

## Open and closed questions

A critical key to a successful interview is to avoid what are known as closed questions. A closed question is one to which the interviewee can answer with a simple yes or no. This is particularly important if the interviewer is not going to appear in vision. Thus, for example:

> Question: *Mr Smith, you are the environmental officer with responsibility for festival litter?*

> Answer: *Yes.*

If the interviewer is not going to appear in vision then the only bit of this interview you can use is the word *Yes* which isn't going to be very helpful. Better to use open questions to which you cannot answer with one word. For example:

> Question: *Mr Smith, can you describe the role of the environmental officer at this festival?*

> Answer: *The environmental officer is responsible for making sure the festival organisers have made adequate provision for the removal of tents. . . .*

There are a number of different techniques for asking open questions. One easy one is to make sure your questions start in such a way that it's impossible for the interviewee to answer yes or no. For example, questions which start:

- *Tell me . . .* or *Can you describe . . .* will always elicit a better answer.
- *Who, what, why, how, when, which*: *Why* is a particularly good word to start with; it will almost always mean your interviewee has to offer some kind of explanation or judgement of an issue, rather than just give you a quick answer.

However, you will need to be careful with these types of questions as they can sometimes be answered too quickly. For example:

> Question: *Who is responsible for collecting the tents?*
>
> Answer: *The litter pickers.*

Again this is not particularly helpful. A better framing might be:

> Question: *Can you tell me how you organise the workforce to collect the tents?*

*Very open questions*

It is possible to ask a question which is too open. These questions tend to leave the interviewee a little confused as to what you really want them to answer. For example:

> Question: *Tell me about waste at festivals . . .*

The interviewee could be forgiven for feeling a little at sea with this question; it's so wide they probably won't know where to start and are more than likely to stumble and ask you for some clarification.

## Controversy

Sometimes, particularly in news and current affairs, the interviewee is giving you one side of an argument. You may have sympathy with his or her view or you may take the opposite view; either way you shouldn't let your own views be obvious and you shouldn't, as an interviewer, become involved in the discussion. This does not mean to say that you shouldn't put the opposing view. You should do this but you need to make it clear that this is not your view. For example:

> Question: *Mr Smith, the pressure group Tidy Britain has argued that festivals like this should be banned as they cause environmental damage – how would you answer their criticisms?*

Even if you can't attribute the counter-argument to a specific person you should always keep a distance from it. For example:

> Question: *Mr Smith, some people have suggested that it would be better to ban festivals like this because of the environmental damage. How would you respond to them?*

## How do you feel . . . questions

Sometimes it's tempting to ask the question *How do you feel . . .* about something. This can be a tricky question to answer. It can put the interviewee on the spot and they might just answer with a few rather banal adjectives. For example:

> Question: *How to you feel about so much waste at these festivals?*
>
> Answer: *Well I think it's terrible really, I think it should stop . . .*

When you come to the edit, the only usable bits are *Well it's terrible really, I think it should stop.* Again that's not going to be very helpful. It might help to be a little more specific:

Question: *What are the consequences for you personally, having to deal with so much waste?*

Answer: *Well for me personally it means a great deal of time is spent and it's awful to watch so much stuff being destroyed when I know there are people out there with very little; I find it quite hard to deal with.*

## Anecdotes

In either television or radio you want your interviews to be engaging and colourful. Your viewer or listener will be much more engaged with your interviewee if they can give examples and anecdotes rather than just rather bland comments. They may not tell you any anecdotes to begin with but this is something you need to winkle out of them with your follow-up questions. For example:

Question: *Mr Smith, what are the consequences for you personally having to deal with so much waste?*

Answer: *Well for me personally it means a great deal of time is spent, and it's awful to watch so much stuff being destroyed when I know there are people out there with very little, I find it quite hard to deal with.*

Question: *Can you tell me the worst instances of waste you have come across?*

Answer: *Well yes, I remember there was one family, they had a six-berth tent and when we found it, it was still set up for supper – all the plates and cups were laid out – there was a pot of tea on the table and salad and condiments all laid out – it was a bit spooky, it looked as if they had just suddenly disappeared – but what had happened is that they had been called away to deal with their vehicle which was sinking in the mud and they had got so fed up by the time they got the car out of the quagmire, they just wanted to get home, so they just left everything and drove off – clothes, sleeping bags, everything was just lying there waiting for this family who were never going to come back.*

## One question at a time

Make sure that you ask just one question at a time. Long, wordy questions which are really about three questions rolled into one will become confusing to all but the most experienced interviewee. They won't know which question you really want them to answer and the answer is likely to be a bit rambling, or they will probably just answer the last question and forget about the others. So, for example:

Question: *Mr Smith, we've heard about the problem you have with the number of tents you've got left over at the end of a festival; can you tell us a bit about how you deal with the tents, who picks them up and what happens to them after you have collected them all?*

You've really asked three questions here: how do you deal with the tents, who does the work and what happens to the tents after they have been collected. Your interviewee will be confused about which of the three questions to answer first; they will more than likely pick on one and forget about the others, but even if they don't, the answers will become rather confused and difficult to edit later. It's better just to ask one of the three questions and then use the other two as supplementary questions.

### Vox Pops

This stands for the Latin *Vox Populi* (voice of the people). It tends to be used when you want to achieve a range of popular opinion on a subject. It is also used in some contexts to give eye witness reports on an event. In this case your interviewees won't necessarily be experts and they won't have been briefed. The questions therefore need to be fairly simple; you are really asking for a quick reaction to something. If the subject is controversial you should make an effort to get a range of opinions to reflect both sides of the argument. You shouldn't be using Vox Pops selectively to support an argument you want to make, particularly if it is a news and current affairs type of programme; you should fairly reflect what you are hearing.

### Start the answer with the question

It can be useful to brief your interviewee to include a little bit of the question in the answer. Again, when you come to edit the piece together it will make much more sense and will avoid you having to use clunky commentary. For example:

> Question: *Mr Smith, can you tell me about the methods you have for getting rid of the 5000 tents you have left here?*
>
> Answer: *Well, first we go through and check that the tents are empty and there are no stray festival-goers.*

This is not a particularly bad question but it may be easier in your edit if you brief the interviewee to add in a little of the question at the top of the answer. For example:

> Answer: *Well we have strict procedures for getting rid of tents at this festival, first we go through and check that the tents are empty.*

When you get to the edit you will find that the second answer gives you more flexibility. You will have less work to do in your commentary to set up what the contributor is talking about.

## Things to avoid before the interview

* **Avoid scripts:** Don't let your contributor read from a prepared speech. It will always come across sounding staged and unnatural. Contributors do sometimes feel very nervous and want to prepare in advance. You should almost always prepare your interviewee: they should know what type of programme it is and the main points of the piece. It will help them if you let them know the areas you are going to want to cover.
* **Don't let contributors wear dark glasses:** (television only) If your contributor is wearing dark glasses it's a good idea to ask them to remove them. It is very disconcerting for a viewer. If they can't see the person's eyes, then they are likely to disconnect with them emotionally and stop watching. As a viewer, you don't have the same visual cues as you do when you are talking to someone in real life. If the shot is a CU or MCU then you won't see much of the body language. The eyes are a very important part of communication.

- **Avoid bright sunlight:** Again for television viewers someone squinting in the sunshine can be very off-putting. Sunlight can also cast quite a dark shadow across the eyes which makes it look as though the interviewee is wearing sunglasses. If you are interviewing someone outside, try to avoid having them face directly into the sunlight so that they squint.
- **Don't let your interviewee eat or drink when talking:** There is nothing more off-putting, particularly on radio, than the sound of someone chewing or swallowing while they are talking. Your interviewees shouldn't eat or drink while they are talking to you. If it's a long interview then it's likely that the interviewee will need some water, but its best that you stop recording in between questions and let them have a drink, and then resume the interview.
- **Don't use swivel chairs or rocking-chairs:** For either radio or television, try to avoid putting your interviewee in a chair that moves. They are likely to be rather nervous and when this happens they are likely to rock or swivel more than usual. This will look very odd on screen and will mean that their voice is constantly getting nearer or further way from the microphone. If they are sitting, make it a firm, fixed chair.
- **Pieces of paper:** Try not to let the interviewee have pieces of paper with notes on in their hands during the interview. On radio they will start to rustle the papers and it will be distracting; on television it looks odd. Often interviewees will have made notes they want to refer to and that's fine, but tell them to put the notes to one side during the answer and refer to them between questions.

## Things to avoid during the interview

- **Don't interrupt the interviewee:** You should not interrupt the interviewee while they are talking. Apart from being a bit rude it will make the piece difficult to edit. You should wait until they have finished the answer and then ask the next question.
- **Don't talk during the interview:** Sometimes when we are holding a conversation we tend to interject with small comments – *mmm yes . . ., oh really . . ., goodness. . . .* You should avoid this during an interview. It will prove very irritating to the viewer or listener. You can smile and nod as encouragement but don't speak. It's sometimes a good idea to warn the interviewee about this in advance; it can look a little odd if they are not expecting it.
- **Don't use camera moves:** (television only) You may want a number of different shot sizes; however, you should always change shot size between questions and not during them. It is very difficult to make an edit on a move, so generally you should avoid any zooms or pans. If you use them you are likely to be stuck with having to use the whole of an answer, however long and boring, and you won't be able to cut anything out.
- **Noddies (if possible):** (television only) Noddies are cutaways of the interviewer, usually nodding or smiling. They tend to be used in the edit if you want to cut out a bit of what the interviewer says. They look very clunky and these days rather old-fashioned. It's also surprisingly difficult to pull off a convincing nod. It is better to think of other ways to cover an edit.

## Things to remember before the interview

- **Communicate:** Do make sure the contributor knows what is going on. If you need to set up the equipment, let them know and tell them how long it's likely to take. Most people are happy to wait but quite like to know what they are waiting for. If you have to change something, like move position, tell them why the change is happening: too much noise, sunlight, etc.

- **Check phones:** Check that everyone has turned off their mobile phones and that there are no phones around that are likely to go off during the interview.
- **Offer reassurance:** Since you are unlikely to be transmitting live you can have as many goes as you have time for at getting the interview you want. Sometimes an interviewee needs some reassurance. You can tell them that if they are unhappy with an answer then it is fine to stop and start the answer again. Under pressure people can quite easily become tongue-tied and flustered, things come out wrong and they quite often want a second go at an answer. Unless there is a very good reason against it, you should let them do this.
- **Check recording levels:** You will need to check that the sound level is OK for recording. Settle the interviewee into a comfortable position and then ask them a few questions unrelated to the interview. You should use their answers to check that everything is recording at an acceptable level. The interviewee and the microphone should be in the position they will be during the recording. If necessary you can move the microphone and then check the levels again before starting to record.

## Things to remember after the interview

- **Get some wild track:** Whether you are recording for television or radio you should get some wild track, sometimes referred to as atmos (atmosphere), usually about 30 seconds to one minute. Earlier chapters have discussed the importance of wild track and you should get some for each interviewee. In television the convention is to point the camera at the microphone which you are recording so that the editor will know what it is. In radio you should just say, *thirty-seconds wild track*, and then record the silence.
- **Thanks:** Do remember to thank your interviewee for taking part and thank them again at the end of the interview. It's also nice after the interview to tell them that you liked the interview, or found it interesting, useful, etc. Even the most confident people like to know that they have done a good job. If you don't say anything they will leave wondering whether everything was OK. If you didn't rate the interview that highly perhaps a little white lie wouldn't hurt.

## Conclusion

Good interview technique is a combination of good research, knowing the types of questions to ask, listening to the answers and developing a good rapport with the interviewee. You will need to have all these elements in place to achieve an effective interview which will engage your audience.

# 18  Recording factual programmes for radio

Quite a lot of the information you will need for recording factual programmes for radio has been covered in other chapters. If you haven't read the chapter on interview techniques you will need to do so. You will also need to read the chapter on the technical aspects of recording sound and the chapter on story structure. This chapter will run through some of the different types of factual programme you get in radio and the different approaches they take.

Radio differs from television in that you have a direct line into the mind of the listener. It is an intimate and personal medium; it tends to be something people listen to by themselves rather than the more collective way they watch television or films. With a radio programme you are much closer to your listener and the listener will have a much stronger bond with a radio station. Audiences will endlessly flick through dozens of television channels looking for the content they want; they are often barely aware of what channel they are watching but with radio the loyalty can be as much to the station as to the programme. Even in this age of digital radio and hundreds of channels, listeners still tend to listen to a station as much as they listen to a particular programme. This puts radio producers in a relationship with their listeners that few television producers can ever approach.

The second important thing to remember is that a radio listener is a more active audience than the television viewer. The listener wants to create an image in their mind as they listen. It's your job as the radio producer to help them create this image. You do this by your imaginative use of all types of sound. It could be the words people are using, it could be the actuality sound, and it could be music. However, you must always be thinking about how to combine sounds together to help the listener create a mental image. Once they can 'see' your programme in their head, they will engage with you and your piece. Unlike the TV viewer, the listener contributes to the programme by creating these mental images, and your job is to stimulate them.

The enormous advantage of radio is its flexibility. It is fast, cheap and can get to places that television can't. When you are dealing with sensitive subjects contributors often feel more comfortable with radio, not least because they can preserve some measure of anonymity but also because there is less equipment to feel anxious about.

## Types of factual programmes

There are many different types of factual programmes on radio; here are some of the most common:

- **News and current affairs:** News bulletins tend to be fairly short. They are read by a newsreader from a studio and sometimes include sound bites, short extracts from an interview or a statement from someone involved in the story. They may also include a despatch. A despatch is a report presented by a journalist or correspondent. The style or choice of story will depend on the station and the audience. Current affairs programmes will have the same 'news values' of balance and right of reply, but they will also have longer 'packages', items from a reporter in the field, interviews and studio discussions. They will have the main 'presenters' in a studio but will also play in either pre-recorded or live reporting material.

- **Magazine programmes:** Magazine programmes are also hosted by a presenter or presenters in the studio. They will also include pre-recorded items that may have been made on location as well as studio interviews or discussions. A magazine programme is likely to cover a particular topic; it may be an arts programme or a consumer programme, for example. Within each programme there will be a number of different items which will relate to the main theme.

- **Discussion/panel programmes:/phone-ins:** This type of programme might have a panel of experts discussing a topic, possibly in front of an audience. The audience sometimes become part of the show by asking questions. It might also be a phone-in, usually based around a particular theme.

- **Documentary:** A documentary could be recorded entirely on location or it could contain studio elements. However, the main difference from a magazine programme is that it will cover only one subject. It could be 30 minutes or even an hour long, but it will all be concerned with the same topic.

- **Radio feature:** A radio feature is a term used for a particular kind of documentary. A feature often combines a few more elements than a straight documentary. It might include things like poetry, song, readings, music, etc. This type of programme has a less hard factual edge to it; it will be more stylised, more personal. It is often, although not exclusively, used when the subject matter is from the field of arts, so will include documentaries about musicians, artists, writers, etc. However, it may also be used to make programmes on all types of subject. They tend to have a much more 'authored' feel to them.

The last two definitions in particular are fairly loose, and many programmes will combine a number of elements in them: not every programme sits happily in any one particular category. However, the above list does cover the main styles of factual radio programmes.

If you log onto the website you will find some links through to different kinds of factual radio.

This chapter will assume that if you have chosen to make a factual piece, you are likely to be making one of the following:

- news item
- package for a magazine programme
- short documentary or feature.

## Tasks

Radio tends to use fewer people than television and much of the time all the tasks can be allocated to one person. However, it's worth thinking about the different tasks that do exist, even if you end up doing all of them. There are of course many different tasks in radio; the ones I've listed below are those that are likely to be most relevant to your project.

- **Presenters**: They are responsible for introducing the programme and linking all the items. They are usually the voice of the programme and the person the listener will remember. They tend to set the tone for the programme.
- **Reporters/correspondents:** These are the people who present the packages; in a magazine programme they may not be referred to as a reporter, they may just be referred to by name. They will do the interviews and write and record the links for the package. In news they would also send a despatch: a short piece written by the reporter.
- **Producers:** Factual radio programmes don't often talk about directors and producers but just about the producer. This person could be the studio producer who will produce the links from the studio and compile the programme together. They may also be the person researching and producing packages for the programme. In a magazine programme the person producing the package may also be the person doing the interviews and recording the links for the package. They will also be responsible for recording the sound on location.
- **Sound recordists:** Sometimes called studio engineers, studio managers and recording managers. These are the people responsible for the technical side of the studio recording. Occasionally you have sound recordists out on location, but this will tend to be for big productions. For small packages the producer is usually responsible for recording all the sound.
- **Researchers:** In most documentaries the producer will do the research and in news it's the responsibility of the journalist. However, occasionally you will get researchers working, usually across daily or weekly magazine programmes.
- **Broadcast assistants/production assistants:** Again this task can have a number of different titles. However, the role is really to help the producer, make bookings, and prepare scripts and anything else that needs doing.

## Documentaries, features and packages

Previous chapters talked about how to structure a factual piece. As a reminder there are three main points around which you build your narrative:

1 hook or tease
2 main piece
3 conclusion.

You will also have researched your contributors and locations and know what you are trying to achieve. When you actually get to the point of recording, there are a number of elements you need to think about.

### *Sound images*

Whatever type of programme you are making, you are trying to create an image in the mind of the listener. The degree to which you will do this will depend on the type of programme you are making. If it is a news piece you will only want to use the sound you have around you; at the other end of the scale a radio feature might use location sound but combine it with lots of other elements – they might even treat the sound somehow. However, creating a sound image is just as important as the interviews or script. If you ignore this element you will end up with something dry and bland which your listener will find difficult to connect with.

### Narrative voice

You will now have to start to think about who is going to tell the story. If you are thinking of this as an item in a magazine programme you will need a studio presenter to introduce the piece. You will also need a presenter/reporter to voice the actual package itself. You may or may not also decide to make their questions audible.

Most documentaries have some sort of presenter. On radio these tend to be presenters with an interest in the subject and the documentary has an authored feel to it. Radio doesn't tend to use the kind of anonymous narrator you sometimes get in television documentaries. Features may have a presenter or there are some types of feature which don't use a presenter at all. This is quite hard to achieve, and storytelling without a narrator is much more difficult, but it can end up as a very creative way to make radio.

### Gathering the material

By this stage you should have done your preparation and have already:

*   researched the story
*   found contributors and briefed them
*   researched sound effects/atmos you can gather
*   researched any additional material, song, music, etc.
*   decided on a narrative voice
*   created a treatment.

You are now ready to collect your material. In radio it's all about building a picture with the sound. If you haven't done so you should read the chapters on interview techniques and on recording location sound. However, for radio there are some more particular considerations.

### Where are you going to do the recording?

Where you do the interview will be significant; you will need to balance the need to get clear sound with the need to build up a sound picture. Let's say, for example, that you are doing a piece on migrant labour in the catering industry. You are doing a subjective piece following the different experiences of three young people coming to the UK in the hope of pursuing a career. They find themselves working in low-paid and difficult conditions. Your piece is looking at the contrast between their expectations and the reality of life in Britain. You have found your three contributors and are happy that they have a good story to tell. You have also decided to interview people from pressure groups, which support people in this position.

Where are you going to do the interviews?

*   You could take your contributors off somewhere quiet where you won't be disturbed and where it's relaxed enough to allow them to talk freely and to describe more intimate aspects of their life. The down side to this is that there is no actuality to help create a sound picture.
*   You could decide to interview contributors in the kitchen. That way you will get a good sense of where they are and what their life is like; you can create an impression of the busy, pressurised conditions in which they work. However, it may be difficult to get a clear recording, since you are likely to have to do lots of retakes as there will be inter-mittent bangs and crashes. You would need to make sure you had a good directional microphone in order to have any hope of getting the sound clear enough. There may

also be issues that the contributors might feel a little constrained about what they can say in a public place, particularly their place of work.

There are two other options you can think about.

- You can record the interview somewhere quiet but record a lot of the actuality sound of the kitchen. When you come to the edit you can mix the two sounds together; this way you will have control over the sound but still get some atmosphere.
- You could do two different interviews, one in each place. The interview in the kitchen would have to be done around the reality of life: what is the young woman doing, who are her colleagues, what are conditions like, etc. You could then do a second, more reflective interview in a quieter place where you might ask your contributor to talk about her feelings about coming to the UK, missing her home, whether she made the right decision, etc. This is a slightly more tricky option; you will need to know that you can make it work in your treatment and that the piece doesn't end up feeling muddled, but it might be another way of getting what you need.

There is no right or wrong answer to this: you will have to make the judgement as to what will work best for your piece.

### Intimacy

Radio is a very intimate medium. It also involves a lot less kit and is much less intimidating. You should therefore be able to get your interviewee relaxed enough to be able to talk quite freely. If you are dealing with a sensitive issue or you are hoping that your interviewee will talk in a personal way then you should allow enough time for them to feel relaxed and build up a rapport with you. Remember to keep eye contact with your interviewee so that they know you are interested in what you are saying. You can nod and smile, but remember not to talk or make any other sound while they are talking as you won't be able to edit it.

### Anecdotes

In radio particularly, you will want the interviews to be as evocative as possible. Remember: it's much more interesting for the listener to hear something which is drawn from the interviewee's personal experience, some sort of story or anecdote rather than bland comments. Remember your follow-up questions: *You mentioned. . ., Can you give me an example of that?* will often help the interviewee to come up with an anecdote.

### Actuality sound

It cannot be emphasised enough how important actuality sound is going to be for you to make a creative and imaginative radio package or documentary. It is every bit as important as your interviews and you need to think about it. Getting good actuality sound is the way you are going to create a picture in the listener's imagination.

As discussed earlier, you may be recording your interview at a location where there is already a lot of sound; even if you have done this already, you should record the sounds around you as a separate track as well. This will give you more to play with when you mix the two together.

Once you have done the interviews you should think about the actuality sound again. Was there anything in the interview which you feel might be complemented by some kind of actuality? For example, in your piece on people working in catering, it may be that you have recorded the sound of the kitchen at work, but in the interview the contributor talked a lot about the customers or her journey to work. You may want to think about doing some extra recordings when you know what they have said. The more personal your piece, the more important this is going to be.

## Acquired material

Acquired material is something you have not written or recorded yourself. It might be a song, poem or a piece of archive. If you are looking to make a short feature rather than a documentary style of programme you may want to involve other elements. However, mixing factual interviews with other material can be one of the trickiest things to get right. If it's not done correctly it can sound very clumsy. The key thing to remember is that the audience needs to be convinced that there is a good reason for using the material and that you have not just thrown it in. The material needs to help move the story along, not just interrupt it. If the material flows naturally out of interviews or commentary, or leads the listener into the next section then it's helpful; if it only tangentially relates to the main flow then it is likely that the audience will start to become confused about what it is doing there and will start to switch off. You need to be consistent about how you are using the material; the audience needs to understand from the outset what type of programme they are listening to and what types of elements they are likely to hear. If you have a piece which is largely a straightforward documentary but just has a poem plonked somewhere in the middle, it will sound very odd. The listener is not expecting a poem in that style of programme and will become confused. If you are combining different elements, try to introduce them early on in the piece and use them a number of times rather than just the once.

- **Sound archive:** This might be an interview with someone who is no longer around, or it might be a piece of actuality sound to evoke a time or place. If it's not obvious then you will need to let the listener know you are using an old interview or sounds from a different era. There should be a natural purpose and it should flow naturally from something said in the interview or lead naturally into an interview.
- **Poetry/readings:** These are most easily used if the subject of the piece is the poet or the author. The readings then have a natural purpose. If the poet or author is not the subject of the piece you will need to be sure that there is a strong link with the rest of the programme and it is something the listener will expect to hear.
- **Song:** This is similar to poetry. If you are using a song with lyrics there needs to be a natural flow. It may be that you are doing a piece about music-hall artists or something about clubbing. The songs are integral to the story itself and will evoke a sense of time and place. However, a song which just loosely relates to the subject but which has no personal connection with the rest of the piece will sound clumsy.
- **Music:** Music is used much less in radio documentaries than on television. Television documentaries quite often have a music track but the viewer will often be only vaguely aware of it. On radio the listener won't block it out and it will be much more evident. Just as with all the other elements the music should be a part of the storytelling, it should have a role.

## Writing for the ear

Writing for the ear is different to writing for the page. You may have a very beautiful written style but, if so, you are likely to have to unlearn some of your techniques in order to write a successful radio script.

Why is it different? When you read something off the page or indeed off a computer screen, you are in charge of how quickly you absorb the information. You may choose to skim something or you may choose to read slowly. Sometimes we do both, skipping the bits that are less interesting and then reading some sections carefully. If there is a word or phrase you are puzzled about, you might pause to give it a little more thought; this is often done quite fleetingly without even being aware of it. However, the choice of how quickly you take in all the information in is entirely yours.

This is not the case with the spoken word. If someone is talking to you then you have much less control over how you receive the information, the speaker is the one who is deciding. When we speak to someone face to face there are a lot visual clues to help: hand gestures, expressions, etc. Indeed, it's often said that when you are speaking to someone only 7 per cent of the information they receive is from the words; the rest is from body language, tone and expression. The speaker is also getting information from the listener. The listener's body language and expression can signal that they are puzzled or have missed the point.

When you are listening to the radio two things have happened. As the listener you no longer have the ability to control the speed at which you receive the words and you have none of the visual clues you would get if you were speaking to someone face to face. You are therefore left with words, tone and intonation. In radio you have to make up for this and adopt a style of writing which will help the listener cope.

### *Write as if you were speaking*

The most important thing to have in your mind is that you should write a script as if you were talking to one person. You are not writing a speech to be performed for a large audience and you are not writing a lengthy essay. You should try and get as close to a conversational style as possible.

If you start to listen to the way people speak, most of the time they don't observe the rules of punctuation that you get in written language. Sometimes after you have done an interview you may want to transcribe (write out) what the interviewee has said. This is quite a time-consuming activity, but you might want to try it just once and it will become obvious very quickly how the spoken word differs from the written word. It's almost impossible to know where to put the commas and full stops, let alone any kind of semicolon or other punctuation. This is because the spoken word relies on lots of other methods to convey meaning. When you come to write a script you can't lose all the punctuation and sentence structure; you will end up with a rambling mess, but you should simplify it as much as possible. If your script starts to have a more conversational style it will be much easier for you to inject the other two important elements of tone and intonation.

- **Tone** is the mood you want to convey. A happy piece will want a bright cheerful voice; a more sombre piece on a sensitive subject might need a more subdued tone. Some pieces might need an urgent sound. It's very difficult to get your voice to sound right if the script is written in a way that is completely different to the way you normally speak.
- **Intonation** is the emphasis you give to certain words; this can significantly affect the meaning the listener gets from what they hear.

Say these two sentences out loud but put the emphasis on the words in bold:

- I really **wanted** the cake.
- I really wanted **the cake**.

The first sentence implies that you are desperate for a piece of cake. The second implies that of all the things on offer it was the cake you wanted. The difference is subtle but important to a listener to help follow the sense of a piece.

## How to create a conversational style

This chapter cannot teach you to write; however, if you follow some of these tips your writing style will automatically become more conversational.

- **Use short, punchy sentences.** Your sentences shouldn't ramble on and generally you should only have one thought per sentence. You should avoid sentences with lots of sub-clauses. If you find yourself with more than one comma per sentence take another look at it. For example, read these two sentences aloud; the second one should feel a lot more natural and flow more easily off the tongue:

  *'Alan, the garage mechanic, works on over 50 cars a week; as a result he has a very good knowledge of different engines.'*

  *'Alan is a garage mechanic. He works on over 50 cars every week. He has an amazing knowledge of any type of engine.'*

- **Use active voice rather than passive.** When we speak to each other we generally use the active voice, since it lends itself to a more natural conversational style. For example:

  | | |
  |---|---|
  | *The door was opened by a young girl.* | Passive. |
  | *A young girl opened the door.* | Active. |

- **Simple language:** Try not to use jargon, unless you are very sure that your audience will understand it. Try to keep your language simple and to the point.
- **Repeating words.** Try not to use the same word twice in a sentence; it can begin to sound a little clumsy. It's better to look for a synonym if at all possible.
- **Use elisions** When we speak we tend not to say phrases like *will not, do not, cannot*; instead we say *won't, don't and can't*. You should use this in your scripting.
- **One listener:** Try to imagine that you are talking to one person; you are not addressing all your listeners, you are just talking to one of them.
- **Practice out loud:** You will need to read your script out loud to hear how it feels on the tongue. Don't be shy about this, don't rehearse in your head or mumble under your breath. You will only really understand whether the script works by reading it out loud in your normal speaking voice. As you practise the words you may start to stumble or find things difficult to say. That's when you need to stop and look again at your script. If you are having trouble saying it, perhaps the writing isn't clear enough or punchy enough.
- **Keep it short:** Generally you don't want to make cues or links too long, usually 30 seconds is long enough but that's not a hard and fast rule; however if a link or a cue

is too long you will start to lose the audience When you write a script you should think in terms of about three words per second, so a 30-second piece will have about 90 words.

Of course good writing is about getting the tone and style right. This will depend on a number of factors:

- **Your audience:** You will need to adopt a tone which you think will appeal to your particular audience.
- **Subject matter:** If you are dealing with a sensitive issue you may want to adopt a different tone to when you are dealing with something more trivial.
- **Your own personality:** Radio presenters bring a lot of themselves into anything they write. It will be really difficult for you to write a convincing piece if it doesn't feel true to your own personal style and your own way of speaking. You need to reflect yourself in the script for it to sound comfortable.
- **Your own creativity:** Remember: you are trying to create a picture in the imagination. There are literary devices you can use to help you do this: metaphors and similes will help to create a picture. However, if you overuse them or use them inappropriately they will start to sound a little false and too 'literary'. Adjectives, particularly ones which appeal to the senses, will immediately start to create an image. Remember: the audience is working with you. A few strong, well-placed adjectives may work better than lots of flowery prose.

## Structure of intros, cues and links

### *An intro or introduction*

This is the piece of script that comes at the top of the programme. It has to do several jobs: it has to hook the listener and help them to understand why they want to continue listening. It will set the tone and mood of the piece. If the introduction is bright and quirky then the rest of the piece will have to follow on along those lines. If the intro is sombre, then this will be the tone for the whole package. It is generally the longest piece of script.

Here's an example:

> *Good morning and we've got a good news story for you as we head off to Stafford to see the graffiti artist who's giving Banksy a lesson or two. We've got some old news; we'll be catching up with a Hollyoaks star, as she tells us how she's getting on a year after her dramatic exit from the programme. And we've got some bad news; we'll be talking to 90s boy band, Ace, about why the tour dates have been put back yet again. That's all coming up here on Essential Radio.*

### *Cue*

The cue into a magazine item or a news item is a bit like a headline: you need to grab the audience's attention. It is similar to an introduction but it generally introduces a specific item or person. It shouldn't be more than three or four sentences long. You can start with the reason why the listener might be interested in the subject matter and then introduce the piece. The last sentence should relate directly to the next thing the listener is going to hear. It should relate specifically to the top of the item. Imagine, for example, that you are doing an item on the teenagers imprisoned after the riots of 2011; the following could act as an intro, with a cue into the first report.

> *The summer of 2011 saw some of the worst riots in Britain for over 20 years. Across the country shops were looted and cars set on fire. The government was swift to punish offenders and over 300 young people under 18 were given prison sentences ranging from four weeks to 18 months. The sentencing was some of the harshest on record. The government said it wanted to send out a signal but what was the effect on the young people caught up in the government's policy of zero tolerance? Were they criminals who got what they deserved or foolish teenagers in the wrong place? Emily Lawson has been to Whitney Young Offenders Institute for girls to talk to some of the youngsters imprisoned after the riots.*
>
> *FX: Kitchen acoustic, sounds of pots and pans, people working in the kitchen.*
>
> *EMILY: In the kitchens here at Whitney Young Offenders Institute, 16-year-old Lauren is peeling potatoes. . . .*

### Links

Depending on the type of piece you are making, the links can be done by a presenter as part of a package or, if the piece may have studio links, read afterwards. Links, like cues, generally have a structure. A link has three main elements. It should get the listener out of the last bit of interview, move the story forward, and introduce the next bit of interview. Thus, for example, let's go back to the story about young offenders imprisoned after the riots. Imagine that the listener has just heard from a young offender, Lauren, recently released, who has been describing her experiences of being in a young offenders' institute and her shock at being given a ten-month sentence for a very minor offence. She tells us that she has lost all self-confidence and feels worthless. Your next contributor is a campaigner from a group wanting prison reform. He will say that this kind of harsh sentencing is detrimental not just to the offender but to our notions of justice. Here is an example of how you might link the two interviews:

> *Lauren's loss of self-worth is one of the most common psychological effects of prison on young women. Her experiences are typical. But for some teenagers this feeling of self-loathing can develop into something more extreme. Peter Morgan runs the charity Worth, which helps teenagers behind bars. He has made a study of the psychological effects of prison on young women in particular.*
>
> Peter: *Well, this kind of loss of self-image can go one of two ways. . . .*

In this example, the first part of the link picks up from the last piece of interview. This allows the listeners a bit of breathing space to catch up and consolidate what they have heard. It also helps the piece feel as if it has a natural flow. The second part introduces a new thought, in this case that loss of self-worth can lead to extreme behaviours. The last part of the link introduces the next speaker and why he is here. Again the last thing the listener hears from the link should lead directly into the next contributor.

### Outro

This is the sign-off, the last piece of commentary before the end of the piece. How you write this will depend rather on what type of piece you have been doing. If the piece has had a discussion you may want to recap. It may be that you will want to leave the listener with a question. Some pieces don't need an outro; quite often radio features don't use them. If you have a strong interview section that might serve as your outro. The main point is that the listener should get a signal that the piece is coming to an end and feel a sense of closure. Pieces which end abruptly when the listener isn't prepared tend to jar and confuse them. They may end up with a slightly dissatisfied feeling about the whole piece, not just the ending.

## Conclusion

Making factual programmes for radio can be hugely rewarding. It's technically much more flexible than television and involves a lot less cumbersome equipment. People can feel less intimidated by talking to a microphone rather than have the cameras looking at them. However, this is not to say that creatively making factual radio is easy. Getting a good piece for the ear is hugely challenging. You have the same structural issues and you need to have a very good written style. Your interview techniques need to be good as you have no pictures to help with any deficiencies in your speakers. You also need to have a good imagination in how you can use sound to tell your story. On the other hand, if well done, factual radio can be immensely powerful.

# 19 Radio drama

This chapter will look at some of the production techniques associated with radio drama; these would also apply if you were making a radio advertisement. While writing and researching a radio play is very different to writing and researching a radio advertisement, the production process is similar. Whichever you are planning for your project you should read the whole of the chapter to understand the techniques you are going to need to use.

## Radio drama

A phrase often quoted by radio producers is attributed to a small boy who supposedly said, '*I like radio – the pictures are better*'. Nowhere is this more true than in radio drama. Radio creates pictures in the imagination and because the listeners create their own image it's a deeply personal and powerful experience.

If you ask anyone who listens frequently to the long-running radio soap *The Archers* they will probably be able to describe to you what each of the characters looks like, they will have a mental picture of the village and they will probably know exactly what the inside of the local pub looks like. They will be able to do this **without having ever seen a single image**. Indeed, those images can be so powerful that listeners often don't like it much when they do see a picture of the real actor: they'll often complain, *No, that doesn't look a bit like Tom Archer*. They have a mental picture of the character and want to stick with it. This tale of country life may not be to your taste but talk to someone who is a fan and you will start to understand how drama on radio can work directly with the imagination.

Since radio creates pictures in the mind, there is no limit to the pictures which can be created. TV and film drama are hugely expensive. Locations, sets, costumes, all cost vast amounts. So except for the very fortunate, writers in TV drama are rather constrained as to type and number of locations. Not so on radio. The writer is free to set the piece anywhere they want to. The sets are created by the skill of the writer and the production team in conjunction with the active participation of the listener. One of the most famous radio comedies *A Hitchhiker's Guide to the Galaxy* has gone through many different iterations since. It's been a book, TV series and feature film, computer game, even a stage show. The initial success of radio was that it skilfully created a humorous sci-fi adventure. It created a fantasy world in the mind of the listener and the locations literally went from one end of the galaxy to the other.

Radio is a writer's medium. There is very little between the writer and the audience. If you like words then this is your medium.

 If you are thinking of recording some radio drama but haven't listened to much of it, log onto the website where you'll find a link to a number of recordings.

## Tasks

Just as with anything else there are several tasks which you should allocate to members of the group when you do your drama.

- **Cast:** People acting in the play.
- **Director/producer:** Usually in radio this is done by the same person.
- **Writer:** You may have chosen to use an existing piece, but if not you will need someone to write the play.
- **Recording engineer:** Different organisations use different titles for this role. But you would need someone to monitor the technical aspects of the recording. Make sure there are no technical glitches.
- **Music and effects:** Sometimes these are added during the editing or mixing process but some directors like to play them in during the performance itself. Some directors think that it helps the actors give a better performance. If this is the case then someone needs to be responsible for playing them in at the right time.
- **Spot effects:** You can get lots of sound effects from libraries or from the internet, but some kinds of effects are difficult to use in this way. Spot effects are effects which are done in the studio at the time of the recording. They are often small, specific effects, for instance someone putting a cup on the table or footsteps. In film this is often referred to as foley.

As with the other types of recordings you may not have a different person responsible for each task; one person may have to take on several tasks, but you will need to know what the tasks are and who is going to do them.

## Radio studio

It's quite possible that you won't have access to a studio. This shouldn't necessarily stop you from thinking about making a radio drama piece. It is quite possible to do the recording without a studio, although there are other things you will need to be thinking about, in particular the acoustics. However, you will also need to make sure that you have the equipment to record the drama itself, so you will need the microphones and some sort of mixer.

However, you may be lucky enough to have access to some sort of studio. A radio studio can comprise one room or two. If it has one room, all the recording equipment will be in the one place along with the microphone. They tend to be used for simple recordings. For the most part radio studios will have two rooms. One is called the cubicle. The cubicle has all the recording equipment, speakers and the mixing desk and computers If it's a digital studio the computer software will control the recording, playbacks and all the editing. The other section is the studio; it will have a microphone, possibly a table and chairs and stands for the script. Radio drama is usually conducted in this kind of studio.

An earlier chapter looked at the different kinds of microphones which you might be using. You will need to know what kind of microphones you have. Are they omnidirectional or directional, for example? This is because you will need to position the actors in front of the microphone to get the best sound and you will need to know how the microphone is picking up the sound. Generally a directional microphone is likely to be more useful, particularly if you don't have a studio to record in. However the clip-on microphones can also be helpful.

## *Stereo*

Radio drama is often recorded in stereo. The idea of stereo in the context of music is quite familiar. In radio drama, using stereo can help create a sense of space. When the listener is creating a mental image of what is happening in the play, the stereo effect will put the characters on the left or right of the sound stage. This will help the listener create a mental image of what is going on. You don't' necessarily need a stereo microphone to get a stereo picture. You can use two mono microphones. These are called a coincident pair and they are usually set up so that they cross over one another (Figure 19.1).

You are actually recording two mono tracks. However, the recording engineer can move the sound around the stereo image and put the voice to the left or right. Stereo obviously opens up a wealth of possibilities to radio drama, but it demands careful monitoring. You need to make sure you have a clear mental picture of the scene and that everyone stays in the correct position. The listener will get very confused if a character starts to jump all over the stereo picture; it will have the effect of making it seem as if they are jumping about in the room.

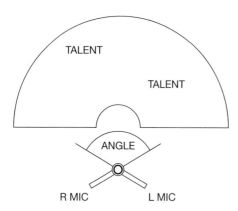

*Figure 19.1* A coincident pair

## Script

You will need to ensure that everyone has a copy of the script. When you lay out the script there are a number of points to remember. An earlier chapter gave you examples of a script layout.

You can also log onto the website and follow the link to see more examples.

- The script should be printed on one side of the paper only. This helps avoid the noise of script rustling as the actors are reading their parts.
- Generally each of the dialogue turns is numbered. The numbers start from one again on each new page. The pages themselves should also be numbered.
- You should also indicate any music or effects (FX) on the script where they occur.
- You should ensure that none of the dialogue turns are split over a page if at all possible. You should never split sentences across a page – it makes it more difficult for the actor to read them.
- If you have several versions of the script make sure everyone has a copy of the final version.

## Creating sound images

In radio drama you are trying to use sound to create an image in the listener's mind. Something which just sounds as if it's being read on the radio isn't really a drama. The sound image you create is every bit as important as the actual dialogue. It is the sound image that will create a sense of mood and place in the listener's mind. There are a number of different elements which go into creating a sound image.

### *Acoustic*

One way of creating a sense of place in a radio drama is to alter the acoustic. In radio drama the acoustic refers to the amount of reverberation (echo) you can hear on the recording. In order to get a sense of acoustic you will need to start listening to how voices sound in different locations.

In an actual location the amount of reverberation depends on the extent to which the sound-waves coming from your voice are reflected back. Sound-waves tend to reflect back if they hit something hard. If they hit something soft they get absorbed or if they don't hit anything at all they just fade away.

You can easily get a sense of this if you use a portable recorder to make some recordings in different locations.

- **Outside, park, playing field:** If you are outside then there is very little for sound-waves to bounce off. This means you get very little reverberation. In radio this is referred to as a **dead acoustic**.
- **Church or large hall:** If you go into any large space with no soft furnishings it has a very echoic feel to it, particularly if you go into an old church, for example, with its wooden benches and stone walls. In radio drama this is called a **live acoustic.**
- **Bathroom or toilet cubicle:** Here you have the hard surfaces for the sound to bounce off but because it is a very small space it will have a different acoustic to a church. It won't have that cavernous echo – it will sound closer. This is often referred to in radio drama as a close or **boxy acoustic.**
- **Sitting room:** This type of space has some hard surfaces but also some softer surfaces. It means that not so much of the sound is reverberated but it is not like the exterior recordings where you have a very dead acoustic. Producers sometimes refer to this as a **bright acoustic**.

Understanding the acoustic of the space in which you have set the script is important, as it forms the basis of the sound world you are trying to create.

### *How to create an acoustic*

If you are using a studio space then most of the time it will have a fairly neutral acoustic. It won't have that reverb where it sounds as if you are in a church; nor will it sound as if you are recording in an open space. A professional drama studio will often have different acoustic areas in the same studio. There will be a dead area, usually created by erecting screens or walls made of material which absorbs sounds and laying carpet on the floor. There may also be a live area where there is a wooden floor and harder surfaces. You are unlikely to have this luxury; however, you can still play with the acoustic.

- **Live acoustic:** Most mixers allow you to add some reverb. This will give you the kind of live acoustic feel. Treat it carefully though: the differences are quite subtle and if you add too much you will make it sound as if the action all takes place in some huge cave.
- **Dead acoustic:** This can be more complicated and a little more makeshift. Sometimes people will bring blankets into the studio space and almost try to create some kind of tent for the actors to work in. The soft blankets or duvets will absorb the sound-waves and give a sense of a dead acoustic.
- **Boxy acoustic:** You would add some reverb but with a shorter reverberation time than for a live acoustic. This gives the impression of being in a smaller space.

## Location recordings

If you don't have a studio and are recording on location you could try to find an acoustic which matches your script. You could try recording outside if the script sets a scene outside. The difficulty of this is that you are at the mercy of everything else going on around you. Dogs barking, cars passing, aeroplanes will all start to become a nuisance. As discussed in Chapter 13, a continuous sound is less problematic than an intermittent sound, but you will need to think about your editing.

Recording inside is more controllable, and it's probably easier to find a quiet space. However, it's worth thinking about the natural acoustic of the room. If you are in a big room with lots of windows and hard surfaces, it will be very difficult to create a convincing exterior acoustic. You would need to construct some kind of dead area with blankets, duvets, etc., and your cast may start to find it a bit comical acting inside some kind of cosy tent you've constructed.

Getting the acoustics right takes quite a lot of practice and a good ear. If you want to play with the acoustic then it's probably best to practise before you have all your cast assembled. You will need to keep trying out different things to hear the different acoustics which you can create and it will take a bit of practice before your ear gets properly tuned in.

## Creating sound image, sound effects

There are two types of sound effects. The first is the type you might find in a library. There are all sorts of online Sound FX libraries where you can get a very good selection.

If you log onto the website you will find links to some libraries.

The first thing you need to think about is the atmos (atmosphere); this might also be referred to as ambience. The earlier chapter on sound discussed the idea of recording wild track. This was to get some of the atmosphere of a room. Even if a room sounds quiet there is likely to be some kind of atmospheric noise. If you want to create a convincing soundscape for your drama you will need to choose some kind of background atmos.

The ambience or atmos is generally the first thing you want the listener to hear. In radio you want to create a sense of place in the mind of the listener. Remember: your listener is actively working with you to create this picture. Give them a lead and they will start to create their own mental picture.

### Specific sounds

It may be that there are a number of specific sounds which you will need to hear at a particular time in the script. This might range from phones ringing, the sound of the TV in the background, dogs barking and cars passing. Again you can find a large range of these sounds from any of the online sites.

When you use this kind of effect you will need to think carefully about where you place them in the sound picture. If, for example, you want the sound of a dog barking in the distance, you will need to make sure that it sounds distant and muffled; otherwise it will sound as if members of your cast are about to be ravaged by a vicious animal.

Some of these sounds can add to your atmos: bells ringing, birds tweeting can add to a sense of being in the countryside. Car horns and so on can add to an urban feel. Others may be specific sounds that are needed and specified in the script.

People differ as to when they add the effects. Some directors like to add them in as they are recording the script. They feel that the actors give a better performance if they know what is happening around them. Other directors like to add them in the edit, as this means they have more control. It can be more difficult to edit a piece if there are a lot of sound effects added during the recording.

## Spot FX

Spot effects are the types of effects which you will add yourself, usually as you are recording. They are the type of effect that is difficult to create from a recording. If, for example, you have a scene set around a dinner table during a meal, you would expect to hear the sounds of knives and forks clinking on plates. You can get your cast to create these sounds or you can have someone beside them doing it. Sometimes the cast find it difficult to hold the script and create the sound. The spot effects are the equivalent of a Foley artist in film or TV drama. In TV and film it's usually only quite big productions that will use a Foley artist and the effects are added in post-production. In radio you can have fun with spot effects, experimenting with different ways of re-creating a sound.

There are so many ways to create spot effects that it's too long to list them here, but if you  click onto the sites listed on the website you can find out more.

Depending on how complicated the sound is, some spot effects are recorded along with the dialogue and others might be laid later. Recording at the same time gets the timings better and for simple effects like clinking of glasses this is probably the way to go.

## Music

Music can be an important component in a radio drama. It is most frequently used to introduce a scene or to segue between one scene and the next. It is sometimes used during a scene but you should be very careful about this as it can quickly become quite irritating. It's probably a good idea in a short piece to avoid too many different bits of music as you piece will quickly sound slightly disjointed. Using one piece of music as the theme will probably work better. Music can help create:

- **Mood/genre:** Listeners tend to be able to identify certain music with certain genres quite easily.
- **Period:** Music can be quite evocative of a period in time.
- **Place:** Music can help to establish where the piece is set – particularly if it's a different culture.
- **Passage of time:** Some music between scenes will help to establish a passage of time.

There are plenty of mood music libraries you can use so that you can easily search and use the type of music suitable for your production. You should remember however that it is *very* difficult to make a good music edit. For this reason people usually add the music after they have recorded the speech. That way if there is any editing to be done it can be done without having to edit any music.

### Silence

Silence can be a powerful effect on radio. You shouldn't be afraid of using silence if the script calls for it. However, it is obvious that you can't let that silence run for too long or the listener is going to think something has gone wrong with the radio.

## Creating a sound image, recording techniques

As well as using sound FX and acoustic to create the sound image, you will also need to use some microphone techniques. In order to do this you will need to figure out what kind of microphones you have. If you refer back to the previous chapter on sound you will know how to check this. In radio drama it's more useful to have a directional microphone than an omni microphone if you only have one choice.

- **Distance:** You can use the microphones to create a sense of perspective. In order to do this you will need to have in your mind a sense of who is the main character in any particular scene. They will then be close to or 'on' the microphone. You may want all your other characters to be equally close to the microphone. If the scene is set in a small space, for instance, people sitting around the dinner table, then you would have all the people equidistant from the microphone. However, you may choose to have your characters at different distances. To do this effectively you will need to have a mental picture in your mind as to where everything is in the scene. If you are re-creating a scene in a large space with people spread around, you would have your main character 'on' the microphone and the other characters slightly 'off' the microphone; i.e. they are placed at a slight distance from the microphone. In reality the distance need not be very far. A small step away from the microphone can make all the difference. This will create a sense that the characters are standing some distance apart.
- **Moving on and off the microphone:** You may want to create the impression of a character arriving or leaving; you can do this with sound effects to some extent – doors opening, footsteps, etc. – but it very quickly starts to sound very slow and clunky, almost comical. A more subtle way is to get the actor to move towards and away from the microphone as they are speaking. They don't have to move very far: a couple of small footsteps are enough to give the listener the impression that the character is moving away somewhere. If you are working in stereo you will also need to decide whether they are going to approach or move off to the left or right of the stereo image. Generally, if a character arrives from the left you would have them leave to the left to avoid confusion in the listener's mind.
- **Projecting the voice:** The extent to which a character projects the voice also con- siderably affects the sound image. Most of the time you would want your cast to deliver the lines in a normal speaking voice. On radio you don't generally need to project in the same way as you do in the theatre. Radio is very intimate and works directly with the listener's imagination, so subtlety is all. However, there may be occasions when you will

want to create a sound picture of two people who are far apart when they are talking to one another. In this case you need to move them off the microphone and get them to project the voice a little, but not too much as you will distort the microphone.

- **Interior monologues:** This is a device which is much more common in radio than in TV. An interior monologue is the character's inner thoughts, something that the rest of the characters aren't privy to. It gives a very intimate feel. To create an interior monologue you need to change the acoustic. Usually you would lose all the effects or have them pulled right back. The actor works very close to the microphone but speaks quietly. It can be difficult to pull this off as it usually ends up with quite a lot of distortion on the microphone. But if the actor can keep the voice quiet and talk across the top of the microphone rather than into the microphone then you can achieve a nice effect.
- **Narrator:** Some radio drama also uses the technique of a narrator. Again when you have a narrator you need to alter the sound space. Usually you would have a neutral acoustic and lose any background atmos.
- **Fading in and out:** Sound which appears suddenly can jar with the listener. Often radio producers will fade in FX; this means that they bring the sound in gradually rather than all at once. The fade doesn't have to be very long but just a second or so to give the listener time to adjust. The same might be true at the end of a scene. Normally it would just be music and FX that are faded in and out – you wouldn't normally fade in dialogue.

## Rehearsals

You will need to offer your cast a chance to read through the script together. You can do this in a reading, away from the studio, just so that everyone is familiar with the script and can raise issues if they wish. However, you will need to remember that rehearsals really only start when you can hear what it sounds like through the speakers. Don't spend too long rehearsing away from the microphone, as it will sound different. If you do a rehearsal away from the microphones it's better to use this as a chance for everyone to discuss the characters or discuss any issues. You may give the cast some kinds of character profiles, a bit of background and you may also want to discuss the relationships their characters have with each other. However, this is not quite the time to discuss the specifics of a performance; this is better done when you are actually hearing it in the studio or on location.

Once you are on the microphone you will have a much better idea of what a performance is going to sound like. Directing a cast is tricky, particularly since both you and the cast are likely to be inexperienced.

A few tips for directing a cast:

- **Be positive:** People feel quite exposed when they are acting and are likely to be sensitive, especially if they are inexperienced. Point out what you liked.
- **Be specific:** If you want something different you will need to tell the person what it is. *Can you do that better . . . ?* is not a very good note to an actor.
- **Talk about the character not the person:** If you refer to the character rather than the actor, you may get a better response. So instead of *You are being too aggressive on that line . . .* say, *I don't think that character would be quite so forceful.*
- **Pacing:** As well as noting how the actors are delivering the words you should think about the speed of delivery. A common fault with inexperienced or amateur actors is that

they tend to speak very quickly. This is usually because they are nervous. It may be that you want to vary the speed of delivery depending on the emotion of the character at the time. Be careful not to exaggerate this: it will sound quite comical if the actor speeds up and slows down continually.

## Rehearse recording

Most drama directors tend to rehearse and then record sections of the script at a time. This allows them to rehearse not just the lines but any sound effects. As the director you need to be thinking about:

- **Performance:** Are the actors conveying the right meaning?
- **Microphone techniques:** Are they at the right distance from the microphone? Are they moving towards and away from the microphones at the right time?
- **Sound effects and acoustic:** Are you building a good sound picture? Remember: if you are playing in the sound effects at the same time as recording the dialogue you will need to **establish** the sound before you start any dialogue. You will need to allow the listener a couple of seconds to register the atmosphere and any other sound FX before you start any dialogue.
- **Fluffs and script noise:** Inevitably you are going to find that members of the cast will get their lines wrong or stumble on occasions. It's also very common to hear extraneous noise on the microphone – quite often this is the sound of the actor turning the pages of the script. If either of these things happens you will need to retake the dialogue. When this happens, make sure that you give the actors a run-up to the bit you need to retake. Get them to redo more than you actually need. This will help you make a more natural sounding edit in your post-production.

As the director, you will also need to make sure that everyone knows what they are supposed to be doing.

- Before you start a recording you should remind everyone what you are going to do. This is where the numbering on the script comes in. You tell them the page number and dialogue turns for the start and end of the take. Thus, for example, *We are going to record from speech 3 on page 8 to speech 6 on page 9.*
- You should make sure that everyone is in the right position with regard to the microphone; if you are recording in stereo they should be reminded which side of the microphone they are on.
- You should remind members of the cast of any moves they need to make, approaching and moving away from the microphone.
- If you are playing in the FX then make sure whoever is doing this is ready.

Just as you do when you are taking a shot for film there is a kind of sequence of commands that you go through to make sure that everyone knows what is happening. So, for example, if you are happy that everyone knows what they are doing you say something like:

| OK studio, stand by for a recording please . . . | If you are in a separate cubicle you will need to say this over the talk back: *Anyone who isn't ready should say so now.* |
|---|---|
| *Running to record . . .* | If you have a recording engineer then they will start the recording. |
| *Recording . . .* | *The sound person confirms that the recording has started.* |
| *Cue FX . . .* | If you are playing in FX then these would be faded in – remember: you will need to establish the FX for a couple of seconds before you cue the dialogue. |
| *Cue dialogue . . .* | Often the cue to the actors is done by a light flashing on and off rather than a verbal cue – if you don't have a cue light you will just need to give a verbal cue. |
| *Cut . . .* | The recording has stopped and the actors know that the scene has finished. At the end of the section you are recording you would normally allow a couple of seconds of atmos or FX to run after the last piece of dialogue. This will help with the editing. |

At this point you will need to decide whether you are happy with the take or whether you want to take all or some part of it again. If you want to run anything again you will need to be clear with everyone why you are running the piece again and tell them anything you would like to have done differently. It may be that there were some extraneous noises or some line wasn't delivered quite correctly.

You may only want to record a few lines again. If you do this make sure you record more than you need both at the beginning and at the end, this will make your edit a lot easier. If you do want to record anything again you will need to repeat the sequence of commands.

Nobody sticks exactly to the script I've suggested but they will do something similar. By using this familiar sequence of commands everyone knows what is happening and becomes focused on their job. It saves a lot of wasted time.

## Mixing and editing

Once you have recorded the material you will need to edit and mix it. You will need to choose the best takes of any particular scene, edit out any fluffs or bits that went wrong and then mix the scene with any music or sound effects.

- **Ingest:** This is the process of loading the material into the editing package. You may have recorded directly into the package, but if not you will need to ingest your material.

You should be careful to keep all your rushes organised and properly labelled; it will save you lots of time in the end. You should also have any music loaded and any sound FX which you didn't play in during the recording.

- **Editing:** If there is any editing to do – removing mistakes, etc. – then you should do all of this first. Editing speech like this can be very tricky. In the chapter on factual recordings there are some tips on editing speech which you should read.

## Mixing

The next thing you will need to do is to lay any of the music or sound FX.

- **FX/atmos:** Remember: you are trying to create an image in the mind of the listener. If you are using atmos, then you should allow a couple of seconds at the beginning of each scene for the listener to absorb the atmosphere before you bring in any dialogue. If you do this the listener will start to create their own mental image. Likewise you should leave a second or two at the end.
- **Music:** Music can be a way of moving from one scene to the next. It creates a pause in the narrative and allows the listener enough time to work out that they are moving from one scene to the next. There may also be diegetic music; music that comes directly from the drama, a radio playing in the background, for example. You may need to treat this type of music and you will certainly have to think about the balance if you want it to sound convincing.
- If you want to add non-diegetic music or incidental music, then the music needs to be there for a reason. What are you signalling with the music? Are you signalling a reflexive mood, are you signalling drama or action? This type of music is much less used in radio drama than in film or TV so you will need to be quite careful about how you use it. The viewer on TV will sometimes barely register the music but on radio it will be much more prominent.
- **Transitions between scenes – fading in and out:** Often in radio drama the FX and music are faded in and faded out. The fade doesn't have to be very long but it can make a smooth transition. However, this doesn't have to be the case. Sometimes the producers will fade the end of a scene but bring the next scene in more sharply. There is no set way of doing this; however, if you are aware of the options you can try different things to see which works best.
- **Pacing:** Not every single second of a radio drama needs to be filled with words. The music and effects help create a mental image and create a mood, and you will need to leave enough space for this to happen. However, you will also need to think about how the pacing is managed. Some dramas demand a quick pace, others need more time for reflection. A lot of this will have been decided in the recording, but you can also use your mix to alter your pacing, particularly in the transitions between scenes.

## Play out

Once you have mixed the piece and done all the final tweaks you will need to play out the material. The format you use will depend on what your particular project requires. However, remember: *always* keep a backup copy and don't delete any of your rushes until you know for sure that you are not going to need them again.

## Conclusion

Radio drama can be a highly creative and exciting art form, particularly if you like the spoken word. Technically it is less cumbersome than film or TV drama and that leaves you all the more time to make something which is much more creatively challenging and polished. There are no limits to the number of locations and characters you can create and no limits to the scope of your story. It's a powerful medium.

# 20 Editing radio sound

The edit in radio is a very important creative process. It is where you will create the sound picture your audience is expecting. What sounds you use, when you bring them in and how long you hold them will all help the listener to create a mental picture. Your listeners should be 'seeing' the programme in their heads. They will do a lot of this for themselves but you will need to give them the cues through your use of sound.

Once you have assembled all your radio material and written your script, you will need to do four things:

1    ingest your material
2    edit your interviews
3    record your script
4    mix the programme.

You will most probably be using a digital, nonlinear system. There are so many around that it's outside the scope of this book to talk you through the actual kit. This chapter aims to talk you through the editing process; this process will be more or less the same whichever type of kit you use.

## Ingest

Ingesting is when you load all the material you have recorded and assembled onto your editing and mixing package. From a production point of view the most important thing is that you label everything properly and organise it so that you can find everything. Just as with the recording, the more organised you are, the more head space you will have to be creative. A little time spent organising your material will mean a lot more time available in the end.

## Editing the interviews

It's usually best to edit your interviews first and assemble all the parts you want into the right order. Clearly when you come to edit your interviews you are looking for the pieces which best tell your story and which will have an impact on your listener. Quite often producers will *tidy up* an interview. This means that they will get rid of *ums, ers* and long pauses. They may also get rid of sentences which were repetitious or where an interviewee stumbled a bit and repeated something. This will have the effect of making your piece flow. It's a bit fiddly and time consuming but worth the effort.

The producer may also do a more substantial edit. They may take the beginning of an answer, cut out the middle and then use the end of the answer. Broadcasters do this all the time. However, you do have a responsibility not to substantially alter meaning by selective editing. For example, imagine you had interviewed someone on the benefits of raising the school-leaving age to 18; you knew that the interviewee was basically in favour of the changes but did also mention that there were a couple of drawbacks. You have a responsibility to fairly represent that person's view. You should not set them up as an opponent of the change and then only use the bits of the interview where they mentioned the drawbacks. This can be quite a difficult balance to achieve.

## Hints on editing

Creating clean sound edits can be tricky. If you don't choose the right edit point you will get a kind of jerky, unnatural-sounding edit and the listener will feel a little disturbed. There are several techniques to help with this.

*   **Breaths:** We are barely aware of it when we listen to people speak but we are drawing breath all the time. When you start to edit speech you will become very aware of it. However, a breath is a natural part of speech and is part of what gives our speech patterns a kind of rhythm. You should be wary of routinely taking out all breath sounds.
*   **Pauses:** If you are cutting an interview, you should leave enough pauses that the speech still sounds natural. You may want to edit out all the *ums* and *ers* but you shouldn't edit all the words so tightly together that they begin to sound unnatural.
*   **Cut at the beginnings of words, not the end:** For example, your interviewee says: *My grandmother was 65 when she . . . or was it 66, I can't remember, no, it definitely was 65 when she first decided to row the Atlantic.*

You will want to edit out the hesitation over the age, so the piece goes: *My grandmother was 65 when she first decided to row the Atlantic.* There are a number of ways in which you could do this and the choice will entirely depend on how the interviewee has said the words and what the intonation sounds like However, imagine that you want to edit out the bits in red. *My grandmother was 65 when she . . . or was it 66, I can't remember . . . no, it definitely was 65 when she first decided to row the Atlantic.* Your cutting points would normally be at the beginning of the first *she* and the beginning of the second *she* rather than at the end of the *when*. You can't be hard and fast about this as it depends on how the words were said, but it's probably best to try it this way first.

*   **Wild track:** You will remember the chapter on recording location sound when we talked about recording wild track of atmos. This is slightly different to the sound you record to create your sound picture. This can be the sound of a silent room. This wild track comes in handy when you are editing speech. Sometimes it's very difficult to get a clean edit and whatever you do the edit sounds obvious and unnatural, or the edit points have to be so tight that it doesn't sound convincing. Sometimes you can add a tiny piece of wild track to create more of a pause between words and you will get a much better effect. Even a silent room has an atmospheric sound and you can hear this most clearly when you start editing. Wild track can also be used at the beginning or end of an interview. The wild track creates a *handle* which you can use to fade in or out on. Again the ear seems a lot less forgiving than the eye and doesn't like abrupt change; even a short fade out of the atmos makes your piece feel a lot more polished.

## Recording your script

This should be one of the last things you do when you are absolutely sure you are happy with the script and know exactly what material it is cueing or linking. On paper you can change your script as many times as you want and it doesn't cost you anything, but once you've recorded it's much less easy to change.

You may be lucky and have some kind of studio space to record in or you may just record the script in a quiet room. If you are not recording in a studio space then ideally you will need to find a room with carpet and soft furnishings. A bedroom can be a good place; there are lots of soft things around to absorb the sound. You really don't want your script to sound echoic or hollow. As with interviews, people will sometimes construct a kind of tent out of duvets or blankets. This creates a less live acoustic. You may not want to go that far but avoid trying to record in a big room with hard floors like a classroom.

## Presenting

Presenting can be tricky: some people love it and some really don't take to it. However, here are a few tips:

- **It's all in the script:** The most important thing about your performance will be the way the script is written. If you haven't written it in a way that is suitable for the ear, you will find it very difficult to get a good performance from anyone. It will very quickly sound wooden and clumsy. Even the most experienced script writers will change and alter the script right up to the last moment. As you start to say things out loud they will begin to feel quite different. This is fine, and if a presenter isn't comfortable with something then you do need to change it. However, you will always need to keep in mind the purpose and structure of the link or cue. Where is it coming from, what do I need to tell the listener, what will the listener hear next?
- **Use your normal voice:** You are not acting here, you should be using your normal voice at your normal speaking level, and you don't need to project as if you were on stage.
- **One person:** You should also be talking to one person and not a crowd of people. Remember: in the mind of the listener it's just the two of you in this conversation; if you start to imagine you are giving a speech it will have the effect of pushing the listener away.
- **Keep up the energy:** You will need to keep energy and liveliness in your voice; if you don't you will come across as rather flat and a little dull. You may start to put people off listening to you. Some people try to consciously smile when they talk. Clearly the listener isn't going to see the smile but some people feel that physically smiling helps keep a bright tone in the voice.

## Mixing the programme

Once everything has been assembled, ingested and edited and you have recorded any commentary, you will need to mix the programme together. This is a creative part of the process and there is any number of ways to mix a programme. However, here are some of the things you will need to think about.

- **Set the scene:** Just as with any other medium you will need to set the scene for the listener. If the top of the piece comes from a studio or a piece of voice-over then there is not a lot of scene to set. However, once you are in a location with your listener you will need to let them know where they are. This is where you should be thinking about your actuality. You should allow a few seconds of actuality before anyone starts speaking; this will allow the listener to absorb the sound and understand what they are hearing. Similarly at the end of a scene, if you are moving from one location to the studio or voice-over or to another location, you should allow the listener a couple of seconds to hear the atmos fade out and a new one fade in. Give them space to understand what is happening.

- **Pacing:** Not every single second of your piece needs to be filled with words. Remember: the listener needs time to absorb what is being said. Of course there are some styles of programming that are deliberately fast paced and that's fine. But just remember: there will be times when the listener will need a moment to catch up with you.
- **Fading up and down:** Our ears tend to feel more comfortable if sound is faded in and out rather than hearing a sharp cut. Thus at the beginning and end of a scene there is usually a fade in and fade out. The fade will usually be on the atmos rather than on anybody actually saying anything. You don't necessarily need to have a very long fade; even quite a quick one will usually be enough.
- **Actuality:** As well as using ambient sound at the beginning and end of a scene, if the style of the piece demands it then don't be afraid to use actuality throughout the piece. It creates a sense of place, and the listeners will use this information to try to picture the scene in their minds; it's a really powerful tool.
- **Music:** Music can be great. However, you will need to make sure that the music really fits into the piece and that you are using it consistently. Too many different pieces of music will start to sound confused. In the mix you will also need to get the balance right between the music and anything else. You will need to think about when you might raise the level of the music and when you might drop it back. Conventionally you would fade music in, bring up the levels for a couple of seconds and then fade it down before you start any speech. Your music and speech must not fight; there should be no confusion in the minds of the audience about what they should be listening to. It's very difficult to use music with lyrics under speech. The listeners will start to wonder whether they are listening to the speaker or to the lyrics of the song, and as a result they won't hear either properly.

## Finishing

Once the programme has been mixed there may be a few final editing tweaks to do but these should be fairly minor. You will then need to finish off. This will depend on what format you have been asked to present your piece in. You will need to play out the piece in the appropriate format. However, you should always keep a backup copy. You should always hang on to all your source material until the piece has finally been submitted and you know there is no possibility of changing it.

## Conclusion

Editing is a very creative process in radio. It's rather like composing a piece of music in some ways: you are looking for the best way to blend the sounds and create a picture in the minds of the listeners. Pacing your piece properly, whether you use a fast or slower pace, will have an enormous impact on the listener. Using music and actuality to mix with your interviews will start to create a sound picture in your listener's mind.

# 21 News and current affairs

News and current affairs is a particular type of factual programme. The process of creating the material is similar to other programmes, although it is usually done much more quickly. However, there are some particular issues with news and current affairs that are worth thinking about.

The term *News* and the term *Current affairs* are often used together. However, they do refer to two slightly different things. News tends to mean a straightforward report on an issue, generally delivered by the studio presenter. It may also include short sound bites from some of the key players in a story; it may also include the voice of a reporter. Some bulletins are very short; others can last for up to half an hour. Current affairs tends to involve a lot more discussion and debate and will include opinions from different sides of any argument.

 If you log onto the website you can hear some examples of news bulletins and current affairs items.

## Accurate, fair and impartial

Whether you are making a news item for TV, print or radio there are several elements which it is vital to get right. Three of the most commonly quoted requirements of a news item are that it is accurate, fair and impartial.

### *Accuracy*

Accuracy is important in all factual programmes but it is particularly important in a news item. Broadcasters can and do make mistakes on occasion but the public is much less likely to forgive a mistake in a news item than in any other type of programme. One of the first duties of anyone involved in the production of news is that their reports are accurate. You should make very sure that you have checked that you have got all your facts correct. You need to be absolutely certain about:

- **What:** What are the facts of the story? Think about the facts that you know and not what people think might be the case.
- **Who:** Who is involved in the story, what is their job/role/name?
- **Where:** Where did the events happen?
- **When:** When did they happen?

You should be able to verify any of the above and be absolutely sure that they are accurate facts, not someone's best guess. Figures and statistics can be difficult. You can't always double-check and sometimes figures on the same issue will differ. If, for example, you were doing a report on truancy, you won't have the resources to literally go and find out how many children are out of school in any one week; however, someone will have the figures. Usually a reporter will attribute those figures, so, for example. *The Department of Education says the number of children out of school in any one week is around 7,000.* This is much better than *The number of children out of school every week is around 7,000.* If that figure is challenged or disputed, then at least your reporting is accurate, even if the Department of Education figures are not.

If you are reporting on events you will need to make sure that the things you say happened have actually happened, and if there is any doubt about the events you will need to make that clear. Thus, for example, if there is an accident on a motorway your report might read: *Seven cars were involved in a motorway collision on the M1 earlier today. The accident was caused by ice on the road.* You need to be absolutely sure that there were seven cars, it was on the M1 and that ice was the cause of the accident. If there is any doubt, then again you should attribute the information and make it clear that there is some doubt, so it could read: *At least seven cars were involved in a motorway collision on the M1 earlier today; police say the most likely cause of the accident was ice on the road.* Your report is accurate, even if it later turns out that there were more cars and that the cause of the accident was something else.

### Fair

Fair is a slightly more complicated concept and is rather more subjective; different people might genuinely hold different opinions as to the fairness of a story. As we've seen, the first four questions for any news story – who, what, when, where – should be accurate. The next three points that a news report can cover are why, how, consequence.

It's much more difficult to be factually accurate about these questions. It may not be at all clear how or why something happened and the consequences may be heavily disputed. For these three areas your reporting must be **accurate and fair**.

It's the job of a reporter to reflect all the sides of the argument and to reflect them as fairly as possible. Thus with your report on the M1 motorway accident:

> *At least seven cars were involved in a motorway collision on the M1 today; police say that the most likely cause of the accident was ice on the road. Road safety campaigners are blaming the local council for cutbacks which have reduced the amount of grit on the road.*

Your report is accurate. There was an accident, it did take place on the M1, the police do think it was ice on the road, and road safety campaigners have blamed the local council. However, the report is not **fair**: you are only reporting one side of that argument. For your report to be fair you will need to get a response from the local government who have been accused of being negligent.

> *At least seven cars were involved in a motorway collision on the M1 today; police say that the most likely cause of the accident was ice on the road. Road safety campaigners are blaming the local council for cutbacks which have reduced the amount of grit on the road. Local government officials responded, saying that they have not cut back on any gritting of major roads or motorways.*

Being fair and accurate can be as much to do with what you leave out as what you put in.

> *At least seven cars were involved in a motorway collision on the M1 today; two of the cars were driven by young women under the age of 20. Police say that the most likely cause of the accident was ice on the road.*

Your report is accurate. However, by highlighting the fact that two of the cars were driven by young women you are somehow implying that their youth and inexperience was responsible for the crash. It's possible that the other five cars were driven by men in their fifties but you haven't mentioned this and so you may leave the audience with a false impression.

## *Impartiality*

Impartiality is slightly different to **fairness**; there are very few journalists anywhere who would be happy to say that their reporting is **unfair.** However, not all journalists would say that their reporting was impartial. In the world of print journalism newspapers have very clear agendas and political alliances. The *Daily Telegraph* newspaper, for instance, is regarded as a right-leaning newspaper, while the *Guardian* would be more left leaning. Both newspapers happily accept their different political bias; however, neither would be happy if they were accused of being unfair.

Broadcasters are in a different position; their news output should be **impartial**, and it shouldn't have any specific political agenda. It is the job of any public service or terrestrial broadcaster like the BBC, ITV or Channel 4 to be **fair** and **impartial.**

### How to achieve impartiality and fairness

1   **Balance:** Have you fairly represented all sides of the story?
2   **Language:** Look at the language you are using, particularly at the adjectives. Does the language imply some kind of value judgement?

## *Balance*

While this is easy enough to say, it's not that easy to do in practice and you will often find yourself having to make judgements. Take the issue of balance, for example. There may be more than two views on a subject, which you will need to represent. There may also be a large body of agreement on any particular subject with only a tiny minority in disagreement. You would need to decide how much time to give to that small minority. They should be represented, but perhaps by allocating equal time, particularly over a long-running story, you may be exaggerating the importance of that point of view. There are times when something is so atrocious that there is no point representing the other point of view; the example which is often used is that of a reporter commenting on a horrific massacre in a war: would they really have gone and got one of the killers to give a balancing view on the atrocities they found? Hopefully though you won't be dealing with any stories of this kind, so you should be looking to make sure that everything you report is balanced. Generally speaking, if there is an issue over which there is some controversy you will need to represent all sides. If an accusation has been made you will need to allow the person who has been accused of something a **right of reply.**

## *Language*

A news report is not the place for your own personal opinion. You should think carefully about your wording, in particular using words which imply judgement or value. You should choose your adjectives carefully. For example:

*At least seven cars were involved in a horrendous pile-up on the M1 today . . .. Road safety campaigners are blaming the incompetent local council for cutbacks which have reduced the amount of grit on the road.*

The words *horrendous* and *pile-up* are quite subjective but some news reports might use them. However, look at the word *incompetent*: did the road safety campaigners actually use this word or was this the reporter's take on it? It's not unknown for some reporters to use this kind of language, but a more balanced way of reporting might be as follows:

*At least seven cars were involved in a collision on the M1 today. Police say it's one of the worst accidents recorded on this stretch of motorway. Road safety campaigners say that the council's approach to gritting has been incompetent and that cutbacks have reduced the amount of grit on the road. Local government officials responded, saying that they have not cut back on any gritting of major roads or motorways.*

Remember: as a journalist you can report **facts** straightforwardly but **opinion** should be attributed to the person who voiced that opinion and should be balanced by any other opinions on the subject. You should not be reporting your own opinion.

Impartiality and fairness come out of an attitude of mind. In a news piece you should not be writing a story to prove a point. You should go into the story looking for *all* of the relevant facts. Once you have them to hand you will need to set out the arguments as clearly as you can, giving weight to all the sides of the issue which you think are important. You should see yourself as the outsider looking at what is going on. The phrase often used is that your report should be without favour.

## Structure of a news report

News reports are about telling the audience who, what, where, when, why and how but they tend also to have a structure:

- headline/cue
- the facts
- interviews and balancing arguments
- concluding remarks.

### Headline

The headline usually comes from the studio presenter. The job of the headline is to grab the listeners and tell them why they want to listen to the rest of the report. The headlines may all come at the top of a news bulletin.

### Cues

Cues are the introduction to a piece from a studio presenter; they will normally then be followed up by a report from a reporter in the field – the job of a cue is to set up the basic facts and to give the listener a reason to carry on listening to the piece.

### The facts

This should be the what, who, when, where of the story. These are the things you know; this is not the place for opinion. The facts should come first before any discussion.

- **Report from a correspondent/journalist:** Some pieces will be reporting the facts; other pieces will interpret the facts and make sense of them for a journalist.
- **Interviews/arguments/discussion:** This can be the place for the why and how questions; it can also look at the consequences or outcomes. The key players will put forward their point of view.
- **Concluding remarks:** The reporter will sometimes bring together the arguments or parts of the discussion and then sign off. This is not the time for a rant or polemic from the reporter but just a drawing together and summary of the arguments.

 If you go onto the website you can hear a number of different news reports. Have a go at deconstructing them.

## Writing and language

Language is also difficult in that you have to strike a balance between making your piece interesting and attention grabbing but not letting your own opinions and prejudices start to colour the piece.

Writing for the ear is dealt with in a separate chapter but it's worth considering it here with specific reference to news. Stylistically, the same three basic principles apply to writing news reports as to writing anything for the ear.

1   **Simple language**. This is not the place for words which obscure meaning. There is no room for ambiguity. The listener only has one chance to understand what you are saying and in radio there are no graphics or pictures.
2   **Short sentences.** Long sentences with lots of sub-clauses can be confusing. It's too difficult for the listener or viewer to keep track of the meaning. As a rule of thumb if you have more than one comma in a sentence have another look and see if it can be broken down into two sentences.
3   **Active not passive verbs.** *The Prime Minister opened parliament today* not *Parliament was opened by the Prime Minister today.*

## Conclusion

News is a very particular type of factual programme making. It carries with it lots of responsibilities. Journalists tend to work under a lot of time pressure and so have to make decisions very quickly. It's for this reason that it's important they fully understand the importance of **accuracy, fairness and impartiality.** This is not to suggest for a minute that other types of factual programmes are unfair or inaccurate; news, however, does come under a particular scrutiny and therefore merits careful attention.

# 22  Editing TV

In any production the editing is every bit as important as the shooting. In a professional world editing time can be very expensive, and most producers and directors will be strictly rationed as to how much time you are allowed to spend in the edit. The amount of time you would be allocated varies according to the type of programme and the type of budget allocated. However, it's rare for anyone to feel that they have enough time; most people feel that they could always do with more editing time. In your project you may not be limited by financial considerations but you may have limited access to equipment and you may have limited time available. It therefore makes sense to try to prepare in advance as much as possible for your edit and make the most of the time you have.

As with cameras there are a huge variety of different types of editing packages, and systems change all the time. Therefore this chapter will not make reference to any particular type of equipment; however, it will assume that you have some access to a nonlinear digital editing system. While they vary slightly, most of them work in broadly the same way and whatever package you are using you will approach the edit in the same way.

## Ingest

Ingesting is the process of loading your footage into the edit package so that you can start to edit. It's a useful point at which start to look at your rushes again and put them into some kind of order. Most edit packages use a system of files or 'bins' as they are often called to store your rushes.

How you order your rushes is up to you. Some people order the rushes by tape number or digital file. However, that means you have to have a comprehensive log of what is in which file and/or a good memory. Another way of dividing up the material is by subject matter. Each of your contributors could be in a different bin. You could have all your PTCs in one bin. The rest of your bins could be made up of material you intend for the different sequences. What you are really trying to do is order the material in such a way as to make it as quick and easy as possible to find the material again.

### Time code

Most video cameras and most edit systems will give your shots a time code. This is usually an eight-digit number showing hours, minutes, seconds and frames. It will look something like 00: 03:13:32. The time code is important for locating your shots. By making a note of your time codes when you log your shots you will easily be able to find them when you start your edit.

## *Viewing and logging*

It sounds obvious, but one of the most important things to do before the edit is to go back and watch what you have shot and make some notes for yourself. You can do this while you ingest the material.

**Logging:** When you log material you should make a note of three things:

- what the shot is
- what the time code is
- digital file or tape number.

### *The shot*

In one sense this is fairly obvious; you will need to describe the shot; the size and any moves. However, you can also make other notes for yourself. If the shot is not usable, perhaps because something went wrong or because the camera wobbled, or any number of other things, then you can mark it as NG or no good. This will save time later; you may choose not to ingest these shots. It may be that you have taken the same shot several times. Each take was OK but may have had good and bad elements to it; you will need to make a note of how each shot differed. There may be something you particularly liked about a shot and know where you would like to use it. Again it's useful to think about this. How you describe the shots and what notes you make will depend on you. Only you know why you like or don't like a shot and how you think it might be useful.

### *Time code*

Once you have identified the shots it's useful to make a note of the digital file number or tape number and the time code. You can use this for reference when you start to make up your script. You can put the time code on your script so that you can easily find the shot when you come to the edit.

### *Digital file or tape number*

Make a note for yourself of what is on each digital file or tape. This will save hours of needless searching. Viewing and logging rushes in this way may seem very laborious. However, it's one of the best ways of becoming familiar with your material. By watching through the material and taking notes in this way the images will start to stick in your mind. Later on in the edit you will start to recall images and it will allow you to be a lot faster and more imaginative about trying out different shots.

## Building your sequences

This is the fun bit and the most creative part of the editing. When you prepared your shooting script you identified the types of sequences you wanted to use and now is the time to start building them. Again, people vary in how they like to approach this. Some people start at the beginning of the script and work through, while others like to build up sequences out of order.

There are endless ways in which you can put shots together and there is no way to give you a rule book about this. However, here are some tips to help you get started:

- **Think sequence, not shot:** Individual shots strung together make for a very bitty edit. They don't draw the viewer in. The viewers want you to tell them something with your choice of shots and thinking of sequences will help you to do this.
- **Lead with pictures:** Often when new directors start making programmes they plaster the whole thing with sync or commentary or dialogue. There is not a moment in the film when someone isn't saying something. This can have a negative impact on the viewers who are struggling to keep up. They have to work quite hard to keep up processing all the images and keeping the narrative going. If you couple this with poor scripting then the viewers will struggle even more and their minds will soon start to wander onto something else and they will lose track completely. You should allow time throughout the film for the pictures to lead. You should lead into any commentary or dialogue with some pictures, giving the viewers time to settle before they start listening. You don't necessarily have to come to a piece of dialogue or sync with the presenter or contributor in vision from the very first word. You can lay some pictures over the beginning and then come to them in vision.
- **Jump cuts:** The term *jump cut* can refer to cuts which don't feel smooth, which slightly jar or disturb the viewer. Unless you are particularly going for that effect you should try to avoid them. The way to avoid a jump cut is never to cut together shots which are too similar. You should also avoid cutting from a wide shot to a closer shot without changing the angle of the camera. You should also avoid cutting from one wide shot to another wide shot without having something else in between; the viewers tend to expect a wide shot to be followed by a sequence of closer shots and if you don't do this they will start to disconnect from the film.
- **Establishing shots:** You will need some kind of establishing shot for each different location you have visited. The establishing shot doesn't have to be the first shot you use in any sequence but you will need to use it fairly early on.
- **Reveals:** Sometimes you will want to tease your viewers a little. You can start a sequence with something they don't understand and then come to an establishing shot to reveal what the viewer is looking at. This can be an engaging way to start a sequence – just don't leave the viewer in the dark for too long!
- **Length of shots:** This obviously depends on the style of programme you are making. Some programmes have very quick fast cuts, others are more leisurely. Remember: the style of cutting needs to feel consistent with the subject matter of the film. If you are making a film about a very sensitive subject, for example, bereavement, and you use a very pacey style of editing and commentary, you can come across as being rather insensitive. On the other hand, slow moves and long shots on a piece can start to be a little boring. As a general rule, though, you wouldn't hold a static shot for more than about five seconds unless there was a very particular reason for doing so, less than one second and it starts to be a bit subliminal. Where there is a move on a shot then it will hold a little longer. There are of course some programmes which don't do this; they will use a very fast style of commentary. However, it's difficult to sustain this approach for very long and it tends to be used for shorter sequences and to create a particular effect.
- **Cutting on a move:** Previous chapters described types of shots including moving shots such as pans and tilts. It was suggested that you think carefully about these types of shots and only use them if you felt you had a good reason. The problem with moving shots is that it's very difficult to get in and out of them when the camera is actually moving. You can get away with it sometimes but too much and the viewers will start to feel something a bit like motion sickness; it disturbs the brain a bit and they will get distracted and stop

watching your film properly. You can of course cut in and out of the shot at the beginnings and ends of the moves when the camera is steady but if you have made your move too long you are left with a rather lengthy and possibly boring shot.

## Effects

Even the most modest edit package usually comes with a number of effects. There are a huge variety of different effects you can add to a shot; the following are some of the most common.

### *Transitions*

There are a number of ways of getting from one shot to the next:

- **Cut:** This is the most common form of transition where you have an instant change from one shot to the next.
- **Mix/cross-fade/dissolve:** These are all terms to describe the same transition, a gradual fade from one shot to another. They have a more relaxed feel than a cut and are useful if you want a meandering pace and contemplative mood.
- **Fade:** The picture fades to a single colour and then the next picture comes in. The colour is only on screen momentarily. The fade to black or fade from black are ubiquitous in film and TV and are used to signal the beginning and end of a scene.

These kinds of effects are similar to camera moves; you should use them sparingly and for a good reason. The different transitions subtly imply something to the viewer. If you use a fade to black it implies to the viewer that you have ended something. It doesn't have to be the end of the film but it is definitely the end of a sequence. A dissolve or a cross-fade implies more of a connection, often between the images; sometimes it may imply a passage of time or move to a different place.

### *Wipes*

One shot is progressively replaced by another shot in a geometric pattern. Pictures can slide on and off, either from side to side or up and down, they can pixelate, or peel on and off. If you experiment with your package then you will quickly get to see them. These can be great tools. However, they are defined effects and they will give your programme a very definite style. If you want to use this kind of effect you will need to use it consistently through the piece and establish your style quite early on. If you just use these effects once or twice through the piece they will start to jar and stick out like a sore thumb. This is not meant to imply that you should overuse the effects; just that you will need to establish the stylistic convention at the beginning of the piece and then stick with it.

- **Slow motion and speeded-up motion:** Most packages will allow you to speed up or slow down your shots. You can do this subtly so that it's difficult to detect or you can do it very deliberately so that it's obvious. Again if you do this there has to be a good reason and it needs to visually make sense to the viewer. Speeding up a shot is almost always done humorously; it's usually because you want to indicate a passage of time. Slow motion gives a kind of dreamy effect, asking the viewers to think carefully about what they are watching. It gives an almost romantic implication. Be careful how you use it.

- **Colour:** Some packages will allow you to play with the colour of a shot. You can *saturate* the colour. This means you are putting more colour into the piece and gives it a very bright, vibrant feel. You can *de-saturate*; this means you take colour out of the piece and it gives it a rather washed-out effect. You can also change the reds, greens and blues individually to create effects. Like all these effects, you will need to be careful to use them consistently, rather than just throw in a few effects for the sake of it. You will need to have a good reason and the effect needs to be a part of the storytelling.

## First assembly, rough cuts and fine cuts

Edits are normally divided into two phases: the first assembly/rough cut stage, and the fine cut stage.

- **First assembly:** This is a very loose assembly of the main building blocks onto a timeline. You will not have done much work on pictures at this point.
- **Rough cuts:** Once you have a first assembly you should start on the rough cut. You should start to put a shape to your piece adding in pictures, cutaways, etc. Once you have done a rough cut you should view the piece again and then make notes for yourself. Then you should go back and refine the piece a bit more. You can make as many rough cuts as you want but hopefully each cut will be a little less rough than the last. For this reason you shouldn't spend too long getting all the fine editing right at this stage. It tends to be a bit of a waste of time, since you are likely to have to do it all over again as you change and refine the piece.
- **Fine cut:** The fine cut is the polishing stage. You should work on getting all the transitions right, getting all the sound levels right and making any fine adjustments to colours. You should only move on to this stage once you are happy that you have the piece as you want it.

## Editing factual

Just as with shooting, the way you approach a factual edit is slightly different to the way you would approach a dramatised sequence. With a dramatised piece you will have a detailed script/storyboard which forms the basis of your edit. With a factual piece you should have your outline script but you will have to use the time between your shoot and the edit to make up your edit script.

### Before the edit

#### Interviews

You will also need to review any interviews you have done. Sometimes interviews are transcribed; this means you have a written version of the interview. Transcribing can be very helpful: it offers a much more efficient way of putting your script together; it's much easier to work from a paper version than from memory. However, transcribing an interview can be very time consuming and you may feel that it's not worth it. If you decide not to transcribe the interview you will need to watch it through and make notes for yourself, just as you did for the shots. You can start to break the interview down into smaller sections; you can either break it down into the different answers or break it down by time. Either way you should be making a note for yourself as to which answers you felt were strong and why. If there are any bits you know you don't want then again it's useful to make a note for yourself about this.

Again, by looking at your interviews and making notes for yourself in this way, you will ensure that you become familiar with your material before the edit. The more familiar you are with the material the easier and quicker you can make decisions in the edit.

*Preparing the edit script*

Your next job is to start to prepare an editing script. For this you are going to need the outline script you prepared before the shoot and you will need all your notes from the log. In your outline treatment you will have a number of things to get you started:

- You will have already thought about the overall structure and narrative of the piece.
- You will have viewed all your rushes and made a note of important time codes.
- You will have an idea of where the interviewees and contributors fit in and what they are supposed to have said.
- You will have all the PTCs scripted.
- You will have a good idea of the type of information you will need in the links.

The edit script will look a little like your outline treatment. It should be divided into three columns, on one side the pictures and on the other side the words, and in the third column you will have a note of time codes so that you know where everything is and you can find it easily. However, now you will have all the pieces of the puzzle to hand and you can put in all the different elements.

## Template 22.1  Factual edit script

| EXAMPLE Edit script | | |
|---|---|---|
| **Festival Fever** | | |
| | *Visuals* | *VO (voice-over)* |
| Digital file 1 Time code 00:15:38 | GVs secret garden festival. Bands, different types of entertainment. | This is the Elusive Festival, one of the hundreds of festivals held in Britain this summer. For three days 3,000 people turn up and pitch their tents to enjoy the music, the atmosphere and the dozens of acts which perform here. As festivals go this is fairly small – nothing like the scale of Glastonbury or Womad. It's peaceful, good-natured and fun. |
| Digital file 3 Time code 00:04:32 | WS from lookout tower to show extent of the festival and the numbers of tents pan left to reveal Karen. | |

|  | *Visuals* | *VO (voice-over)* |
|---|---|---|
|  |  | And yet, once the festival is over, the organisers will spend at least three weeks clearing up the 35 tons of rubbish left behind. |
| Digital file 2 Time code 02:12:22 | Karen is in the middle of the festival, surrounded by tents and party-goers. | PTC (Piece to Camera) Karen: I've been going to festivals like this since I was 16. They are part of the British summer now. Festivals like this are a place for creativity. Not just musicians, but artists and craftsmen and women, dancers, performers, all come and find audiences at this kind of festival. I've seen the way they feed creativity. But I've also seen what they leave behind, not just the rubbish but the enormous amount of waste – some 500 tents will get left behind, tables, chairs and over 1,000 sleeping bags. All of them just thrown away. |
| Digital file 7 Time code 00:41:08 | We meet the festival-goers as they are having breakfast, cleaning out their tents, etc. | VOX POPS Families, groups of teenagers: *No . . . I don't take my stuff when I leave . . . we just buy a cheap tent and then leave it. The problem is when it rains and it all gets wet and muddy you can't get it packed up and, if you do, it's too heavy to carry.* *I was here last year – we left most of our clothes – you just buy a load of cheap T-shirts before you come and then wear them and then leave them – it's just like part of the ticket price. I left the tent – it was my dad's and he was pretty pissed off but that's just how it is.* |

|  | *Visuals* | *VO (voice-over)* |
|---|---|---|
| Digital file 3<br>Time code<br>00:09:56 | GVs of last year's festival. People packing up to go.<br><br>WS from tower to show the number of tents left. | VOICE-OVER:<br>Small festivals like this don't provide much in the way of facilities, they can't afford to put down walkways or have much in the way of washing facilities. So if it rains, everyone just gets muddy, and not many people want to take their mud home. But that means a lot of work for those left behind. |
| Digital file 6<br>Time code<br>00:13:24 | Russell is on observation tower – in the background we can see the vast expanse of the festival behind him. | INTERVIEW Russell Jones:<br>*We employ about 300 people for about three weeks to clear up the mess. Most of them are people who've been at the festival and stay on afterwards to earn some money. We don't have much in the way of machinery, most of it's done by hand. I can't believe how much gets left behind. It causes us massive problems. It's so expensive we just can't afford it, not just paying all the litter pickers but the amount we have to pay to get rid of all the rubbish means we're not sure if we can keep going with the festival. We've tried recycling but even that is just too expensive for us.* |
| Digital file 5<br>Time code<br>00:19:38 | GVS Picking litter, cleaning toilets, collecting rubbish. | VOX POPS Litter pickers:<br>*We were at the festival and then we stayed on to clear up, it's good money but if you get caught slacking then you get fired straight away.*<br><br>*You can pick up loads of stuff here. I get all my clothes for the year just by doing this. I got these boots that someone left – I don't know why, they aren't even dirty, there's so many sleeping bags – but it is such a waste.* |

|  | Visuals | VO (voice-over) |
|---|---|---|
|  |  | You get loads of people coming to festivals like this and they think they are all environmentally friendly and that and they just eat veggie burgers and stuff and then they go and just dump all their stuff. |
| Digital file 5 Time code 00:16:32 | We find Karen by a piece of heavy crushing machinery. We see waste being loaded into the crusher – we see a line of vans waiting to unload the waste. | PTC (Piece To Camera) Karen: This is where it all ends up – here at this recycling centre. Each ton of rubbish collected costs the festival £300 to dispose of. With 35 tons of rubbish each year that's a lot of money. |

## The edit

### *First assembly and rough cut*

People vary a lot in the way they approach an edit and you will find the way that suits you best. However, to start you off I'll propose one method that you may find easy to adopt.

- **Sync:** These are your pieces of interview. Start the edit by pulling out the bits of interview you have chosen and put those in the timeline. You should be watching all the bits of interview. Often you will find that something that looks fine on paper sounds terrible and your sound edits won't work at all. On the other hand, you may find that something you thought wasn't that good turns out better than you thought. At this point don't get too picky or do too much fine editing. You are likely to be moving things around a lot, so for the moment just pull things out and put them in the right order.
- **PTCs:** If you are using PTCs you should put them into place now. Don't get hung up on finding cutaways or anything; just put them into the timeline as they are.
- **Guide track:** You will need to record your links as a guide track. Remember: this is not going to be your final commentary. Commentary tends to change all the time and it's one of the last things you will put on. However, you will need some sort of guide commentary, your best guess at this point as to what the commentary will eventually be. Not everyone will do this. Some people prefer to build a sequence of images and then write the commentary. However, whichever way you do it you will be rewriting commentary a lot and at this point the guide track is really there to give you an idea of length and to indicate the sequences you are going to need.
- **Build your rough cut:** You can now start to build your sequence of images. Remember: you are looking for sequences not individual shots and you should be leading with your pictures.
- **Timings:** Once you have all the above in place it will give you an idea of the length of your piece. If you find that once you have laid down all the elements above your piece

is much longer than this length then you should start to think about making some cuts now. You will save yourself a lot of time which you could spend cutting sequences tht just end up having to be junked for length. If you are under length then you will need to think about what more you should be be adding in. However, at this point you don't need to have it exactly to length; once you start adding in your pictures it will begin to get much longer. Ideally, your piece shouldn't be more than about 10 per cent longer than your ideal duration.

- **Refine and recut:** Go back over your cut to start refining. You may want to change the bits of interview or build up more pictures; you will probably want to change the commentary as your picture sequences build up.
- **Feedback:** Get feedback; you will need to hear a reaction to the piece from someone who doesn't know it.

## Commentary writing

Good commentary writing is a difficult task. Writing commentary for TV has a lot in common with writing for the ear in radio but it also differs. In radio the words help to create the picture but in television the words should be at the service of the pictures.

In the chapter on writing for the ear there was a discussion on ways to make your writing work for the ear and not the eye. If you haven't read this section then you should do so before starting your commentary. There was also a discussion of the different types of commentary you might have to write. In TV there are the same basic types of commentary.

- **Introduction:** This is the section of commentary which sets up the piece and engages the viewer. It brings the viewers in and tells them why they should listen to the rest of the piece.
- **Cues:** A cue is mostly used in TV when the programme has a studio presenter. The cue from the presenter is the script which introduces the viewer either to a package, a kind of filmed insert to a studio programme or hands over to another presenter.
- **Voice-over links:** In a factual piece this type of commentary moves the story along. It will move us perhaps from one subject to the next or from one stage of the narrative to the next. It may lead from one interviewee to the next.
- **Authored commentary:** Some programmes have a more 'authored' feel to them. Instead of an anonymous voice-over, there may be a presenter in vision who also does the links and the piece has a more personal feel. They may be an acknowledged expert in the subject or they may be undergoing some sort of personal experience. This type of programme may not have any interviewees but may be all scripted commentary. Natural history programmes tend to be done in this way.

In television you will need to balance the commentary with the pictures. Too little and the viewer won't know what's going on, too much and the viewer quickly gets a sense of information overload. Viewers can't keep up with watching the images and listening to all the commentary; they will start to miss bits and lose the thread of what's going on. The most skilful writers get this balance just right: they put the words at the service of the pictures, giving enough information but letting the pictures do most of the work. Like almost anything else, writing good commentary is subjective and creative, but here are some tips to help:

- **Don't** describe what's happening in the scene. If the viewer can see it you don't need to spell it out.

- **Don't** paint by numbers. You have put in your guide track, PTCs and sync but this does not mean that you have to literally interpret or illustrate everything exactly. You should be building the best sequence and then adjusting the commentary to fit the pictures, not the other way around.
- **Don't** plaster commentary all over your piece. At the beginning of a sequence let the pictures establish themselves before you bring in any commentary; only say as much as you need to.
- **Don't** let your commentary and pictures fight each other. While you don't want to describe what is happening in a scene, at the same time you don't want to be talking about something completely different, so that the viewer has to try to mentally make the two things fit together.
- **Fix the picture:** If it's not immediately obvious what the viewers are looking at and why you will need to let them know quickly, otherwise they will be trying to figure it out and won't be listening to your commentary. Even if it is obvious, you shouldn't throw them off course by starting you sentence with something completely unconnected.
- **Lead into picture sequences:** It's not always easy to do this, but if you can set up your commentary so that it leaves you an opportunity to follow with a sequence of shots without the need for more commentary, then you will find you have a stronger piece. Thus, for example, in the piece we looked at earlier on waste at festivals, you have decided to open your piece with some shots of the festival in full swing but you also want to talk about waste.

Example 1

| Images | Commentary |
|---|---|
| WS Band performing on stage | Waste is one of the most difficult problems that confront the organisers of Britain's festivals. |
| MS people at festival enjoying themselves | Thousands of people attend festivals every year. |
| CU people dancing, CU people in exotic costumes, drinking, eating, laughing | But with so many people, there is a huge clearing up job to be done. |
| Bins overflowing | 8,000 tons of rubbish has to be burned or destroyed each summer. |

In this example you will open the shots by looking at a festival, but the first word you use is 'waste'. You have said 'festival' but right at the end of the sentence. The viewers are confused, not because they can't recognise that they are looking at shots of a festival but you have opened your commentary with a completely unconnected word, and they will then start to wonder why.

Example 2

| WS band performing on stage | Summer, and Britain's festival culture is in full swing. |
|---|---|
| MS people at festival enjoying themselves | This year some two million people will attend a festival. |
| CU people dancing, CU people in exotic costumes, drinking eating, laughing | Festivals bring together music, art, creativity and just plain fun but they bring something else. . . . |
| Bins overflowing, ZO (zoom out) to reveal empty festival site with abandoned tents | Waste – thousands of tons of waste. |

The audience know what they are looking at and your opening words aren't confusing them. The words *full swing* mean that at that point you could happily show shots of the festival without the need to say anything else. Again at the end, you have finished the link with the words *thousands of tons of waste*. The viewer will now happily watch any number of shots of rubbish and waste without you having to say anything else. Instead of telling a story with words, you are leaving space for the pictures to tell the story.

## Laying commentary

Laying the final commentary is one of the last things you will do. This is because it's likely to change any number of times during the edit process. However, once you have got your piece together you will probably want to re-record the final commentary and lay it. You may have been recording bits and pieces as you go along but if you re-record it all at the end and lay it fresh it will probably sound a lot better than lots of pieces recorded at lots of different times.

## Music

Music in factual programmes is obviously determined by the type of factual programme it is. Some types of factual programmes have no music; the closer it is to a news programme the less likely it is to have music, which might seem a bit frivolous. However, other types of programmes will use music, either music recorded on location or music which is added later, sometimes both. Choice of music is obviously quite an individual thing; however, here are some hints:

- Music does significantly impact upon the mood or feel of your piece, so make sure you have chosen something appropriate.
- Generally speaking, music with lyrics isn't going to work terribly well. The words of the song tend to clash with what's happening on screen, unless they are specifically about the topic of the programme.
- Music with lyrics should never be used under commentary, as they will definitely 'fight'.

- Music is like pictures and sound FX. The viewer needs some time to register the music, so always lead the music in advance of any commentary.
- You will need to dip the sound quite low under any commentary.
- As a general rule, it's harder to make music work under interviews or PTCs.
- Fighting rhythms: If you are using a lot of music you will need to make sure that the rhythm of the music isn't fighting the rhythm of your cuts. If you have a slow piece of music with lots of very fast cuts it may start to feel a little odd and vice versa. Sometimes editors will try to cut the pictures with the beat of the music.

### *Laying music*

Again, as you build your edit you can add music to see how you like it, but you should avoid doing any kind of fine tweaking of the music until you have finished the picture edit; otherwise you will find yourself having to do it all over again.

### Editing dramatised sequences

In a dramatised sequence the process is slightly different. You will already have a script and if it's a music video you will have a kind of script in that you have the song. However, just as with a factual programme you will want to make the pictures do the work. Just as with a factual programme you will need to look at your material before you start to edit so that you become familiar with it. As you ingest you can start to organise the rushes. Often directors and editors organise the shots according to the scene, the shot size and the character in the shot.

**Let the pictures do the work:** Just as with a factual programme you don't want your entire piece to be dialogue from start to finish. You will need to allow space for pictures to do the work. You will need to build in time for this. It can be at the beginning or end of a scene, or during the scene if the dialogue can accommodate it, but don't forget: building visual sequences is an important part of the process.

### Continuity editing

In most conventional drama we tend not to notice the cuts very much; sometimes directors want the viewer to be very aware of the cuts but at other times they want the cuts to be barely noticeable. This kind of editing is known as continuity editing. If you want your cuts to be less noticeable there are some things you can do:

- **Changing shot sizes:** The least noticeable changes in shot size happen if you make the changes slowly. So you go from a wide shot to a mid-shot and then to a close-up.
- **Changing angles:** If you are moving from wide shot to mid-shot, you would normally choose a different camera angle. The angle should change by at least 30 degrees. If you use the same camera angle you get a **jump cut**, and this tends to disturb the viewer more.
- **Match the shot sizes:** If you have more than one character in a scene, once you have moved in from your wide shot to a mid-shot or close-up, you should try to keep the shot sizes and framing the same on both characters.
- **Matching angles:** If you want to preserve the sense of two people talking to one another you will need to have the correct corresponding angles. So when you make the cut the eye lines should match and appear to be looking at one another.

- **Action cuts:** An action cut is a cut which you make while a character is performing some sort of action. Thus, for example, your character may be reaching for a door handle. You may for some reason want to direct the viewer's attention to the door handle so you may cut to a close-up on the door handle just as the character turns the knob. This kind of cut can be quite tricky to get right. If it's a fraction out it will look a little odd to the viewer. Of course, it also depends on the shot having been right to start with. You will need to make sure that the action is at the same point in both shots when you make the cut. Editors will normally have both shots up on the screen at the same time and will adjust them more or less frame by frame to make sure they match.
- **Crossing the line:** Remember the crossing the line rule: nothing will disturb the viewer more quickly than if you start disrupting the geography of a scene.

## Other points for drama editing

- **Cutaways:** These need to be motivated by the action or dialogue. If you use a cutaway, the viewer is going to assume that you have done so because you are trying to signal something or because you are sharing what the character is seeing/doing. If the cutaway has no purpose then the viewer will try to figure one out. Viewers will start to try to work out why you are showing them the cutaway and will become confused. While this is happening they are not listening to the rest of the scene and you will have lost their attention.
- Of course there are lots of directors who don't keep to this pattern; they may deliberately choose to ignore it so as to create an effect on the viewers, possibly to remind them that they are watching a film, not real life.
- **Pacing:** Pacing refers to how long or short you make the shots between the cuts. Pacing your cuts really depends on the type of piece you are making. However, it's worth remembering a couple of points.
- **Static shots:** Generally shots don't last for more than about six or seven seconds before the viewer expects something else to happen. Shots which last for less than a couple of seconds can start to feel a little uncomfortable in a normal scene, it may feel somewhat jerky. Of course, lots of directors do use very short shots, particularly in a montage (lots of quick shots put together). However, the viewer cannot sustain this pace of shot change for very long.
- **Moving shots:** These tend to last a bit longer providing that there is a good reason for the move. Alternatively, if there is a lot of movement happening in front of the camera you can sustain the shot for longer.
- **Speeding up the pace:** If you speed up the pace of your cuts during a scene it creates a sense of urgency; it will start to feel as if some sort of climax is about to happen. This is fine so long as it fits in with the narrative of your piece.
- **Slowing down the pace:** This has the opposite effect. If you have had some fast action demanding a lot of attention from the viewer, then slowing down the pace of the edit will allow the viewer some time to catch up.
- **Cutting dialogue:** How you choose to cut your dialogue will significantly affect the quality of the finished product. Something may have been beautifully shot and acted but if the editing is poor the whole piece ends up looking quite shoddy. Here are a couple of tips to help:

  1  **L-shaped editing:** You don't need to cut to the person speaking immediately as they start talking. It can often create a smoother edit if you allow the character to

say the first few words under another picture and then cut to the character. You can download the template off the website.

## Template 22.2 L-shaped editing

| Non L-shaped edit | | L-shaped editing | |
|---|---|---|---|
| **Dialogue** | Cuts | **Dialogue** | Cuts |
| **Character A:** Do you want to go to the cinema this evening? I really want to go and see that film Jenny went to see the other night, it sounded so good. | | **Character A:** Do you want to go to the cinema this evening? I really want to go and see that film Jenny went to see the other night, it sounded so good. **Character B:** Oh no . . . not tonight. | |
| **Character B**: Oh no . . . not tonight. I'm so tired I just can't face the thought of getting into the car and fighting all that traffic – can't we just stay in? | **CUT TO B** | I'm so tired I just can't face the thought of getting into the car and fighting all that traffic – can't we just stay in? **Character A:** But you always say that. | **CUT TO B** |
| **Character A:** But you always say that. You are never not tired – even if you've just been around the house all day you say you are tired and don't want to go out. | **CUT TO A** | You are never not tired – even if you've just been around the house all day you say you are tired and don't want to go out. **Character B:** That's not fair | **CUT TO A** |
| **Character B:** That's not fair – we went out last week, and I'd been at work all day and really didn't want to go at all | **CUT TO B** | – we went out last week, and I'd been at work all day and really didn't want to go at all. | **CUT TO B** |

2 **Reaction shots:** If there is a long piece of dialogue from a character you may not want to keep the shot on the character who is speaking for the whole of the speech. You could cut to the person the character is speaking to for a **reaction shot**. You will get a sense of how the second character is reacting to the person who is talking. You can do this at a particularly dramatic point in the dialogue if it seems right. If you think back to the section on shooting drama, this is why you should run the scene a number of times and film reactions as well as dialogue.

## Music

You may want to lay some music on your drama and this will play an important part in the edit. There will be two types of music you are likely to want to use; both of these will be added during the edit.

1   **Diegetic music:** Music which is actually supposed to be a part of the scene, something the characters are supposed to be able to hear, something coming from a radio or CD, IPod, etc.
2   **Non-diegetic music/incidental music/title music:** This is the type of music that the characters are not supposed to be hearing, which adds to the atmosphere of the piece. With this type of music you will need to make sure that the music is not fighting with the dialogue. Most of the time the music is either faded out under dialogue or kept very low so that it doesn't detract. Music is more often used over sequences with no dialogue.

Music is generally one of the last things to be added. You should sort out all your picture cuts first and then lay the music. If you lay the music first you are almost certainly going to have to change it radically as you change the pictures, and you will waste a lot of time.

**Music videos** are slightly different. In this instance the music is the thing you are trying to feature, so you will probably find it easier to lay the music first and then cut the pictures to fit the music.

**Trailers** are a kind of hybrid. They are likely to use more music than the programme or film they are trailing. The music is often a way of holding the piece together. A trailer uses lots of different extracts from different parts of the film or TV programme, but having a single piece of music running underneath gives the piece cohesion and holds it together.

## Voice-over/commentary

This isn't often used in dramas, although you do sometimes get a kind of 'narrator' voice coming in. It's commonly used if a story is told in flashback and you hear the voice of the person telling the story. It's used quite sparingly, usually only at key moments in the drama. Trailers also sometimes use a voice-over commentary. As with factual programmes this is something you would lay properly at the end of the edit, although some directors will use a guide track or rough version of the commentary to help time the piece.

## Fine cut

Once you have got all the pictures right, either for a documentary or a dramatised piece, and you are happy with the music and commentary, you can then move to finishing the piece off and doing the fine cut. This is the point where you will do any fine tweaking. You may want to adjust the sound levels and sound edits to make them smoother. You can add any effects or transitions you want to use. This process can be quite fiddly, so you will need to leave yourself enough time at the end to polish the piece. However, you will need to be sure that you are happy with the overall piece before you start this process. You can waste a lot of time if you start doing fine editing before you are settled on your rough cut.

The last process is the play out. You will have been given a format on which you are expected to deliver the piece, so you will need to 'export' the piece onto this format. Clearly you won't want to play out your piece until you are absolutely sure that you have got the piece you want. Normally you would not delete the project from your edit package immediately. If there was some kind of disaster you might need to come back to it, but once you have played out then you have finished the actual production work.

## Conclusion

The edit is a creative part of the production process; every bit as creative as the shoot itself. It's important not to underestimate the amount of time you will need to spend on your edit. Just like the shoot, you will need to organise yourself if you are going to get the best out of your available time. It's also really important to get feedback and to **listen** to the feedback: that first reaction to your piece is a really important one.

# 23 Feedback and evaluation

## Feedback

If you are working in a professional TV environment you would almost certainly expect to get feedback during the edit. Feedback usually comes from the people responsible for commissioning the material in the first place, or from the producers, series producers and executive producers. It's quite common at this point for directors to be asked to make changes to the piece.

Feedback is an important part of the edit process and can be very helpful. As you work on a piece you become very close to it, you know the material inside-out, and you know the rest of the story. However, the audience isn't going to know this. They are going to see the piece once and they will need to be able to understand it first time around. Having someone come and look at your piece helps you to understand how your viewer will react. Shots or interviews which make perfect sense to you may not be so comprehensible to someone who hasn't been intimately involved with the production. Getting feedback can feel uncomfortable, especially if you have put a lot of work into something, but remember: you are making this piece for the audience, so you will need to get an idea of how they are going to react.

### When to get feedback

There are normally two points during an edit when it's useful to get feedback. The first is at an early rough-cut stage. The first assembly is usually too soon for most people but it won't hurt to get some feedback then if you want to. However, you shouldn't leave it too long before you get feedback. When you ask someone to view the material you should explain where you are up to in the edit; if they are experienced they will know not to worry about little things, but if they are not experienced you may need to warn them. The second point at which to get feedback is when you have laid your commentary, music and effects but before you have actually spent time on all the fine editing.

### Giving feedback

You may be asked to give feedback on someone else's work. If you do then you will need to make sure your feedback is constructive. There is not much point in an edit telling someone that you think the location was wrong or you didn't like the presenter they used. This is not something that they can easily change. You will need to stick to offering feedback on things that can be changed.

- **Narrative structure:** Does the piece make sense to you, can you understand it? You should be able to follow the narrative quite easily without having lots of things explained to you; viewers won't have that luxury.
- **Pacing:** Does the piece feel too fast or too slow to you? Are you getting information overload or conversely are you getting bored?
- **Sequences:** Is there a steady buildup of pictures and sequences or are there too many single shots? If it's a radio piece are you getting a sense of place?
- **Cuts:** Are there any cuts which feel odd or which jar?
- **Pictures and sound:** Do you have enough pictures and sound to add colour and drama? Is the piece too speech heavy?
- **Clashes:** Are there moments when the pictures and the commentary don't fit, or where the music and pictures don't fit?
- **Music:** How does the music feel with the piece? Does it seem to complement what's happening on the screen?

## Evaluation

At the end of your project you are likely to be asked to write some sort of evaluation. The aim of the evaluation is generally to reflect not just on the production process but the degree to which the project has fulfilled its original remit. There will be a number of ways to approach this; however, the information you have been collecting through the production process here will help you to evaluate the project effectively. It will be useful here to refer back to the folder where you have collected all the various documentation. If your production has been made over the course of a few months then it's sometimes difficult to remember everything, but your notes should help you at this point.

### *Brief, target audience and genre*

It's likely that you were given a specific genre and a specific audience for your piece. A part of your evaluation will be to demonstrate how effectively you researched your audience and genre. Any of the notes you make on evaluation need to relate back to the original brief. If you are going to describe a production process or a creative decision, you will need to describe it in terms of how it helped you to fulfil the brief you were given.

#### *Background research*

The first part of the evaluation should be to describe the kind of research you did to familiarise yourself with the genre. You will have looked at films, TV or radio programmes similar to the one you are making. Chapter 3 on research suggested a number of questions you should ask yourself. The notes that you did at the time on this chapter can form the basis of your evaluation.

Make a note of all the pieces which you watched as part of your background research. What did you notice which was typical of the genre you are creating? For example:

- **Use of shots:** Think about the chapter on shot sizes, moves and framing; what do you notice about the director's choices?
- **Sound:** What was the background sound like, and how did it affect your reaction to the piece?

- **Lighting:** Was the lighting naturalistic or was the director creating a mood with the lighting? How hard or soft were the shadows?
- **Editing:** What kinds of edit decisions were made? Was the cutting fast or slow? Was it 'naturalistic' or was the director trying to tell the audience something through the choice of cuts?
- **Pacing:** Is the overall impression fast or slow?
- What did you notice about the mise-en-scène? The use of location, costume, makeup?

*Critical evaluation*

- Story: Who was telling the story? In a factual piece, was it an objective approach or did the piece have a more authored feel? If it was a drama from whose perspective was the story told?
- What can you say about representation in the pieces, particularly in regard to gender, race and social class?

## Production research

You will need to demonstrate how you applied your research to your own project.

- **Creative thinking session:** Start by referring back to the notes on your creative thinking session. Here, the notes you took, however scribbled, will be useful. What ideas did you all come up with, why were some rejected? How and why did you decide on your final project? How did you stay focused on the brief? You should make the connection between the idea you eventually agreed on and the research you did initially on your genre.
- **Creative choices:** You will then need to talk about the choices you made during the production. Again, you will need to relate the choices which you made back to your original research. There are three questions to ask yourself: what choices did I make? Why did I make them? How did they relate to my research into the conventions of the genre?
- **Audience:** Who did you decide was your audience? What do you know about this audience which might relate to how you made your piece? Did this have any effect on the choices you made?
- **Reception:** Where and how would you expect your media to be consumed? Is it likely to be at home or in a public theatre/cinema? Would your audience have expectations of this particular genre of work? If so, what might there expectations be? If you want, you can create the kind of user profile which we discussed in Chapter 7 on advertising.
- **Narrative:** What kind of narrative devices did you employ – character, location, plot? Even if it was a factual piece you can think about your story, your contributors and the locations you choose.
- **Narrative voice:** How did you tell the story? Did you have a presenter, or just a voice-over for a factual piece? If it was a dramatised piece, from whose point of view did you tell the story? Did you use any devices like interior monologues or voice-over?
- **Structure:** How did you structure your piece? Did you include elements of story structure? If so, how?
- **Representation:** You could reflect on representation. Did you consciously try to use any particular stereotypes? Think about any representations you may have had of age,

gender, ethnicity or disability. Were these representations typical of the genre or is this something you brought to the project? If they are typical of the genre you could give some examples.

### Technical choices

Think about the choices you made about **sound**. Think about the different types of sound you used.

- There will have been the background sounds, things that were going on around you over which you had no control.
- You will have made deliberate decisions to record some types of sound, actuality and atmos.
- Did you add any sound effects? If so, what type and why did you add them?
- You may have added some music to the piece, in which case how did you decide what to use?

Think about the types of **shots** you decided to use and the type of filming you decided to do.

- Did you use a particular stylistic device, for example, handheld shots, to give a sense of 'veritas'?
- You may have chosen to use a lot of angled shots, high, low or oblique angles. If you did, why did you choose to do it that way?
- Did you choose a lot of moving shots? If so, why did you make that choice?
- Did you choose to use a lot of close-ups which might create a more intimate or sometimes claustrophobic feel or did you go for lots of wide shots which might distance the audience?

How did you approach the **lighting**?

- Did you use any lighting or did you use available light?
- If you used available light how did this affect did the kinds of shots you could take?
- If you chose to use lighting, was there any particular effect you were attempting? Did you want to create a naturalistic setting or did you try to create some kind of atmosphere with the lights?

## Production

In this section you may want to reflect on the practical aspects of the production.

- Decisions: How did you come to decisions as a group? Did you have a group leader or were decisions made by consensus?
- Teamwork: How did the team dynamic work? Was there a good working relationship or were there lots of arguments?
- Tasks: How did you identify the tasks and how did you allocate them?
- Time: How did you plan your time on the production?
- Production plan: Did you make or use a production plan?
- Shooting/recording days: How did you go about setting up your recording days? Who did what on the day?

- Risk assessment: Did you identify any risks on the shoots or recordings? If so, what did you do about them?

## Feedback

There are different kinds of feedback. There is the type of feedback you get while you are in the process of making the programme. There is also the type of feedback you get once the piece is finished.

- **Feedback in production:** The first part of the chapter discussed the importance of taking on board feedback. You could talk through the feedback you got in the edit. At what stage did you ask for feedback? How useful was the feedback? Was it specific, was it given at the right time, could you use the feedback to make the programme better? If so, what did you do?
- **Feedback after the production:** What kind of feedback did you try to get after the production was finished? Who did you show the piece to and were they the target audience? What kinds of reaction did you get? Did your audience understand the references you were making in the piece? Was the response the one you intended from the audience or did you get a different response? If so, how did it differ?

### *What went well?*

You could mention the aspects of your production which you think went particularly well. You should also indicate why you think they went well and how they relate back to the initial brief. You should also try to indicate why you think something was successful. Was it because of the research you put into it, for example, was it because you had the opportunity to rehearse or practise something before doing it for real, or were you just lucky?

   If you are talking about the practical aspects of the shoot, how did this enable you to deliver on your creative objectives? Perhaps you were able to create a very effective lighting set-up, but you should also indicate how this helped to deliver your creative ambitions.

### *What would I improve?*

You could think about some of the aspects of the piece you were less happy with. You could talk in terms of your creative vision for the piece – were there aspects of the vision which you couldn't achieve? If so, why not? Was it for practical reasons? Was your vision too ambitious? Did it just not work out the way you thought? To what extent were you happy that your creative vision was right in the first place? If there were problems with the practical side of things, what went wrong? Was it something you might have predicted?

### *What new skills did you develop?*

Think about how you developed during the project. What new skills did you develop? If you had any kind of preliminary exercises set before you started your project you could talk about anything you learned from the first exercise which you applied to this production.

- **Practical skills:** Shooting, recording, editing, lighting.
- **Team skills:** Team building, leading a team, creative thinking skills.

- **Creative skills:** Creating a vision, communicating the vision, putting that vision into practice.
- **Critical skills:** Learning to deconstruct pieces of media and to understand the component parts. Ability to describe and distinguish between different genres.

## Conclusion

Writing a good evaluation is all about explaining how the decisions you took related to the original brief you were given. What did your research tell you and then what did you do about it? Keeping good records as you go through the production process will mean that writing your evaluation at the end will be a fairly simple task. You should not be afraid to talk about the challenges you met along the way, but always talk about the approaches you took to overcoming them. Don't be modest: if you think something worked well and you were pleased with it then say so!

# Glossary

**Acoustic**   the amount of resonance in a room.

**Acquired material**   anything included in the production that you have not recorded or shot yourself.

**Action**   cue used by the director to cast or presenter to start once the camera is rolling.

**Actuality sound**   in radio the sound naturally occurring in a location.

**Ambient sound**   the sound or ambience of a room – this could just be the silence.

**Aperture**   the setting on a camera which controls the size of the iris and changes the amount of light coming into the camera.

**Backlight**   a light behind the object in a camera frame. Gives depth to the image.

**Big close up(BCU)**   very close shot of a person or object.

**Blocking**   the process of setting the action in a scene, usually drama.

**Camera left/right**   position of an object in the frame of a camera from the point of view of the camera.

**Camera microphone**   a microphone that is either mounted on top of a camera or is integral to the camera.

**Cans**   headphones.

**Caption**   on screen text.

**Cardioid microphone**   microphone that picks up more sound from the front and side than from the rear.

**Casting**   choosing actors for roles.

**Close up (CU)**   close shot of a person or object.

**Closed questions**   questions that only invite a very short answer.

**Colour balance**   method of combining the three primary colours correctly.

**Commentary**   narration added to a programme.

**Continuity**   the process of ensuring that props, costume and positions of objects and people remains consistent throughout the filming of a scene.

**Continuity editing**   the process of editing in such a way that the viewer perceives the action as continuous.

**Contrast**   the difference in the brightness of a scene.

**Copy**   term used in advertising to describe the written/spoken element of the advertisement.

**Copyright**   the rights that an individual or company might hold to reproduce written work, artistic work, recorded material, stills or music.

**Crash zoom**   using the zoom lens at high speed.

**Credits**   list of people involved in a production.

**Cross-fade/dissolve**   gradual mix of one shot or audio track to a second shot or audio track.

**Crossing theline** moving the camera across an imaginary line of action and disrupting the viewer's sense of the geography of a scene.

**Cut** two different shots put together in an edit.

**Cutaway** shot that takes the viewer away from the main action. Often a shot that shows some detail or illustrates the main action.

**Cue** signal to start action.

**Dead acoustic** acoustic with little or no reverberation.

**Depth of field** the measure of the areas of a shot that are in sharp focus.

**Dissolve/cross-fade** gradual mix of one shot to a second shot.

**Dolly** camera equipment used for moving the camera while in use.

**Dubbing** mixing and laying the soundtrack for a TV programme.

**Edit** cutting different pictures and sound together.

**Establishing shot** wide shot giving a general view of a location.

**Exposure** the amount of light entering the camera. Usually expressed as an f/stop.

**Exterior** any filming or recording done outside.

**Eye line** the height or direction of a person's gaze on camera.

**F/stop** the mechanism on a camera that changes the amount of light through the lens by changing the size of the aperture.

**Fade in/fade out** gradually bringing in or taking out of an image or sound.

**Fade to black** gradually fading out an image until there is only a black screen.

**Feedback** response to your production from teacher/peers.

**Feedback (audio)** howling noise from a microphone.

**Fill light** diffuse light used in conjunction with a key light to fill out shadows.

**Fine cut** the polishing stage of an edit.

**Focal length** the distance over which images remain sharp in a shot.

**Following action** filming technique of filming the action as it happens rather than directing it.

**Frame** single image of a video field.

**Framing** composition of an image.

**Freeze frame** shot from a video that is used as a static image.

**FX (sound effects)** sound added to a programme that is neither spoken word nor music.

**Guide track** rough version of commentary or music laid during the edit as a 'guide'.

**Gun microphone** very directional microphone.

**GVs (general views)** shots used in factual programmes to show the viewer the location or subject of the programme.

**Handheld shots** shots that are taken without having the camera mounted on a tripod but held on the hand or on the shoulder.

**Handles** a few sections of a static shot at the beginning or end of a move.

**Hard lighting** the type of lighting that produces strong shadows.

**Hazard** something that might be a safety risk on a shoot or recording.

**Headroom** framing a shot so as to ensure that the person in the shot has enough space above the head and is also not too low in the frame.

**High angle** shot in which the camera is above the object looking down on it.

**Hyper-cardioid microphone** directional microphone picking up a small range of sound than a cardioid microphone.

**Incidental music** music added to create mood or drama in a scene, not heard by the characters.

**Ingest** process of loading footage or recorded material onto the edit package.

**Interior**   any filming or recording done inside.

**Interior monologue**   inner thoughts of a character in a drama, not heard by the other characters.

**Jump cut**   cut between two shots of the same subject that make it appear to jump around the screen.

**Key light**   the main light used in any set up.

**L-shaped editing**   mostly used for editing dialogue, the practice of cutting to a character speaking slightly after their dialogue has started.

**Lapel microphones (Lavalier, neck microphones)**   microphones that can be clipped onto a person and if necessary hidden.

**Line of action (180 degree line)**   imaginary line connecting the characters in a scene that serves as a guide as to where to place shots in order to keep the geography of a scene clear in the mind of a viewer.

**Links**   commentary used to link one section of a programme to the next.

**Live acoustic**   acoustic with a lot of reverberation.

**Location**   any place you are recording or filming that is not a studio.

**Logging**   process of watching or listening to rushes and making notes.

**Long shot (LS)**   a shot of a person that shows their whole body.

**Looking room**   framing a shot so that a character has space to the left or right in which to 'look' and is not perceived by the viewer to be too close to one side of the frame.

**Magazine programme**   type of TV or radio programme that contains a number of different items linked by a presenter or presenters.

**Medium close up (MCU)**   shot that shows the head and shoulders of a person.

**Mid shot (MS)**   shot that shows the head and torso of a person.

**Mix**   the mixing together of sound.

**Mood music**   music that has been specially composed to be used as incidental music.

**Mute shot**   shot taken without any sound.

**Oblique angle (Dutch tilt, canted angle)**   shot composition that involves tilting the camera to one side.

**Observational documentary**   type of documentary that 'observes' the subject rather than narrates a story.

**Ominidirectional microphone**   microphone that is not directional and records all sounds equally.

**Over-the-shoulder-shot**   camera angle that shows action from the point of view of a character or person in a scene and which also shows a small section of their head and shoulder.

**Pan**   swivelling the camera horizontally.

**Popping**   distortion on the microphone caused by exhalation of breath.

**POV shot (point of view)**   camera angle that shows the action from the point of view of a character or person in a scene.

**PTC (piece to camera)**   piece of commentary delivered by a presenter in vision.

**Radio microphone**   wireless microphone connected to the recording device by transmitters.

**Reaction shot**   during dialogue a shot of the person being spoken to. It could also be reaction to some action or event they are watching.

**Recce**   visit to a location prior to a shoot or recording.

**Reflector/bounce**   card or screen used to reflect or bounce light back onto the subject in a shot

**Reveal**   shot that 'reveals' something to the audience as it develops

**Reverse shot**   shot that creates a reverse angle to the previous shot.

**Right of reply**   term used in news and factual programming to give each side of a controversy the opportunity to put forward their point of view.

**Risk assessment**   document detailing the perceived risk associated with a shoot or recording and the proposed action to mitigate the risk.

**Rough edit/cut**   the first assembly of an edit.

**Rule of thirds**   photographic term referring to the guideline that if a picture is divided horizontally and vertically into three, then the eye is most easily drawn to the intersections between the horizontal and vertical lines.

**Rushes**   unedited material that has been filmed or recorded.

**Schedule**   document that details all the information needed for a shoot or recording.

**Shooting ratio**   the ratio of material that has been collected to material shown in the finished programme.

**Shotgun microphone**   highly directional microphone.

**Singles**   hots that depict just one person.

**Soft light**   a light that does not cast strong shadows.

**Sound level**   the volume of sound.

**Spot FX/foley**   sound created and added to a particular point in the action of a drama.

**Stills**   photographs that are incorporated into a programme.

**Stops**   settings for the aperture on a camera.

**Storyboard**   set of drawings that outline the sequence of shots in a scene.

**Sync**   term used in editing for interviews, vox pop where the speaker is in vision.

**Take**   attempt to film a shot.

**Tease**   term used in factual programmes to refer to the opening section designed to grab the audience's attention.

**Telephoto lens**   lens with a long focal length that allows you to film objects in the distance.

**Tilt**   swivelling the camera vertically.

**Time code**   digitally encoded signal that uses hours, minutes, seconds and frame number to identify individual frames.

**Timeline**   timetable for the production allocating periods of time to specific tasks.

**Track/dolly**   moving the entire camera while filming.

**Transitions**   moves/effects between shots or scenes.

**Treatment**   outline of a programme which describes the main elements but which is not the finished script.

**Tripod**   a mounting for the camera, usually three-legged with adjustable height.

**Two shot**   shot that depicts two characters.

**Voice-over**   commentary from a narrator when not in vision.

**Vox pop**   practice of getting a series of short unprepared comments from the public on a subject.

**Whip pan**   Swivelling the camera horizontally at speed.

**White balance**   the process of allowing the camera to correct the colour in accordance with the lighting conditions. Achieved by allowing the camera to focus on something white.

**Wide angle lens**   lens that creates a wide view of a scene.

**Wide shot (WS)**   shot that shows all the action of a scene.

**Wild track**   ambient sound that is recorded separately from the pictures or the main recording and is used in the final edit.

**Zoom lens**   lens that can vary the focal length.

# Bibliography

## Books

Crisp, Mike (1998) *Directing Single Camera Drama*, Focal Press
McLeish, Robert (2005) *Radio Production*, Focal Press
Stewart, Peter (2006) *Essential Radio Skills*, A & C Black
Watts, Harris (1984) *On Camera*, BBC Books

## Websites

### 180 degree rule

180 degree rule: http://en.wikipedia.org/wiki/180_degree_rule180 degree rule, YouTube videos:
http://www.youtube.com/watch?v=BBPw9C57TuU&feature=related
http://www.youtube.com/watch?v=oFmgdhBMNP0&feature=related
http://www.youtube.com/watch?NR=1&v=ya02fT1q18k
http://www.youtube.com/watch?v=y4wX_dmh8_g&feature=related    http://www.youtube.com/watch?v=oNOT9iHDSXU
http://www.youtube.com/watch?v=HdyyuqmCW14
Cinematography, 180 degree rule – Film School Online: http://production.4filmmaking.com/cinematography4.html
Crossing the line: http://www.mediacollege.com/video/editing/transition/reverse-cut.html
Crossing the line – The Joy of Film Editing: http://www.joyoffilmediting.com/index.php/archives/2095/
P1-02:Thriller Opening 2010/11, the 180 degree rule: http://02thriller11.blogspot.co.uk/2011/01/180-degree-rule.html

### Advertisements

Analysis of advertisements: http://www.aber.ac.uk/media/Modules/MAinTV/analad.html
Best ads – TV, print, outdoor, interactive, radio: http://www.bestadsontv.com/
Best radio advertising: http://www.bestadsontv.com/best/radio
Biz/ed, identifying consumer types: http://www.bized.co.uk/educators/16-19/business/marketing/lesson/consumer1.htm
How to analyze an advertisement – Center for Media Literacy: http://www.medialit.org/reading-room/how-analyze-advertisement
How to make a radio commercial in just six minutes: http://www.youtube.com/watch?v=ennwKIL3xiw&sns=em
Producing radio ads to promote your business – for dummies: http://www.dummies.com/how-to/content/producing-radio-ads-to-promote-your-business.html

The top ten keys to creating great radio ads: http://www.strategicmediainc.com/radio-advertising-articles/the_top_ten_keys_to_creating_great_radio_ads.html

Writing effective headlines in advertising copy: http://www.web-source.net/david_garfinkel4.htm


### Depth of field

Depth of field: http://www.luminous-landscape.com/tutorials/understanding-series/dof.shtml

Depth of field in your video: why and how to use it: http://www.izzyvideo.com/depth-of-field/

Understanding depth of field in photography: http://www.cambridgeincolour.com/tutorials/depth-of-field.htm


### Directing the camera

Directing: http://www.urbanfox.tv/creative/sequences.html

Directing actors – five top tips: http://www.raindance.co.uk/site/index.php?aid=2367

Following action: http://www.open-channels.eu/tutor/film/followingaction.html

New director tips/directing actors – Lights Film School Filmmaking blog: http://www.lightsfilmschool.com/blog/new-director-tips/646/

Shooting sequences (video): http://www.metacafe.com/watch/1463654/shooting_sequences_part_1/

Shooting a short sequence: http://www.urbanfox.tv/creative/sequences.html

Television production handbook: http://www.tv-handbook.com/Editing%20and%20Program%20Continuity.html


### Framing and moves

Camera angles: http://www.mediaknowall.com/camangles.html

Camera shots: http://www.mediacollege.com/video/shots/

Filmmaking techniques: http://www.youtube.com/watch?v=d1japIhKU9I&feature=related

Five deadly sins of amateur video: http://www.youtube.com/watch?v=etVxvl6mcJ8&feature=related

Grammar of television and film: http://www.aber.ac.uk/media/Documents/short/gramtv.html

Rule of thirds: http://digital-photography-school.com/rule-of-thirds

Traditional film camera techniques: http://www.siggraph.org/education/materials/HyperGraph/animation/cameras/traditional_film_camera_techniqu.htm

Twelve basic shots – G.R. Claveria: http://www.grclaveria.com/12_Basic_Shots_CLAVERIA.html

Types of shots: http://digital-lighting.150m.com/ch07lev1sec1.html


### Interviews

Interview techniques for radio: http://ezinearticles.com/?Interview-Techniques-For-Radio&id=2189018


### Lighting

Cinematography, tips for video lighting – Film Look Training: http://www.youtube.com/watch?v=MJdt5Y9p28c

How to shoot with available light: http://digital-photography-school.com/how-to-shoot-with-available-light

How to shoot in direct sunlight: http://digital-photography-school.com/how-to-shoot-in-direct-sunlight

How to use light diffusers in photography, video: http://www.ehow.com/video_4412411_use-light-diffusers-photography.html

Techlearning, Light right – a crash course in lighting, video: http://www.techlearning.com/article/
light-right-a-crash-course-in-lighting-video/41240

Three-point lighting in 3D Studio MAX: http://www.secondpicture.com/tutorials/3d/three-
point_lighting_in_3ds_max_01.html

Three-point lighting simulator: http://www.mediacollege.com/lighting/three-point/simulator.html

Three-point lighting tutorial: http://www.3drender.com/light/3point.html

White balance: http://www.scrapjazz.com/topics/Photography/Lessons/587.php

How to white balance your camcorder: http://camcorders.about.com/od/videorecordingtips/ht/
htwhitebalance.htm

How to white balance your videocamera: http://www.mediacollege.com/video/camera/white-
balance/

Introduction to white balance: http://digital-photography-school.com/introduction-to-white-balance

## Music videos

Three types of music video, Matt Keil: http://www.mattkeil.com/2010/09/three-types-of-music-
video/

## News and current affairs

BBC College of Journalism – ethics and values homepage:http://www.bbc.co.uk/academy/college
ofjournalism/standards

BBC College of Journalism – Impartiality: from seesaw to wagon wheel: http://www.bbc.co.uk/
academy/collegeofjournalism/standards

BBC College of Journalism – Radio reporting on the road: http://www.bbc.co.uk/academy/college
ofjournalism/how-to

Newswriting for radio: http://www.newscript.com/

## Risk

Risk management, frequently asked questions: http://www.hse.gov.uk/risk/faq.htm#q1

## Sound

Audio tutorials: http://www.mediacollege.com/audio/

Audio for video: http://www.videouniversity.com/articles/audio-for-video-part-1-tape-formats-and-
hardware/

BBC College of Production, television skills, clear sound, recording drama: http://www.bbc.
co.uk/academy/collegeofproduction/videos/tv/clear_sound_recording_drama_tv

Editing and programme continuity: http://www.tv-handbook.com/Editing%20and%20Program%
20Continuity.html

Frequency response: http://www.mediacollege.com/audio/microphones/frequency-response.html

Radio sound effects: http://www.greatnorthernaudio.com/site_map.html

Microphones: http://www.hrelp.org/archive/advice/microphones.html

Recording good sound for film and video: http://www.iofilm.co.uk/io/mit/001/good_sound.php

## Story structure

Documentary storytelling article – New Doc Editing: http://newdocediting.com/client-resources/
resources/

Sequencing: http://masteringmultimedia.wordpress.com/2008/02/14/sequencing-the-foundation-of-video-storytelling/

Structure of a music video: http://www.icateens.org/content/structure-music-video

## *Storyboards*

Storyboard frames: http://en.wikiversity.org/wiki/Lesson_4_Storyboard_Frames

Storyboarding basics on Vimeo Video School: https://vimeo.com/videoschool/lesson/4/storyboarding-basics

## *Writing and scripting*

How to write a script for a documentary: http://www.desktop-documentaries.com/how-to-write-a-script.html

Writing to pictures, the basics: http://www.slideshare.net/AdamWestbrook/writing-to-pictures-the-basics

# Index